C000080236

|5

Credit: Jenny Matthews / Network

WEBSITE NEWS UPDATED WEEKLY
WWW.INDEXONCENSORSHIP.ORG • CONTACT@INDEXONCENSORSHIP.ORG
TEL: 020 7278 2313 • FAX: 020 7278 1878

Editor-in-chief Ursula Owen • **Editor** Judith Vidal-Hall • **Web Managing Editor** Rohan Jayasekera
Eastern Europe Editor Irena Maryniak • **Editorial Production Manager** Natasha Schmidt • **Publisher**
Henderson Mullin • **Development Manager** Hugo Grieve • **Membership and Promotions** Tony Callaghan
Events Co-ordinator Ruairi Patterson • **Project Manager** Aron Rollin • **Director of Administration** Kim
Lassemillanté • **Volunteer Assistants** Lala Amiroeddin, James Badcock, Ben Carrdus, Gully Cragg, Avery
Davis-Roberts, Hanna Gezelius, Monica Gonzalez Correa, Canan Gündüz, Andrew Kendle, Agustina Lattanzi,
Ramsey Nasser, Gill Newsham, Shifa Rahman, Neil Sammonds, Katy Sheppard, Nick Sloboda, Tom Tàbori,
Mike Yeoman
Cover design Sheridan Wall • **Design and production** Jane Havell Associates • **Printed by** Thanet Press, UK

CONTENTS

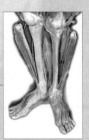

DEATH TAKES MANY FORMS
URSULA OWEN

Disturbing things are happening to the world's demography. While a child born today in the West can reasonably hope to live to perhaps 100, in Africa 9,000 people a day are dying of Aids and life expectancy is falling alarmingly. Statistically, a 16-year-old in Botswana can expect two decades of adult life, just half that of her parents. There are villages in Malawi that are in effect orphanages. Alex de Waal looks at the social and political implications of all this and tells the story (p87) of the spread of Aids in Africa through armies, where HIV levels are two to five times greater than they are in the general population.

Death takes many forms, and this issue of *Index* explores some of them, and their hidden stories. In the rich West, we can afford to have big and troubling debates – the right to death and the right to life – which must seem unthinkable in other parts of the world. AC Grayling argues for the right for an individual to choose when and how to die (p26), while Mary Kenny (p35), acknowledging that 'edge of life' questions are difficult, reflects on her opposition to abortion and support of the death penalty. And how do we price individual lives? Peter Pringle (p93) compares the £80 million spent so far on the Saville inquiry into Northern Ireland's Bloody Sunday with the miserable compensation paid to the families of the 13 dead; he worries, too, about how much of the evidence is still stamped SECRET.

Our regional file looks at India and Pakistan – both countries which, from time to time, casually threaten to use nuclear weapons in a war over Kashmir that has already cost 80,000 lives (p136).

There are other forms of dying we discuss. Carl M Cannon (p40), looking at the death of innocence, asks why it took more than 15 years for the paedophile priests scandal in the US to come properly to the world's attention. Stacy Marking examines the disorderly phenomenon of book-burning (p63), while Helena Drysdale tells us about the death of a language – with its loss of collective memory, a culture buried; and warns us about the 40 or so endangered minority languages spoken in the EU (p69).

Even nations die: Aminatta Forna, returning to Sierra Leone (p75), walks through buildings that symbolise the gradual crumbling of systems, organisations, services and the cohesive set of values that bind a nation together. Yet in Romania, as in much of Eastern Europe, Irena Maryniak discovers ghosts and myths of communism still unburied (p49), silence competing with truth for the public ear. ❏

THE VOICE OF HATE

HAROLD EVANS

VIRULENT ANTI-SEMITISM PERMEATES ALL
LEVELS OF MUSLIM SOCIETY. INSIDIOUSLY
PROPAGATED BY SCHOOL TEXTBOOKS AS WELL
AS BY THE ARAB MEDIA, IT THREATENS ANY HOPE
OF AN ENDURING PEACE IN THE MIDDLE EAST

Just before he was given the boot by President Bush, Yasser Arafat made an extraordinary offer – extraordinary because it was not one of the specific demands Bush was about to make, extraordinary because Arafat acknowledged a hidden horror: the indoctrination of the delusional young people who carry out suicide bombings. In a six-page private memorandum he sent to President Bush and Arab capitals outlining his 100-day plan for reform, Arafat said he would 'renounce fanaticism in the educational curricula and spread the spirit of democracy and enlightenment and openness'.

There is a lot under the stone Arafat has lifted. Fanaticism has been bred into the suicide murderers and millions of young people throughout the Arab nations with scant attention by media, governments, academia and churches in the civilised world. The Palestinian schools, financed by Europe, are open sewers in terms of the hatred they seed not just of Israel, but all Jews and all their friends. Dr Ahmad Abu Halabiya, former rector of the Islamic University in Gaza, speaks the message: 'Wherever you are kill the Jews, the Americans who are like them and those who stand by them.'

Arab leaders come to Washington and London and Geneva with formulas for peace while at home they feed their populations with similar incitements. It means that even if by some miracle there is agreement on the shape of a Palestinian state there will be no peace in the Middle East for a generation. The Israelis may find it in their hearts to forget or forgive the suicide assassins; the Palestinians may find it possible to put behind them the humiliations of occupation. But the political conflict over Palestine is only one aspect of the fanaticism that has been fomented. It adds up to the dehumanisation of all Jews and it has been manufactured and propagated throughout the Middle East and South Asia on a scale and intensity that is utterly unprecedented. This is something relatively new in the Islamic world.

There was more tolerance for Jews in the Islamic empire than ever there was in Christian Europe.

I was aware, as we all are, that the Palestinians hate the state of Israel. What has surprised me is the virulence of this new anti-Semitism throughout all the Muslim countries. It is frenzied, vociferous, paranoid, vicious and prolific, and is only incidentally connected to the Palestinian conflict. Hope, the familiar bromide, seems to have little to do with it. The moment of high hope following Camp David saw a surge, not a diminution, in the tide. It is a singular phenomenon; there is nothing comparable to it in relation to Arabs or Muslims.

Everyone talking about Palestine or terrorism is talking in a vacuum, for nothing can be understood without a proper appreciation of the way minds have been poisoned. We all threw up our hands in horror about Le Pen – it is always satisfying to find fault with the French! – but the world turns a blind eye to worse. A single skinhead assault on a synagogue in Europe is news, but not the unremitting daily assault on Jews waged from Morocco to Cairo to Damascus, from Baghdad to Tehran, the Gaza Strip to Karachi.

The paradox is that the world is connected as never before in terms of the flow of current, but many of the wires are lethally bare. The culture of religious fanaticism that has spawned and condoned terrorism and drives the new anti-Semitism is insensible to reason. Jonathan Swift recognised our dilemma more than 200 years ago: 'You cannot reason a person out of something he has not been reasoned into.' The consequences of unreason are rather more severe than they were in Swift's time.

What we are up against is best illustrated by what the Jews did to the World Trade Center. Everyone in the Muslim world knows that 9/11 was a Jewish plot to pave the way for a joint Israeli–US military operation not just against Osama bin Laden and the Taliban but also Islamic militants in Palestine. On the day of the bombing, 4,000 Jews were absent from the World Trade Center; they had been tipped off not to go to work. I thought this *canard* had long ago vanished up its own orifice but it was being retailed with all sincerity by a Pakistani taxi driver last week in New York of all places – which proves nothing except that he happens to be an accurate representation of a now unshakeable Muslim conviction. Millions and millions and millions believe this rubbish, as a Gallup poll has found after questioning people in nine predominantly Islamic countries: Pakistan, Iran, Indonesia, Turkey, Lebanon, Morocco, Kuwait, Jordan and Saudi Arabia, representing about half the world's Muslim population.

Some 67% found the attacks morally unjustified, which is something – why not 100%? – but they were also asked whether they believed reports that groups of Arabs carried out the bombings. Only in West-aligned Turkey was the answer Yes, but it was close, 46% to 43%. In all the other eight Islamic countries, the populations rejected the idea that Arabs or al-Qaida were responsible. Repeat: that is a poll just a couple of months ago, after millions of words from reporters and exultant videos from the Osama bin Laden show. The majorities are overwhelming in Pakistan, Kuwait, Iran and Indonesia – in Pakistan only 4% accept that the killers were Arabs. Thomas Friedman of the *New York Times* reported last month from Indonesia, the world's largest Muslim state, that nobody has any doubt about the Mossad conspiracy.

Who could be crazy/malign/misguided enough to disseminate such fabrications? The effluent is from official sources and newspapers and television in Arab states, from schools and government-funded mosques, from Arab columnists and editorial writers, cartoonists, clerics and intellectuals, from websites that trail into an infinity of iniquity. The appearance of modernity in the Arab media is illusory. More important than the presence of the hardware is the absence of the software, the notion of a ruggedly independent self-critical free press. CNN will film US bomb damage in Afghanistan. Al-Jazeera and the Middle East stations would never dream of talking to the orphans and widows whose loved ones were blown apart by a suicide bomber. An Arab critic of the USA and the coalition is always given the last word.

How could people be so susceptible to misinformation? Well, conspiracy theories simplify a complex world. They have the advantage that the absence of evidence is itself proof of plot: missing records at Pearl Harbor, missing bullets in Dallas, missing bodies in Jenin. Preconceptions are outfitted in fantasy. Contradiction by authority is mere affirmation of the vastness of the plot: so he's in it, too. Conspiracy and rumour bloom especially where the flow of news and opinion is restricted and especially where illiteracy is high.

But there is another explanation for the potency of lies today. It is the aura of authenticity provided by technology, by the Internet. John Daniszewski of the *Los Angeles Times* asked Ayesha Haroon, an editor of the *Nation* in Islamabad, why they blamed Israel. 'It is quite possible that there was deliberate malice in printing it,' she admitted, but she went on: 'I also think it has to do with the Internet. When you see something on a computer, you tend to

*Kyriat Arba Settlement, Palestine/Israel 1995: Jewish right-wing settlers
with a portrait of Baruch Goldstein who massacred 29 Muslims in 1995.
Credit: Abbas / Magnum Photos*

believe it is true.' Here in our new magic is a source of much misery. An Indonesian visiting the Islamic stronghold of Jojjakara, according to Friedman, was alarmed by the tide running for jihad against Christians and Jews. Internet users are only 5% of the population, but these 5% spread rumours about Jews to everyone else. 'They say, "He got it from the Internet." They think it's the Bible.'

The smear that defiles the Jews who died in the World Trade Center, which millions perceive as reality, owes its original currency in September 2001 to one website. It is called InformationTimes.com, 'an independent news and information service', whose address was given as the Press Building in Washington, DC. So I thought it worth asking the editor-in-chief, Syed Adeeb, for the evidence. He was hard to find. Directory assistance had no entry for Information Times, Info Times or the editor-in-chief.

El Fawwar refugee camp, West Bank 1986: mother of suicide Ibrahim Sarahney with a Hammas portrait of her son, who was responsible for the 1996 bombing at Ashkelon. Credit: Larry Towell / Magnum Photos

Bryan Curtis of Slate was told they had no such tenant; email messages were bounced back. When I spoke to Curtis in May, he told me he had been bombarded by anti-Semitic responses. He also got a threatening legal letter but when Slate's lawyers tried to reply the evanescent litigants were on the lam again. This week I did reach Adeeb in Virginia, so I asked him for his source. He told me it was the television station Al Manar in the Lebanon. When I asked whether he had any qualms relying on Al Manar because it was a mouthpiece for the terrorist group Hezbollah which exists 'to stage an effective psychological warfare with the Zionist enemy', Adeeb's reply was, 'Well, it is a very popular station.' He clearly believed his story; when I mentioned that there were names of Jews who died in the towers, he conceded that one or two might have died, but he found it sinister that nobody could tell him just how many Jews did die there. He volunteered that he was a US citizen, and that some of his best friends were Jews. Adeeb's approach to the world speaks for itself in his headlines:

- Israelis with bomb material arrested in Washington
- Israeli mafia controls US Congress
- Crazy Hindu terrorists threaten America
- FBI and CIA should investigate the Israeli lobby
- Barbarous Israeli soldiers rape and torture 86 women in Nablus, Palestine

I asked for the source of that rape story and was referred to the Labour MP for Birmingham Selly Oak, Lynne Jones. I checked. Jones did indeed put the atrocity in circulation, quoting an email from an Anthony Razook in Nablus, but she was careful to say 'this report has not been authenticated'. Such qualifications evaporate in the endless laundering of information.

Once upon a time stories like this would circulate on smudged cyclostyled sheets that would never see the light of day. But now Wizards of Oz like Adeeb, with this spurious authenticity of electronic delivery, have a megaphone to a gullible world. In the 1930s, Cordell Hull complained of print and radio that a lie went halfway round the world before truth had time to put its trousers on; nowadays it has been to Mars and back before anyone is half-awake. At the end of the line of incendiary headlines and the careless propagation of email there is Danny Pearl, tortured and butchered because he was a Jew and a reporter.

Unfortunately, reporting and comment in the West all too often, for the best of motives, ingenuously reinforces the anti-Semitic mindset. Israel is supported, in Lenin's phrase, like a rope supports a hanging man. Equal weight is given to information from corrupt police states and proven liars as to information from a vigorous self-critical democracy. The pious but fatuous posture is that this is somehow fair, as if truth existed in a moral vacuum, something to be measured by the yard like calico. Five million Jews in Israel are a vulnerable minority surrounded by 300 million Muslims who, for the most part, are governed by authoritarian regimes, quasi-police states, which in more than 50 years have never ceased trying to wipe it out by war and terrorism. They muzzle dissent and critical reporting, they run vengeful penal systems and toxic schools, they have failed in almost every measure of social and political justice, they deflect the frustrations of their streets to the scapegoat of Zionism and they breed and finance international terrorism.

Yet it is Israel that is regarded with scepticism and sometimes hostility. Take the battle of Jenin. The presumption in the feeding frenzy in the best newspapers in Europe and in hours and hours of television was that the Palestinian stories of 3,000 killed and buried in secret mass graves must be true, though the main propagator of this story, Saeb Erekat, has been shown time and time again to be a liar. The *Guardian* was even moved to write the editorial opinion that Israel's attacks on Jenin were 'every bit as repellent' as Osama bin Laden's attack on New York on 11 September.

Every bit? Every bit as repellent? Did we miss something? Was there some US provocation of Osama comparable to the continuous murder of Israeli women, children, the old and the sick – 19 victims at Passover? Was something going on in the World Trade Center as menacing as the making of bombs in Jenin, known proudly to Palestinians as Suicide Capital? In fact, there was no massacre, no mass graves. Human Rights Watch has since put the death toll at a total of 54, including, on their count, 22 civilians – the Israelis say three. Some Palestinian militants in fact claim Jenin as a victory in the killing of 23 Israeli soldiers.

Of course, the press certainly had a duty to report the Palestinians' allegations of massacre; it was entitled to raise questions and express alarm in the editorial columns. But truth did not lie in the balance between competing statements, and it was ill-served by hysteria. Big stories like this demand special rigour in the reporting, restraint in the language, scrupulous care in the headlining, proper attribution of sources and, above all, a sense of responsibility: 'genocide' is too agonising when real for it to be devalued by its use as small change. To describe suicide bombers as 'martyrs', as a recent British headline did, is to endorse a barbarity; Palestinians can call bombers martyrs if they like but it is a defamation of historic martyrs who gave their lives to save others, not to kill randomly and for financial reward for their families. Words, said Churchill, are the only things that last for ever. We should all have as much care with the explosive power of words as we expect airports to have with our luggage.

Let me reject the sophistry that to question such matters is to excuse everything done under the guise of protesting against anti-Semitism. It is not anti-Semitic to raise questions about Jenin, any more than it is anti-press to raise questions about the reporting. It is not anti-Semitic to report and protest against ill-treatment of Palestinians. It is not anti-Semitic to consider whether Sharon's past belies his promises for the future. It is not anti-Semitic to deplore the long occupation, though it was originally brought about by Arab leaders in instigating and losing three wars.

It *is* anti-Semitic to vilify the state of Israel as a diabolical abstraction, reserving tolerance for the individual Jew but not the collective Jew; it *is* anti-Semitic to invent malignant outrages; it *is* anti-Semitic consistently to condemn in Israel what you ignore or condone elsewhere; it is, above all, anti-Semitic to dehumanise Judaism and the Jewish people such as to incite and justify their extermination. That is what we have seen thousands and thousands of times over on a preposterous scale.

The European Community recently voted more millions to the Palestinian Authority. Corrupt as it is, one sympathises with its claim on our sympathies for the relief of suffering and poverty, but should it not have been made a condition that the PA must cease using European money for racist propaganda through its schools, its mosques, on television and radio, in political rallies and summer camps? The fanaticism Arafat offers to renounce – as a bargaining chip, not a moral principle – is the fanaticism stimulated by his Palestinian Authority which, among other enlightenments, makes educational films of little girls singing their dedication to martyrdom. The degree of infection was manifest at Al-Najah University in the city of Nablus where the students put on an exhibition entitled 'The Sbarro Café Exhibition'.

The Sbarro Café was the pizza parlour where a Palestinian suicide bomber murdered 15 people taking a meal. The show, according to the Associated Press and Israeli media, included an exhibit with pizza slices and body parts strewn across the room. The walls were painted red to represent scattered blood.

It is hard looking for sanity to put in the picture – even in the Department of Psychiatry at Ein Shams University in Cairo. Here is Dr Adel Sadeq, who is also chairman of the Arab Psychiatrists' Association, on suicide bombings: 'As a professional psychiatrist, I say that the height of bliss comes with the end of the countdown: ten, nine, eight, seven, six, five, four, three, two, one. When the martyr reaches "one" and he explodes he has a sense of himself flying, because he knows for certain that he is not dead. It is a transition to another, more beautiful world. No one in the Western world sacrifices his life for his homeland. If his homeland is drowning, he is the first to jump ship. In our culture it is different . . . This is the only Arab weapon there is and anyone who says otherwise is a conspirator.'

Next patient, please!

The Muslim world's relentless caricatures of the Jew are boringly on the same one note: Jews are always dirty, hook-nosed, money-grubbing, vindictive and scheming parasites. They are barbarians who deliberately spread vice, drugs and prostitution, and poison water. Among the fabrications:

- Israeli authorities infected 300 Palestinian children with the HIV virus by injection during the years of the intifada.
- Israel poisoned Palestinians with uranium and nerve gas.
- Israel is giving out drug-laced chewing gum and candy intended to make women sexually corrupt.
- Jews use the blood of gentiles to make matzos for Passover (*Al Ahram*, Cairo). Last April, state-funded San Francisco students put out a poster of a baby 'slaughtered according to Jewish rites under American license'.

Incredibly, the Arab and Muslim media, and behind them their states, have resurrected that notorious Bolshevik forgery, the Protocols of the Elders of Zion. This supposedly occult document, which reads like something discarded as too ridiculous for the script of Mel Brooks's *The Producers*, is the secret Zionist plan by which satanic Jews will gain world domination. It has had more scholarly stakes through its heart than the umpteen re-enactments of Dracula, but this bizarre counterfeit is common currency in the Muslim world. A multimillion 30-part series was produced in Egypt by Arab Radio and Television. With a cast of 400! And not as satire.

It is the Protocols that inspire Hamas, the Islamic Resistance Movement, to teach their children that the Jews control the world's wealth and mass media. According to Hamas – and who will be there in the classroom or on the street to raise a question? – Jews deliberately instigated the French and Russian revolutions and World War I so that they could wipe out the Islamic caliphate and establish the League of Nations 'in order to rule the world by their intermediary'. When I checked on the website Palestine Watch, by the way, to report on what they were telling the world about Israeli propaganda, I drew a blank, but there it described Hamas as seeking nothing other than peace with dignity, forbearing to mention the small matter that Hamas is dedicated to the destruction of the state of Israel.

Apart from the volume and intensity of the multimedia global campaign, there has been an ominous change in political direction. Arab frustration with the recognition of the state of Israel after World War II has, for decades, been expressed as 'why should the Arabs have to compensate the Jews for the Holocaust perpetrated by Europeans?'

Today the theme is that the Holocaust is a Zionist invention. It is expressed with a vehemence as astounding as the contempt for scholarship.

- A typical columnist in *Al-Akhbar*, the Egyptian government daily, on 29 April: 'The entire matter [the Holocaust], as many French and British scientists have proven, is nothing more than a huge Israeli plot aimed at extorting the German government in particular and the European countries. I personally and in the light of this imaginary tale complain to Hitler, even saying to him, "If only you had done it, brother, if only it had really happened, so that that the world could sigh in relief (without) their evil and sin."'
- Hiri Manzour in the official Palestinian newspaper: 'the figure of six million Jews cremated in the Nazi Auschwitz camps is a lie', a hoax promoted by Jews as part of their international 'marketing operation'.
- Seif Al-Jarawn in the Palestinian newspaper *Al-Hayat Al-Jadeeda*: 'They concocted horrible stories of gas chambers which Hitler, they claimed, used to burn them alive. The press overflowed with pictures of Jews being gunned down . . . or being pushed into gas chambers. The truth is that such malicious persecution was a malicious fabrication by the Jews.'

Clearly here is a consistent attempt to undermine the moral foundations of the state of Israel and it is espoused by a number of supposedly moderate people. The former president of Iran, Ali Akbar Hashemi-Rafsanjani, had this to say on Tehran Radio: 'One atomic bomb would wipe out Israel without trace while the Islamic world would only be damaged rather than destroyed by Israeli nuclear retaliation.'

The brilliance of the whole campaign of anti-Semitism is its stupefying perversity: the Arab and Muslim media and mosque depict Israelis as Nazis – even the conciliatory Barak and the hawkish Sharon are alike dressed up in swastikas with fangs dripping with blood – but media and mosque peddle the same Judeophobia that paved the way to Auschwitz. How can you talk to someone who conducts all discourse standing on his head screaming? People in the West who adopt the same murderous metaphor for Israel, and I heard it often on my recent visit to Europe, may be regarded as a joke in their own country but that is not where the action is. They are moral idiots but they lend credulity to malevolent liars in the Middle East.

By comparison with the phantasmagoria I have described, it seems a small matter that without exception Palestinian school textbooks, supplied by the PA and funded by Europe, have no space in the maps for the sovereign state of Israel, no mention of its 5 million people, no recognition of the Jews' historic links to Jerusalem.

The Palestinian claim to a state is unanswerable and with wiser leadership would have been flourishing for years. It is tragic that the cause is now being so ruthlessly exploited with 'Jew' as a code word for extremist incitement of hatred of the USA and the West. This is jihad. It is aimed at us all, at Europeans who 'look like' Americans because they believe in liberal democracy and are infected by US culture. But its first victims are the Palestinians and the frustrated masses of the Muslim world. Their leaders have led them into ignominy in three wars. They have failed to reform their corrupt and incompetent societies. It is convenient to deflect the despair and anger of the street to Israel and the Jews who supposedly control the West, but terror and hate have a way of poisoning every society that encourages or tolerates it. When Bernard Lewis observed 16 years ago that anti-Semitism was becoming part of Arab intellectual life 'almost as much as happened in Nazi Germany', he added the comforting thought that it lacked the visceral quality of Central and East European anti-Semitism, being 'still largely political and ideological, intellectual and literary', lacking any deep personal animosity or popular resonance, something cynically exploited by Arab rulers and elites, a polemical weapon to be discarded when no longer required.

But that was before the current electronic efflorescence of hate, before the brainwashing I have sketched, before 9/11. Habits of mind tending to approve terror are becoming ingrained in the Muslim world, sanctioned by the lethargy and prejudice in Europe: those Palestinians who danced for joy on 9/11 and those students who staged the grisly exhibition of pizza parlour murders were not al-Qaida, but their acceptance of terror as a substitute for politics does not augur well for the future of their country or the possibilities of peaceful political dialogue in any of the Arab states. ❑

Harold Evans, a former editor of The Sunday Times *and* The Times, *was most recently president of Random House, New York, and editorial director of the* Daily News, Atlantic Monthly *and* US News & World Report. *He is the author of* The American Century *(Knopf, 1998)*

An abridged version of the thirtieth anniversary Index on Censorship *lecture delivered at the Hay-on-Wye Festival this year*

ALL CHAOS ON THE MEDIA FRONT

EVE-ANN PRENTICE

THE DEMOCRATS ARE IN POWER; SLOBODAN
MILOSEVIC AND HIS PROPAGANDIST JOURNALISTS
ARE GONE. OR ARE THEY? ASSUMPTIONS THAT
ALL IS WELL WITH A NEW, DEMOCRATIC SERBIAN
MEDIA ARE FAR FROM THE TRUTH

A human hip bone was found on the roof of a jazz club behind Serbia's RTS state television headquarters on the morning after a NATO bomb tore into the building in central Belgrade. Sixteen people perished – mostly young doormen, technicians and make-up girls.

It was April 1999, and the West's bombing campaign against the former Yugoslavia was at its height, Slobodan Milosevic was still firmly in power and most people regarded it as the blackest moment in a dark era for the journalists of Serbia, caught between the rigid control of the state and the alienation of the West.

There were deep suspicions in Belgrade that the Milosevic regime was content to see the building bombed, to score propaganda points. Some suggested that the regime's intelligence services sometimes discovered in advance which buildings were on NATO's hit list and pointed out that none of RTS's senior editors or managers was in the studios at the time.

Today, the former head of RTS, Dragoljub Milanovic, is serving ten years in jail for 'causing grave danger to public security' by failing to evacuate the building when the NATO conflict erupted; Slobodan Milosevic is standing trial in The Hague on war crimes charges; the erstwhile opposition is in power in Serbia; and most people in the West probably think that all is set fair for the media in Europe's newest democracy.

Sadly, this is not the case.

What is left of Yugoslavia after a decade of civil wars is made up of Serbia and Montenegro, and the media in both republics face deep problems. In Serbia, German companies have bought shares in important outlets including the old pillars of communism, the state newspaper *Politika* and the popular tabloid *Blic*. Now thousands of journalists and other media workers on newspapers and radio and television stations know they will have to lose their jobs as part of an inevitable and much-needed slimming down of these and other media institutions.

There are also widespread grumblings that the new governing Democratic Opposition of Serbia is interfering too much in the media, with some comparing the Serbian Prime Minister, Zoran Dzindzic, with Tony Blair because of his perceived penchant for complaining when coverage of him or his policies is less than glowing.

The air of unease is not helped when media barons of the Milosevic regime, such as Zeljko Mitrovic and Bogoljub Karic, are still in place, albeit embracing the new regime with vigour. Mitrovic founded TV Pink, a station beloved by Milosevic's wife, Mira Markovic, while Karic – once a close adviser to Milosevic – is the man behind BKTV.

Milosevic had used two main tactics to control information – fines and threats against those who failed to toe the party line – while at the same time trying to create a young generation that was apolitical and did not ask questions.

'Hundreds of television stations dedicated to pop music and fun gave the message "forget politics – enjoy life",' says Stevan Niksic, editor-in-chief of the independent *Nin* magazine in Belgrade who was himself arrested by the Milosevic regime. 'This gave the impression of multiplicity, of choice, when in reality all the technical facilities to broadcast belonged to the state.'

Today, TV Pink is still there, broadcasting a diet of glamour, rock music and occasional Western series such as *Only Fools and Horses*. Mitrovic is often seen enjoying the hospitality at Western embassy receptions.

In Montenegro, the situation is more volatile. Television and radio journalists are furious at changes to the broadcasting laws which they see as paving the way for government interference, especially as Montenegro has its own elections in October and November. Amendments to the existing media law will shorten the pre-election media blackout, increase the ability of the management at state television to dismiss editors and limit the space the media may give to coverage of the activities of high-state officials.

Laws on broadcasting and the transformation of state radio and television into a public broadcaster, which were prepared in collaboration with international experts, had still not been put into effect in August. The Council of Europe and the Organisation for Security and Cooperation in Europe held a series of exasperated meetings with the politicians and the media during the summer, in an attempt to resolve the crisis.

The International Federation of Journalists said it was 'concerned about attempts by Montenegrin politicians to manipulate media through a series of changes to law that may threaten editorial independence'. Aidan White, the IFJ's general secretary, says: 'Politicians must not play political games with media. Elections are the crucial test of democracy and journalists must be able to work without interference. The public has the right to be informed without censorship or political tinkering with their news media. It's time for political leaders to suppress their desire to massage the media message. We need a clear signal that Montenegro is committed to media policies that guarantee the citizen's right to know, that support ethical and independent journalism and that are in line with European standards.'

White is more optimistic about Belgrade, where a new law aimed at bringing the broadcast media into line with international standards was passed by parliament in July: 'It's better to have something on the statute books than nothing at all,' he says. However, he adds a word of caution about Prime Minister Dzindzic's growing reputation for interfering in the media: 'Within recent memory, Serbian journalists have had to live in an all-pervasive atmosphere of fear and intimidation. Dzindzic is unfortunately stepping on to the old-style path of control. This needs a response from the international community.'

There is also unease about the looming lay-offs. 'The fact that German companies have bought into the media suggests normalisation – unfortunately, though, it's a pretty ruthless market out there,' says White.

When 50% of *Politika* was sold to the German company Westdeutsche Allgemeine Zeitung earlier this year, the first public reaction was a 'slight taste of bitterness', says Serbian journalist Alesandra Jelesijevic-Raskovic. '*Politika*, as the oldest Serbian daily, is a kind of a national symbol and the German occupiers during World War II banned it. Some members of the Ribnikar family [the newspaper's founders] were arrested by the Germans.'

But surely life is better now than under Milosevic? Jelesijevic-Raskovic thinks that not enough has changed: 'If you are asking me are there any changes in the media since Milosevic's departure, my answer would be: I don't see any. During the last ten to 12 years there was a lot of pressure, a lot of threats, sometimes lives were at stake. There is still pressure, there are still threats, editors and journalists are sued for provoking "mental suffering", there is still no free access to information. It is a little better than it used to be, but not much. There is a funny relationship between politicians and journalists: they fought to remove Milosevic from the throne and to bring themselves on it; we fought to remove Milosevic from the throne – full stop.'

Giovanni Porta, head of the media department at the OSCE in Belgrade, says: 'Under the old regime it was a crazy system, a crazy situation. Now there will have to be a lot of lay-offs and a lot of tough decisions. The main problem is changing people's mentality.'

The state broadcasting company RTS employs 7,600 people and many will have to go. Streamlining RTS 'in all probability implies major lay-offs', says an OSCE statement. 'The average age of employees is 49 years, most of whom are not qualified for the jobs they now hold.' The organisation adds: 'The state of repair of transmission facilities, still analogue, is very poor and under the very best-case scenario it needs to be completely overhauled into a digital system, in all likelihood involving foreign investment or a joint venture.'

Federal Information Minister Slobodan Orlic admits the problems are enormous. 'The transformation of our media will be very painful,' he says. 'We have 641 print media, 253 TV stations and 504 radio stations; the simplest way to describe it is as chaos.'

In the calm before the inevitable redundancy storm, life goes on in Belgrade; the jazz club behind the bombed RTS headquarters comes alive after midnight with late-night revellers. Most of the club-goers pass within a few feet of a stone memorial to the memory of the 16 who died. It is etched with the single word: *Zasto?* (Why?) ❑

Eve-Ann Prentice is a freelance journalist. She wrote this story for Index from Belgrade

ARAB NATIONALISM: ALIVE OR DEAD?
MOHAMMED HASSANEIN HEIKAL

MILITANT ISLAM HAS PASSED ITS PRIME,
ARGUES EGYPT'S LEADING WRITER
AND INTELLECTUAL. THE FORCE TO
BE RECKONED WITH IN THE FUTURE IS
A NEW BRAND OF ARAB NATIONALISM

Mohammed Hassanein Heikal is a powerful man: he has occupied the centres of power in Egypt and watched them shift over the past 50 years. He was editor-in-chief of the monolithic Egyptian daily newspaper *Al-Ahram* from 1957 to 1974 and Nasser's right-hand man and chief adviser. He still writes prolifically for Egyptian and western newspapers and, when cited, is routinely described as 'the most influential political commentator in the Middle East'. The West's nightmares these days are full of Islamic fundament-alists; we perhaps forget the other great Arab political movement of the twentieth century. For 20 years, between the 1950s and 1970s, Egypt was the spiritual home of Arab nationalism, Heikal one of its last surviving represent-atives. Here he talks to *Index* about the state of Arab nationalism and whether it provides an alternative to political Islam.

With the decline of the Ottoman Empire in the late nineteenth century, Arab thinkers began to conceive of a new social order. Pan-Arabism emerged out of the caliphate's failure to provide a workable model of society along Islamic lines. A generation of Arab intellectuals born in the 1920s and 1930s – Heikal's generation – turned to the West for inspiration. The new pan-Arab model was resolutely secular, inspired by Enlightenment ideals: Arab nationalism, the intellectual heir of pan-Arabism, was crystallised as a political movement by a Syrian Christian, Michel Aflak, who founded the Ba'ath (Arabic for Renaissance) Party in Damascus in 1940.

When Nasser took power in 1952, leadership of the Arab world shifted from the Levant to Egypt: the heady dream of Arab nationalism as separate from either western or Soviet influence was anchored in massive legal and land reforms, which appeared to give Egypt back to the Arabs, and culmi-nated in the Suez victory in 1956. Nasser inspired a generation of Arab leaders: Saddam Hussein studied in Cairo during the 1950s. As a historical moment, the heyday of Arab nationalism was vibrant but short-lived. The

United Arab Republic – Egypt and Syria – collapsed only eight months after its invention in 1958; Egypt lost the 1967 war and eventually accepted Israel in 1979. 'That generation was wasted,' Heikal says.

'I remember the beginning of the 50s. The average age in the cabinet was 35. Take a man like Nasser: he was 37 when he took power. I was editor of *Al-Ahram* at the age of 32. Society was in a state of mobility: everyone was young.' That youth, with its dreams, is now lost. 'We are now facing a similar situation to the Soviet Union's stagnation when the Communist Party was completely bankrupt.'

Heikal describes Egyptian – and by extension Arab – history in 30-year blocks. From 1945 until 1974, the dream of Arab nationalism still held. 'Until the end of the war [the October War of 1973] things were boiling. In 1974, we felt that it was time to breathe peacefully, in the words of Sadat.' But that pause for breath came to suffocate change. 'The 30 years until now have been complete stagnation under the pretext of stability. Now look at the average age of leaders in the Arab world. Mubarak is 75. The average age in his cabinet is 76.'

The USA desires a stable ally in the Middle East and Sadat saw the profit in fulfilling US desire. Sadat and Mubarak strangled political change in Egypt in order to retain massive US funding for their regimes: Egypt receives US aid second only to Israel. 'Mubarak has been vice-president and president since 1975 – more than a quarter of a century in power,' Heikal says. 'Staying in power is too much. Ideas need carriers: they need people. Even if these people have ideas, they are by now out of date. This scares me.'

Although Egypt is considerably closer to the USA than other Arab states, the same process of stability and stagnation encompasses the entire Arab world. 'Gaddafi is the youngest of the Arab leaders and he has been in power since 1969: one-third of a century. He became leader at the age of 27, so for more than half of his life he was in power. And this is not a monarchy.' The Egyptian sociologist Saad Eddin Ibrahim, condemned on 29 July to seven years' imprisonment on trumped-up charges of tarnishing Egypt's image abroad, receiving foreign funding without government permission and embezzlement, has described the Arab states whose republican leaders tend towards monarchic rule as *gomlokiyas*: the word is a mixture of the Arabic words for republic and monarchy; an English rendering would be something like 'republonarchy'. Heikal continues: 'Under Queen Elizabeth, there have been at least 11 prime ministers. The catastrophe here in the Arab world is that the kings rule.' In the Arab world, monarchs and leaders of republics are the same thing.

The 1973 war began this process of stagnation. In return for Sinai, Egypt recognised Israel and accepted that the geographical fantasy of a complete Arab nation was dead. Arab nationalism militates against acceptance of Israel as a legitimate state. 'The problem with Israel is that it cuts the Arab world in two. It is a wedge between tides trying to latch together. There is an Arab–Israeli crisis without Palestine,' Heikal contends. In accepting Israel, Sadat tied Egypt to the USA. 'After Sadat's *infitah* [open-door] policy the new generation were shocked. There were huge demonstrations on 18 and 19 January 1977 which were severely crushed by Sadat.' Sadat's policies killed off Nasser's Utopian dreams: 'The consequence of this is disappointment followed by frustration for the younger generation.'

The rise of Islamic violence in Egypt during the 1980s and 90s, beginning with the assassination of Sadat in October 1981 and culminating in the Luxor massacres in November 1997, arose from this mixture of disappointment and repression. 'Frustration leads to hallucinations of a religious solution, all sorts of illusions, as people search for a way out, a way to renew.' Heikal gestures towards Afghanistan: 'People under the slogans of Islam, being fed by the CIA and corrupted regimes of Saudi Arabia, fighting the wrong battle in the wrong place under the wrong slogan. This is the symbol of the tragedy of a lost generation.'

As a secular Arab intellectual, Heikal inevitably dismisses Islam: he rejects the idea that the rise of militant Islam is the new face of the Arab world, insisting that militant Islamism is a western fantasy. 'The phobia we now see in the US is self-destructive. Something horrible happened on 11 September. But it is not enough to say that there was a crime. That administration in the US has tough questions to answer: they should blame themselves first. You can't cover your responsibilities by turning the US into a police power. That state of mind is a hysterical reflex. Who did it? I am not sure. There were Arab elements, but not Arabs alone. Osama bin Laden is part of the hysteria. He and his type were the creations of the Cold War. It is not an enemy to be feared: you gave them the Stinger. It is easy to create a monster for the other man but once the other man is finished, what do you do with the monster? Dr Frankenstein had to kill him in the end.' Heikal, like the US and European left, turned the question of 11 September back towards the USA: 'If we want to change, let us understand. Hysteria is not change. The insistence on bringing everyone to account before this hysteria of 11 September is delaying changes.'

Heikal stands as one of the last dreamers of the old dream of Arab nationalism, and his replies are brewed in that heady mix of Utopia and brisk political reality. Did he think Arab nationalism was dead? 'There is a difference between losing a battle and failing in life. It was not the invention of anybody – it was a movement. We were detaching ourselves from the body of Islam. The Arab world has one language, one geographic expanse, one law – sharia. For 14 centuries sharia was always the basis of law. We have the same books, the same cinema and this geographical proximity. This is a complete region in everything. We have no Alps, no Manche.' Heikal's version of sharia appropriates the Islamic body of law for secular social purposes and his image of a complete Arab state omits many things – the Copts, for example – but nationalist dreaming is defined by its exclusions as much as its contents.

Heikal is 79, his views those of his generation who turned west and came back home with a new Enlightenment liberal and nationalist vision of statehood. Fouad Ajami's 1998 *Dream Palace of the Arabs* is an elegy to that generation: 'A political culture of Arab nationalism, which had nurtured them, which had come to them sure of itself and been accepted whole and unexamined, had led down a blind alley and been made an instrument and cover for despotism and a plaything of dictators.' Like Heikal, Ajami – a younger man, but the intellectual heir of the same hopes – dismisses the Islamic threat: he insists that 'we must not exaggerate the threat of the theocratic challenge'. Unlike Heikal, however, he argues that Egypt's role is over.

For Heikal, there is still hope in Egypt as the playground of the old nationalist dream. 'There is a generation waiting in the shade,' he sugggests. 'I see now the seeds of something else growing. A new generation is realising there is a different world and they are formed by the Internet. You can't easily dismiss the formative effect of a viewer every day being able to see BBC, CBS, Arab networks.' He is still advocating a turn to the West, but now it is to the Internet rather than the Sorbonne. Heikal's pride in the Arab world, his easy overview of 50 years of complex history and his faith in modern technology's redemptive force – the same technology that allowed 11 September's bombers to cause such havoc and that brings 100 different flavours of pornography into every US home – are at the same time strikingly modern and at ease with the old Arab nationalist model. ❏

Mohammed Hassanein Heikal was interviewed by Daniel Swift in Cairo

VARIETIES OF DEATH

DEATH TAKES MANY FORMS, NOT
ALL OF THEM A MATTER OF THE
PHYSICAL BODY. BOOKS BURN,
NATIONS FAIL, HOPE DIES WITH
LONG WAITING. THE RIGHT TO DIE
CONTENDS WITH THE RIGHT TO
LIFE AND THE RIGHT TO KILL

Taxo, Mexico 2001: Day of the Dead
Credit: DDB Stock / Andes Press Agency

'IF ALL ELSE FAIL . . .'

AC GRAYLING

THOSE SUFFERING FROM INTOLERABLE ILLNESS
STILL HAVE MINDS OF THEIR OWN AND THE
RIGHT TO SAY WHEN, WHERE AND HOW THEY
WILL LEAVE THIS LIFE. NATURAL JUSTICE, AS
WELL AS THE INSTITUTION OF HUMAN RIGHTS,
CONFERS THIS RIGHT

A debate about the right to die would have seemed odd to people in imperial Rome. Suicide and assisted suicide were commonplaces, and often enough grateful ones, for the citizens of that epoch. If a slave held a sword for his master to run into or fall on, or if a servant or family member helped mix poison into wine for someone ready to depart – or required to depart, for emperors gave senior figures the option of ending their own lives, in cases of capital sentences – there was no question of either the principal or the assistant in the case being held blameable, either morally or in law. On the contrary, anyone who helped in such a task was more likely to earn his contemporaries' praise.

Christian ethics brought about a complete change in the acceptability of such practices. The idea that life is sacred because 'God-given' introduced a proscription on the taking of life that has been construed in blanket terms when viewed from the perspective of practices such as abortion, infanticide and euthanasia, although (and inconsistently) it has otherwise admitted of many exceptions, as in war, killing in self-defence, and the execution of criminals and heretics. Nor has there ever been a principled extension of the 'sanctity of life' thesis to non-human creatures (using 'creature' in the theological sense to denote something brought into existence and, in the case of animals given conscious life, by a deity) despite the fact that the grounds for proscribing killing in the human and non-human cases are identical – unless one adds theses about souls as inhabiting only human animals.

There is a continuity between Christian ethics and Jewish thought in this respect. According to orthodox interpretations of *halacha* (Jewish ethics), the preservation of life is such an important duty that it justifies even non-observance of the Sabbath and the eating of non-kosher food. The length and quality of life are irrelevant considerations, because life is of infinite value, and (as one source puts it) 'any fraction of infinity is infinite'. Individuals do not have unlimited personal autonomy and cannot dispose of their lives and bodies as they will; both have been given by a deity for a purpose which it is not open to the individual to question or obstruct.

The idea that the individual is heteronymous with respect to his or her own life and body – that is, without a final authority to decide what will happen in it or to it – is key to the Judaeo-Christian view. The secular ideal of personal autonomy in these respects contrasts directly with it, and lies at the root of several of the core provisions of human rights instruments now widely accepted. The problem of 'the right to die' arises directly from the conflict of intuitions between the lingering Judaeo-Christian view and the secular morality underlying human rights thinking since the eighteenth-century Enlightenment.

The question addressed in the following paragraphs is whether, from the perspective of ethics, the conception of human rights enshrined in human rights conventions – and for convenience let us take a specific one, the European Convention on Human Rights (ECHR) – should be interpreted as recognising that individuals have (a) the right to choose when and how to die and (b) the right to suitable assistance in cases where they are not able to carry out their wishes to die on their own behalf (for example, when paralysed or similarly incapacitated). These questions were directly at issue in the important case of the late Diane Pretty, who sought to have both the above recognised as correct applications of the ECHR in the English courts, but was denied; and who thereupon, but equally unsuccessfully, sought remedy in the Strasbourg court.

The relevant Convention rights at issue are those that accord the right to life, the right to be protected from inhumane treatment, the right to privacy, and the right to freedom of thought and belief (respectively Articles 2, 3, 8 and 9 of the ECHR). The case to be argued here, contrary to the opinions severally made in the English and Strasbourg courts, is that Articles 2 and 3 singly, and all four of the specified articles jointly, give individuals the right to choose when and how to die.

The grounds on which I shall argue this are: first, that a right to life itself includes, when fully understood, a right to die; second, that if an individual is denied the chance to end his life before it becomes intolerable he would in effect thereby be subject to inhumane treatment; and third, that an individual's rights to privacy and freedom of belief give him the autonomy to decide what to do with his own life, subject to the proviso that he does not thereby harm others in the enjoyment of their rights.

The first question is whether the right to life includes the right to die. The judges in the English Divisional Court considering the case of Diane Pretty concluded that it could not do so because 'death is the antithesis of life'. It is not clear whether they therefore took Article 1 implicitly to deny a right to die, for they did not develop a jurisprudence of the 'antithesis' point; but it is at least clear that their intention was to say that a right to life does not include or imply a right to die.

This judgement raises a crucial point, and arguably involves a crucial error. It is important to distinguish between the state of death and the act of dying, to recognise that dying is a process that happens in the course of life, albeit in life's final stages, and to see that all an individual's rights are fully engaged, in this particular connection, with the manner, timing and circumstances of his dying. Once an individual is dead only residual rights remain – for example, in relation to wishes expressed and testamentary depositions made prior to the individual's decease, as affecting his estate and such matters as the form and place of the disposal of his remains.

With this distinction – between death as a state and dying as a living act – in view, it can be noted that important errors follow from failing to observe it. Although death is indeed the antithesis of life, dying is not. As an act of living, dying is one of the most important events in life, and because it can be pleasant or painful, timely or untimely, tragic or desired, it is integral to the character and quality of a person's life as he himself experiences it. We do not experience death, which is not an activity but a state – a state of non-existence indistinguishable from being unborn. But we might very much experience dying, and just as we hope that most of our acts of living will be pleasant, we likewise desire that the act of dying should be so too – or if not pleasant then at the very least not frightening, painful or undignified.

The second and a closely allied point is that 'life' in the phrase 'the right to life' is not mere existence. It is existence with at least a minimum degree of quality and value. In the main meaning of ECHR Article 1, it means a life in which an individual is protected from arbitrary power and threat, is free to seek opportunities and to exercise choices, to enjoy the rewards of his endeavours in peace, and to seek and foster personal relationships – and which, to the degree reasonably possible for anyone in this world, is free from distress and pain. But these protections are there to ensure that it is not enough for a state or another individual to fulfil its obligations under the article merely by providing enough food and water to an individual to keep him alive, if he is otherwise deprived of fundamental amenities, opportunities and decencies. Thus, if someone is kept chained in a box, but fed and watered regularly, this would not be regarded as sufficient of a life for Article 1 purposes to be satisfied. That is one reason why Article 2 exists, to reinforce the sense in which the life to which human beings have a right is a life of a certain minimal standard and value. The life to which a 'right to life' is accorded is thereby a life of a certain kind; and that point is central to the question of whether an individual has a right to terminate his or her own life when it has ceased to have, and to have a renewable potential for, that minimum standard.

As these points imply, mere existence is not automatically a good. If it were, no life-support machine would ever be switched off, and contraception would be outlawed because it limits the sheer accumulation of human numbers. There are indeed people, familiarly enough, who oppose contraception and euthanasia on precisely the grounds that (respectively) the generation and the continuation of life are of such importance in their own right that they are not outweighed by considerations of the quality of life involved. This is precisely the Judaeo-Christian point already mentioned. But it takes only a moment's thought to see the questionable character of this view. The tendency of any argument which does not qualify the concept of the right to life as the right to a life of a certain minimum value is to place quantity of life at the same or a higher level of importance.

Moreover, the English judges in the Pretty case assumed that death – the state of non-existence that follows the life process of dying – is in itself an evil. Naturally, most healthy and reasonably happy people wish to avoid or at least delay death, so that they can continue to enjoy their avocations, their pleasures and their important relationships. But for those who suffer and wish to cease suffering, death is not an evil but a welcome prospect. A life genuinely worth living is one in which neither dying nor death is an evil, but comes at a time and in a manner which completes the value of that life. Since death is inevitable, treating it as an evil to be delayed at any cost is a further error – and it gives rise to the poor argument that says that no one could possibly disagree that considerations of the quality of life should be subordinate to those about quantity of life.

The third question is whether the idea of rights to privacy and freedom of thought amount to a right of self-determination – the right, in other words, to decide how one will live one's life (always granting that no one has a right to live and act in ways that interfere with the rights of others). And, obviously enough, these rights do indeed amount to a right of self-determination, for they protect the autonomy of personal life, and leave the great questions of life to individuals themselves – whom to love, whether to have a family, how to behave in private (consistently with the interests of others), and the like.

The question of when and how to die is one of these questions, even though most people answer it by leaving the time and manner of their dying to chance. But in fact it did not take the recent advent of the ECHR in England for people there to acquire the right to choose in this respect, for it was already implicitly acknowledged. The passing of the Suicide Act in 1961, at last making it lawful for a person to end his own life, in itself implied an acceptance of an individual's entitlement to decide the time and manner of his life's ending. It did so by leaving to an individual's own free choice whether to continue to live or to die. A permission is not automatically the same thing as a right, but in this case the legalisation of suicide was premised on recognition of claims of autonomy – in short, that a suicide's own choice in the matter is an autonomous one – and this in itself constitutes attribution of a right.

THE SUICIDE ACT IN 1961 IMPLIED AN ACCEPTANCE OF AN INDIVIDUAL'S ENTITLEMENT TO DECIDE THE TIME AND MANNER OF HIS LIFE'S ENDING

The point is reinforced by the implicit granting of a right to die to patients who request that measures to sustain their lives be discontinued, as in the case of patients who request that their life-support machines be turned off. A case contemporary with the Pretty case was heard in the High Court, involving an application from a patient – referred to as Miss B – wishing to have her life support discontinued. Her request was granted, despite being opposed by the medical supervisors of her case. Granting her request is tantamount to recognising her right to choose whether to live or die. This case, and the implications of the Suicide Act 1961, and the validity of 'living wills' requesting that aggressive life-saving or life-sustaining treatments not be used in certain cases of illness or accident, jointly constitute acceptance that a right to die exists on its own merits.

Washington, USA 1997: disabled support groups protest against physician-assisted suicide.
Credit: Washington Photos / Camera Press Digital

However, an anomaly created by the 1961 act, an anomaly that has particular consequences for cases like that of Diane Pretty, is that although it is lawful to take one's own life, it is unlawful for anyone to help one take one's own life. The anomaly in this connection therefore is that it is unlawful to help someone do something lawful. The reason is that the Suicide Act rightly seeks to prevent murder under the disguise of assisted suicide; but because it does so by a blanket prohibition, making the aiding, abetting or encouraging of suicide a criminal offence under any circumstances, it has put anyone placed similarly to Pretty in the impossible position that he cannot attain the lawful end he desires. In the light of the foregoing argument, this thereby denies such an individual one of his fundamental rights.

Many confusions surround the debate about assisted suicide and euthanasia, but the main one is that most people fail to distinguish properly between them. 'Euthanasia' literally means 'a good death', and in that sense everyone hopes for euthanasia in the end, usually, by preference, a naturally occurring easy and painless death after a healthy old age. A suicide or assisted suicide might go wrong, if not properly carried out, and result in suffering for the subject, and thus not count as euthanasia in the literal sense.

Euthanasia has come mainly to mean deliberate acts or omissions that result in someone's death; as when an elderly patient with pneumonia is not given antibiotics or when a life-support machine is switched off, allowing someone in a long-term persistent vegetative state to die. This is called 'passive euthanasia' and is regarded as lawful and acceptable. Active euthanasia takes place when someone is given death-inducing treatment of some kind.

There is, in fact, no moral difference between the two kinds of euthanasia, because deliberately not doing something is as much an act as doing something. The concept in theological ethics of 'sins of commission and omission' embodies a recognition that equal responsibility attaches to deliberate withholdings and choices not to act, just as it does to failing to act when action is required. In that central respect, passive and active euthanasia are the same. They both involve deliberate choices, and they both have the same outcome.

It is a matter of sentiment that passive euthanasia seems more acceptable. This point is more obvious when one recognises how often active euthanasia is in fact performed. Failure to shorten the suffering of a patient in agonising or terrifying terminal phases of an illness is so cruel that, in reality, few medical practitioners allow themselves to stand aside. To do so would be to treat people with less consideration than is typically accorded to animals, for we regard it as a kindness to animals to end their lives swiftly and easily when their suffering is otherwise unrelievable. But happily for human victims of pain or distress, in hospitals all over the world, every day, doses of painkillers are raised to fatal levels when needed, the legitimacy of the exercise protected by the 'doctrine of double effect', which says that because the doctor's primary aim is to alleviate suffering, the life-shortening side effect is inescapable and therefore acceptable.

But as with the distinction between passive and active euthanasia, this is a conceptual convenience. Stating that one's intention is to relieve pain rather than to hasten death in such cases is a conceptual sleight of hand, given the empirical certitude that the latter will result. In any case, hastening death is the ultimate form of pain relief, and is therefore comprehended in the treatment to relieve suffering.

In discussions of physician-assisted death, whether direct in the sense of passive and active euthanasia, or brought about by 'double effect', the point is frequently made that medical practitioners are bound by their professional code of ethics to seek to save, protect and promote life, or at least to minimise the suffering incident on accident or disease. In the USA, appeal is still made to the clause in the Hippocratic oath that states: 'To please no one will I prescribe a deadly drug, or give advice which may cause my patient's death.' The principal meaning of this is that the practitioner vows not to bow to (say) family, political or other kinds of third-party pressure to end the life of someone who does not wish to die. But some translations bear a reading that says a practitioner will not accede to a patient's request for death either, and this is the form of reading appealed to by opponents of medically assisted suicide. But clearly, a practitioner who refused to help a patient die who was in great, unrelievable and interminable (other than by death) pain, would be failing in his Hippocratic duty to succour the patient; so the appropriate reading of the relevant clause in the oath is arguably the third-party one alone.

Nevertheless, there is a real concern for medical practitioners, whose primary *raison d'être* is to save life, ameliorate suffering and cure ills and injuries. For this reason, a practical or institutional innovation might be suggested. This is that there should be a medical specialty of thanatology (I here coin a word from the Greek *thanatos*, meaning death), that thanatologists should work within a careful framework of law and under the supervision of a hospital ethics committee, so that every occasion of thanatological treatment is approved in advance, monitored during administration, and properly recorded afterwards. Since only thanatologists will be involved in the work of helping those sufferers to die who have elected such treatment and show a stable and intelligent intention to carry their wishes through, all other medical practitioners will continue to work under the assumption that their sole concern is to save life, cure ills and palliate suffering. Apart from anything else, this will clarify the very grey area in which many medical practitioners now work, given the frequency with which they knowingly, and for compassionate reasons, administer life-shortening treatments.

In The Netherlands, a careful law now exists to permit active euthanasia and assisted suicide, and in the US state of Oregon (despite the recent Federal intervention of the US Attorney-General, which failed in the courts) an equally careful law permits physician-assisted suicide. Every year in Oregon, a report is issued describing the numbers and circumstances of those who have availed themselves of the law, and it makes instructive reading – not least because in the majority of cases it meant that sufferers were able to die at home, with their families and friends around them, in relative peace.

Those who object to voluntary euthanasia and assisted suicide point out that there is excellent hospice care for people with terminal illnesses, where they are looked after in ways that palliate suffering and allow death with dignity. It is certainly true that the hospice movement offers outstandingly good terminal care, and that modern medications greatly enhance their ability to provide it. But the existence of palliative care is not invariably the choice of clear-minded but terminally suffering individuals. They might wish to die when still alert, unaffected by palliative medications and therefore able to interact in full consciousness with their families; able, furthermore, to bid them farewell properly. They may not wish to endure the helplessness and distress of the last stages of their illnesses, whatever is available in the way of pain control, psychotropic medication and psychological support. Despite their afflictions, such sufferers are still persons with minds of their own, and rights, who wish to make choices about their own affairs, and above all to say when, where and how they will leave the life which, for all the satisfactions it might otherwise have brought in personal terms, is drawing to an end so cruelly. Natural justice says that this is their right; and so does the concept and institution of human rights on the interpretation suggested here. ❏

AC Grayling is reader in philosophy at Birkbeck College, University of London

FORCES OF LIFE AND DEATH

MARY KENNY

THE TANGLED WEB THAT LINKS THE
RIGHT TO LIFE, TO DIE AND TO KILL

Soon after the bodies of Holly Wells and Jessica Chapman – the murdered Cambridgeshire ten-year-olds – were found, I wrote an article for the *Daily Mail* in which I said I was a reluctant advocate for the death penalty in certain rare instances. Although it troubled my conscience to write this piece, I wrote it from conviction: I truly believe that the existence of a death penalty for particularly heinous crimes is a fitting act of justice that illuminates, with drama and catharsis, what a dreadful thing it is to deprive a person, perhaps particularly a young person, of her life.

Moreover, I also believe that there can be a redemptive element, for the offender, in accepting the death sentence. It seems to me that this occurred in the case of the Oklahoma bomber, Timothy McVeigh. His execution in 2001 both underlined the enormity of his crime and brought a mystical sense of a just payment being exacted for what he had done. It also brought what Americans call 'closure'. I also had it on good authority that in his final hours McVeigh asked for a priest to confess his terrible sin and ask for pardon before dying.

In several radio programmes I did after the *Mail* piece, I was asked how an opponent of abortion could justify the death penalty? After all, the Pope has repeatedly condemned capital punishment, almost as part of the 'pro-life' package.

Some pro-life Christians do accept the death penalty – the MP Ann Widdecombe is one – arguing that while the unborn child is innocent, the convicted murderer is not. Others disagree. The late Lord Longford not only opposed the death penalty absolutely; he believed every individual has the capacity to repent and remake his life. He practised this belief by befriending Myra Hindley, the convicted Moors murderer, until the end of his life. Similarly, Sister Helene Prejean (played by Susan Sarandon in the film *Dead Man Walking*) has brought 'pro-life' views to a special ministry for men and women on death row (*Index* 3/2001).

Yet few people are totally consistent on the question of taking human life. When I was asked how an anti-abortionist could favour the death penalty, the question might as easily have been put the other way: how can a pro-abortionist, or a pro-euthanasist, condemn the death penalty? Significantly, two people scolded me for my discourse on hanging: one was a feminist friend, a champion of 'the right to choose' in abortion, who regards state execution as 'repellent'. The second was Ludovic Kennedy, who reprimanded me for holding 'Old Testament' views. He is, of course, one of Britain's leading advocates of voluntary euthanasia. It seems as paradoxical that those who support choice in abortion and euthanasia are most vehement in their opposition to the death penalty for especially heinous murder.

Perhaps the consistent point of argument, among the 'right to choose' lobby, lies in that very word: choice. You may terminate life if that is a voluntary, individual choice. That the infant in the womb has not made this choice is dismissed by the claim that the unborn is not a person, which is true in a social sense – it doesn't have a social security number or other social connections – but is untrue in the scientific sense, because it does have a unique DNA. And anyone who has observed a late abortion – as I have – can see that the foetus puts up a fight to survive, shrinking away from the lethal needle that extracts the amniotic fluid. If it had a choice, the foetus signals that it would choose to live.

With voluntary euthanasia, there is not only choice but also, as with suicide, the affirmation of individualism. Thomas Szasz, the libertarian secularist, has written: 'A man's life belongs to himself. Hence he has the right to take his own life, that is, to commit suicide.' Perhaps that is the essence of the libertarian and secularist viewpoint. It could never be the Christian or, I think, the larger religious viewpoint, because the religious view of life – even at its most tentative and vague – holds to a 'higher power' to which we must answer. In euthanasia and suicide, there also exists a social dimension: suicide usually leaves great grief in its wake. Only a childless orphan on a desert island could commit suicide without someone else being affected by the act. (I have never felt the same about Anna Karenina since interviewing a train driver who had had a suicide under the wheels of his engine.)

With euthanasia, there are several far-reaching external implications: the effect on others, the impact on the medical and caring professions, and the utilitarian (and financial) incentive created to bump off elderly people who, by living on, may be eating up their descendants' inheritance. I have a friend who rather hoped to inherit her widowed mother's house, eventually. The widowed mother grew feeble with Alzheimer's, and had to be cared for. Her

Twelve-week-old aborted foetus: from the Prolife Alliance party political broadcast banned in 2001 by the BBC. The ban was overturned on appeal this year.
Credit: Courtesy Prolife Alliance

house was sold to help pay for medical and nursing expenses. The elderly widow lived just long enough to use up the cash made available by the disposal of her property. On a purely utilitarian level, it would have been more beneficial to everyone to have given the bewildered Alzheimer's patient a lethal injection at the start of her long and expensive decline. And that, precisely, is the danger.

I accept and acknowledge that these 'edge of life' questions are difficult: there are no easy answers. It is not possible, and maybe not desirable, to achieve 'consensus' on everything: for consensus usually means less free debate, and free discourse is essential for thought. I also accept that there are many inconsistencies, and these exist on all sides of the argument. For example, although I cannot accept that voluntary euthanasia is a 'right', at another level I do accept impulsive mercy killing: the soldier on the battle-field who takes his gun to put a merciful end to his mortally wounded comrade is carrying out an act for a good and compassionate intention. Just as, while I think suicide should generally be regarded as wrong, the Captain Oates situation is a heroic example of an altruistic suicide.

Although there are these inconsistencies on all sides, what divides opinion, at its most basic, is the religious cast of mind and the secularist mentality. I once thought this need not be. I remember saying to an elderly and wise Monsignor that a person could be an anti-abortionist and an atheist. You could come to a purely rational conclusion that the unborn was entitled not to be deliberately killed because it was a human life. 'You could,' he said. 'But, on the whole, you wouldn't. It only makes sense in the context of the faith.' And I now see that this is so. Only this notion that the spark of life is somehow divine and must be respected as such, will, in the final analysis, sustain the pro-life argument. Where this leaves me with my reluctant advocacy of the death penalty, I do not quite know. But this is among the many mysteries of life's divine dream. ❏

Mary Kenny is *the author of* Goodbye to Catholic Ireland. *She is writing a biography of William Joyce, the last man to be hanged for treason*

COFFIN MODELS ARE DEAD SEXY

An Italian funeral home is using scantily clad models in its publicity materials in a bid to make the afterlife a little more tempting – for its male customers at least.

The website of the Rome-based funeral home and coffin factory Cisa features photographs of its hand-crafted caskets topped with scantily clad females sipping champagne or reclining seductively on the tops of coffins.

'We wanted to make the whole idea of picking your coffin less serious, maybe even make people laugh a bit,' Giuseppe Tenara, one of the partners, told Reuters news agency in Rome, as relayed by Yahoo!

Cisa has followed up on its theme by offering browsers an online girlie-and-coffin calendar: the model sitting on a coffin and overlooking 11 September is wearing a bikini-top made out of a US flag. 'Some people are scandalised, but we just explain we're trying to raise a laugh,' Tenara added. ❏

RJ

CONTROVERSIAL CROSS-SECTION

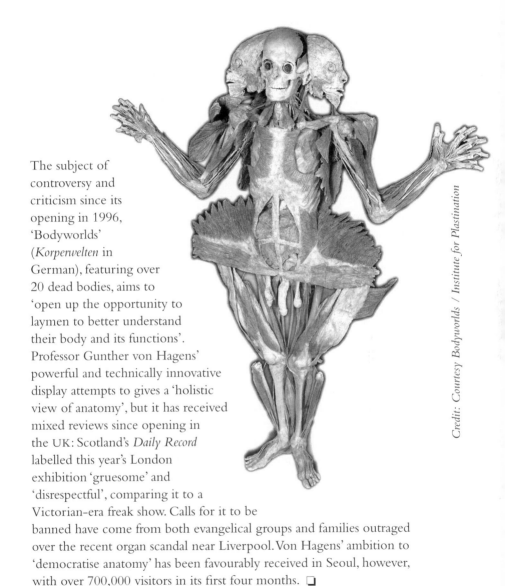

Credit: Courtesy Bodyworlds / Institute for Plastination

The subject of controversy and criticism since its opening in 1996, 'Bodyworlds' (*Korperwelten* in German), featuring over 20 dead bodies, aims to 'open up the opportunity to laymen to better understand their body and its functions'. Professor Gunther von Hagens' powerful and technically innovative display attempts to gives a 'holistic view of anatomy', but it has received mixed reviews since opening in the UK: Scotland's *Daily Record* labelled this year's London exhibition 'gruesome' and 'disrespectful', comparing it to a Victorian-era freak show. Calls for it to be banned have come from both evangelical groups and families outraged over the recent organ scandal near Liverpool. Von Hagens' ambition to 'democratise anatomy' has been favourably received in Seoul, however, with over 700,000 visitors in its first four months. ❑

Natasha Schmidt

www.bodyworlds.com. Also see www.indexonline.org/news/20020809_britain.shtml

SEX, LIES AND CENSORSHIP

CARL M CANNON

HOW DID AN OLD STORY LIKE THE PAEDOPHILE
PRIESTS SCANDAL COME TO DOMINATE THE
FRONT PAGES OF THE US AND INTERNATIONAL
PRESS THIS YEAR, AND WHY DID IT TAKE SO
LONG TO DO SO? ASKS A JOURNALIST AT THE
FOREFRONT OF THE INVESTIGATION OVER A
DECADE AGO

The last few months have been bittersweet for the handful of journalists, led by the incomparable Louisiana writer Jason Berry, who reported extensively in the mid-1980s on the widespread problem of sexual abuse by priests – and the cover-up by the Church hierarchy. At the time, our stories attracted some measure of attention: Berry was interviewed by radio and television outlets around the country, wrote op-ed pieces for numerous big-city dailies and won a Catholic Press Association award. Karen Henderson of Cleveland's *Plain Dealer*, who wrote about problems in her diocese and beyond, won a public service award from the Associated Press. All three of us were nominated for a Pulitzer: Berry for his 1985 reporting; Henderson and I two years later. The zenith of media attention probably came on St Patrick's Day 1988, when Berry and I were featured guests on a dramatic hour-long look at this issue on *The Phil Donahue Show*. Berry also wrote a powerful and superbly documented book, *Lead Us Not Into Temptation: Catholic Priests and the Sexual Abuse of Children*, published to critical acclaim in 1992.

Yet, as any of the journalists who covered this issue concedes, this scandal did not explode full-blown into the public consciousness as we thought it might and as it has this year. The possible reasons continue to trouble us. What's changed?

To journalists, the story behind the story has become well known in the past few months: a Catholic priest in Boston named John J Geoghan serially molested young boys for years while his superiors responded by periodically shipping him off for therapy, then recycling him into new parishes without warning parents there. A crusading alternative paper, the *Boston Phoenix*, documented this pattern; a powerful establishment daily, the *Boston Globe*, fought successfully for open access to court records and, in the process, revealed that the primary concern of Church authorities in the Boston diocese was not the welfare of the child victims but how to keep a lid on the scandal.

It's not too much to say that this story sounds like a remake of a horror movie. In 1984, the Geoghan role was played by a Cajun priest named Gilbert Gauthe. The diocese was not Boston but Lafayette, Louisiana; the beleaguered bishop not Cardinal Bernard F Law, but Gerard Frey. The crusading alternative weekly was the *Times of Acadiana*; the establishment news outlet that broadened the story was the *National Catholic Reporter.*

But in New England, it seems, events move slowly. Geoghan was not even the first priest in the Boston circulation area to be convicted of serially molesting boys. In 1993, a priest named John R Porter admitted to molesting 28 boys in Fall River, Massachusetts, 50 miles to the south. And Geoghan was not defrocked until 1998, even though his crimes were first reported to Church authorities as early as 1972 – and the archdiocese was reeling from his lawsuits by 1993. Geoghan was first charged with moles-tation in Waltham, Massachusetts, on 19 December 1995, but the *Globe*'s first story didn't run until July 1996 when a parishioner sued, saying that Geoghan had molested her three sons.

In the ensuing five years, a close reading of the Boston media reveals little evidence that the furore generated by this episode would be any different from that surrounding the hundreds of other Catholic priests arrested or sued in the previous two decades. By the year 2000, the story seemed out of gas. The *Globe*, for one, mentioned Geoghan only five times that year.

In March 2001, however, Kristen Lombardi of the *Boston Phoenix* published a 7,000-word blockbuster that put together the scope of Geoghan's abuse and the extent to which the local church hierarchy, including Law, was complicit in allowing it to continue. She followed that with a hard-hitting piece in August called 'Cut-throat Tactics', detailing how the Church, instead of ministering to the victims of sexual abuse by priests, confronts, intimidates and bullies families when they come forward to report it. By then, the *Globe* was hard at work on the story, as was the *Boston Herald*. The *Globe* struck gold when it fought successfully for access to the previ-ously sealed court records in the civil suits against Geoghan. The paper published an initial story in July 2001 documenting how Law had conceded under oath that he knew about Geoghan's activities as long ago as September 1984. It followed that up with a lengthy two-day special report in

January that put the entire Geoghan saga on the record. That piece broke the bank.

Since then, the Boston media have reported on the scandal every day. Who hasn't? Feeding frenzy is too mild a phrase to describe this year's coverage of the issue. The story cannot be escaped. It's on local television news, network news and cable news. Fox News did a March special on it; so did CNN. PBS did two. The headline on the cover of the 1 April issue of *Time* magazine asks: 'Can the Catholic Church save itself?' By April, the *New York Times, Los Angeles Times* and *Washington Post* were running stories every day. The 12 April *Los Angeles Times* featured five separate stories on the scandal, including one on an accused priest attacking a news photographer in the halls of the Santa Rosa, California, courthouse. These aren't incremental stories, either. Their tenor can be summed up by the March headline of an *LA Times* piece: 'Scandal Shaking Catholicism to Core'.

The scandal is on the front page of the *USA Today* delivered to your hotel room, and in unlikely places. The conservative, pro-Catholic *National Review* did a cover on 'THE SCANDAL'; *Sports Illustrated* ran an item on a former major-league ballplayer, Tom Paciorek, who came forward (originally in the *Detroit Free Press*) to say he and his brothers were molested by their parish priest as teenagers. The tabloids informed us that three books are in the offing, including one by Jimmy Breslin.

The apogee may have come at Easter, Christianity's holiest time. This very fact might be a hint of how the times have changed. When I wrote about this subject 15 years ago, my editors were so sensitive to the exigencies

Opposite, left: Cambridge, Mass., USA 2002: Maryetta Dussourd, mother of three children who claim to have been abused by Geoghan. Credit: AFP Photo / Jessica Rinaldi

Opposite, right: Boston, USA 2002: Cardinal Bernard Law. Credit: AFP Photo / Jim Bourg

Left: Middlesex Superior Court, Cambridge, Mass. 2002: John Geoghan listens to the judge before being sentenced. Credit: AFP Photo / The Boston Globe

of the Christian calendar that they waited until after Christmas to launch our series. No one has any such compunction today, as the coverage during the eight days on either side of Holy Week demonstrated.

Down in New Orleans, Jason Berry watched all of this unfold with more than an academic interest. So did I, along with others who'd covered this issue before. Although the details were familiar, such stuff never loses its power to shock. I couldn't help but wonder what Gilbert Gauthe's many victims, now grown men, thought of all this.

At the same time John Geoghan was engaging in oral sex with boys while instructing them to close their eyes and repetitively recite 'Hail Marys', Gauthe was forcing altar boys in Louisiana repeatedly to submit to and perform anal or oral intercourse with him, often molesting several boys in one family. Estimates of the number of his victims, some of whom were as young as seven, ranged upwards of 100. Geoghan swore boys to secrecy by telling them what they did was 'confessional'; Gauthe, who often carried firearms, warned at least one boy that if he said anything Gauthe would harm his parents.

Inevitably, though, some of these boys did tell their parents. Diocesan authorities simply transferred Gauthe to another parish – and another, and another. The string ran out in a bayou village in Louisiana called Henry, in 1983. Church officials responded by refusing to tell parishioners – even the parents of boys suspected of being molested – why Gauthe was sent away. They advised parents who did come forward to keep silent. No priest or vicar from the Lafayette diocese ever called the cops. After Gauthe was arrested, the parents sued the diocese. In the course of litigation, Frey admitted there was a second paedophile priest in his diocese.

'When I read the civil deposition of Bishop Gerard Frey admitting there was a second paedophile priest I thought: This is Watergate! – the bishop covering up,' Berry recalls. He wrote about it for Lafayette's *Times of Acadiana* only after being rebuffed by *Vanity Fair, Rolling Stone, Mother Jones, The Nation* and the *New York Times* Sunday Magazine. Berry also contacted Thomas C Fox, then the editor of the *National Catholic Reporter*, who agreed to run his stories. Berry's last piece for the Lafayette paper in January 1986 revealed that Frey had recycled seven sexual offender priests over the years. In that issue, *Times of Acadiana* editor Richard Baudouin ran an editorial calling for the removal of the bishop and the local vicar-general, prompting the diocese to organise an advertising boycott.

In those years, I was a Washington correspondent for the San Jose *Mercury News*. One day in the spring of 1987, I was on home leave when national editor Bob Ryan asked if I had any ideas for in-depth stories or investigative projects. I said that I was convinced that the situation in the Lafayette diocese was not isolated – that it was part of a national pattern and that a day of reckoning was coming for the Catholic Church.

Ryan was an honest, hard-nosed newsman who backed up his reporters, but he was sceptical of what I was telling him. And why not? It was shocking then; it's shocking now. So I told Ryan I thought I could find half a dozen dioceses where cover-ups of sexual molestation had gone on. He said evenly that if I found six instances where diocesan authorities had covered up sexual abuse of children, it was definitely a pattern – and a national story.

Before I did my first interview, I did a Lexis-Nexis search. The tool was somewhat new, and reporters didn't use it much. I found a dozen instances in the clips, usually small wire-service stories, in which priests had been accused of molesting children or adolescent boys. I made phone calls to those places, usually locating a cop or a helpful plaintiffs' attorney (lawyers are the unsung heroes of this scandal) and discovered that, typically, parents had called the police or hired a lawyer only after being stonewalled by Church authorities. I had found my pattern before leaving my office. In time, I would identify some 35 priests in more than two dozen dioceses, not six, who'd been recycled after abuse allegations. I spent three months on the story, travelling to dioceses all over the country to nail it down. The *Mercury News* published my stories on 30 and 31 December 1987, and sent them out on the Knight Ridder national wire. What I found was that Church officials:

- sent offending priests away for therapy, but allowed them to return to parish work or duty in a church school or hospital without notifying parents or enacting safeguards to keep them away from children;
- ignored complaints of abuse, often attempting to discredit the parents, even in cases in which they knew of previous allegations against the priest;
- failed to inform civil authorities of allegations of child abuse, although existing state law required them to do so in most states;
- refused to seek out likely victims when a case surfaced and fought to make sure settlements remained sealed.

My story described an internal report for US bishops that estimated that the cost of paying damages to the victims would exceed US$1billion in the coming decade. The report's authors – priests Thomas Doyle and Michael Peterson, and lawyer F Ray Mouton Jr – were seen as alarmists inside the Church, but their warnings were right, as was my hunch about the Church's day of reckoning. What I didn't imagine was that it would take 15 years before it occurred.

The reasons the story took so long to gain traction are varied and complex, and it takes a while to sort them out. There isn't one explanation, there are many, and they interact with each other in a way that might serve as a cautionary tale to investigative reporters and editors.

First, the original problem with this story was simple scepticism that anything so horrible could be condoned by the hierarchy of a Church that has done so much good in the world. Feeding into this scepticism was the fiasco of the 1993 accusations against Cardinal Joseph Bernardin in Chicago. The abuse allegation against Bernardin was the product of therapy-induced hypnosis delving into the controversial area of 'recovered memory'. The accuser's own lawyer must have initially been sceptical – he polygraphed his own client – but he filed a suit anyway while making an exclusive arrangement for CNN to get the story first and timing it to coincide with the national bishops' conference in Washington, DC. Bernardin denied the charges immediately and forcefully: 'All my life, I have lived a chaste and celibate life,' he said. 'Everything that is in that suit about me, the allegations, are totally untrue, they're totally false.' His vehement denials threw up red flags to journalists with experience reporting on the issue. Four months later, the lawyer withdrew the suit.

It must be said that, by 1993, any editor who'd looked at the sexual abuse issue squarely should have had no doubts about the scope of the scandal. But for those who shied away from taking on a powerful institution, for those who were looking for a reason not to have to write about it and for those in the Church and in the press who just couldn't believe such a thing could be so widespread, the Bernardin case gave them an out.

A second, related reason the story did not have resonance 15 years ago is that even those in the media who understood the dimensions of the scandal were constrained by the very nature of the subject matter. You were not just taking on a powerful and popular institution, you were writing about a crime that seasoned police reporters often tiptoed around.

My original *Mercury News* series ran in the middle of the week, not on a Sunday, and below the fold in what is the deadest news week in the year. My editors gave me time to report it and they published it. But it wasn't as if we were proud of it. Bush's appalled gut-level reaction was my paper's – and, in a way, my own as well. When my editors urged me to wrap up the follow stories by early spring so I could cover the 1988 presidential campaign, I protested only mildly. I wrote about the issue intermittently until 1990 – additional victims kept calling me, but we acted as though we had 'done' the story. For his part, Berry got a cool reception at many of the magazines he approached. Henderson's editors moved her off the story and sent her to a suburban bureau. Even after our appearance on the Donahue show, Berry's book proposal was rejected 30 times before he won a contract.

What's different now? One factor, says *National Journal* media critic Bill Powers, is the increased willingness in journalism to write about sexual issues, even distasteful ones. 'I think one reason this story is finally taking off can be summed up in two words: Monica Lewinsky,' Powers says. 'Before that scandal, the news media were still very chary about any stories with explicit sexual conduct . . . It's hard to remember this now, but ten years ago it was strange and really pretty shocking to see detailed discussions of sex acts in the newspaper. In the post-Monica world, that sort of thing is business as usual and shocks nobody. This is a very significant cultural shift, one that I think made it possible for paedophilia in the Church finally to go front page, above the fold, and become the enormous story it always should have been.'

It's instructive to recall the initial reaction of then *New York Times* Washington Bureau Chief RW Apple Jr to Paula Corbin Jones's sexual harassment suit against President Clinton. 'I am not interested in Bill Clinton's sex life as governor of Arkansas,' Apple said. 'I'm certain there are a lot of readers who are interested in that and there are lots of publications they can turn to to slake that thirst.'

But this point leads to a third reason the priest story finally caught fire: in 2002, this story broke in news outlets with real power. Put simply, on issues pertaining to the Catholic Church, the *Boston Globe* is a publication with the clout to set the agenda for elite East Coast media outlets. Kristen Lombardi herself, although she writes for the *Boston Phoenix*, is quick to give credit to the competition.

Lombardi also believes that the fact that this happened in Boston, the fourth largest archdiocese in the nation, made the story impossible to ignore. No one understands this better than Tom Fox, now publisher of the *National Catholic Reporter*, who has probably dealt with this issue longer than any media executive in the USA. In a piece done by religion writer Kelly McBride for the Poynter Institute's website on this very point – why this story is big now – Fox observed: 'The light and the heat that comes from that kind of exposure that the East Coast media gives to a subject is substantial and feeds on itself.' Fox adds that getting the secret deliberations of a cardinal out in the open was a revelation. 'It's like the Nixon tapes,' Fox says. 'Anyone can see from the documents the course [of the Church] was not pastoral, it was defensive and legalistic.'

To be sure, one can go too far with this argument. A search of the database shows that the *New York Times* covered the issue continually, if sporadically, starting as early as 4 May 1986. In my attic, I found a dog-eared *Times* clip dated 10 February 1988 that cites my original series – and even quotes from it: 'The church's reluctance to address the problem is a time bomb waiting to detonate with American Catholicism.'

This caveat, in turn, leads to another explanation of why this story is so big now: the dearth of institutional memory. Journalists usually don't sweat this lack of institutional memory. How many stories are truly new anyway? Or, as editor Dale Cockerill, an old-timer at the *Mercury News* when I was there 20 years ago, used to quip, 'That story is so old it's new.' This dynamic applies to this story. And though that means that some of the coverage can be jarring because it lacks context, the inverse is true as well: this scandal is all the greater precisely because the story has been around so long. In other words, there is simply no excuse for a bishop not to have figured that when he gets one of these cases, the only possible ethical response is to remove the priest immediately; call the cops; make an honest effort to find all the victims; deal with the problem publicly, even if that means opening your diocese to further lawsuits; treat the kids and the parents – and all the other parishioners – humanely. That this wasn't being done ten and 15 years after the 1985 Doyle/Mouton/Peterson report and half a dozen years after the bishops in the early 1990s adopted guidelines for dealing with this problem made the story more horrific, not less.

Lombardi put it this way: 'As I was digging into this issue last year, I often found myself pondering this one nagging question: Why is this still happening in the Catholic Church? Why do we still see victims come forward, only to experience a hostile reaction from Church officials, only to then seek out a lawyer and then suffer from the Church's aggressive legal tactics? Why are there still cases of pedophile priests in the Catholic Church after all these years? Isn't it time that the Church has wised up about clergy sexual abuse? After all the knowledge that the Church has had and accumulated, this problem should have been addressed – if not eliminated – by now.'

I certainly assumed the Church had dealt with this issue. I'm told today that some dioceses did and that others (such as Boston) may grudgingly have improved their approach to dealing with new allegations but never quite came clean with their old cases – and are now paying the price. To journalists who've come to this issue recently, it may seem inconceivable that Church officials would put a premium on keeping this issue quiet instead of dealing with it. But there is a context for that, too.

In the mid-1980s, theologically conservative Church officials were trying to avoid 'The Conversation': that is, a candid discussion of the subculture of homosexuality in the priesthood and the related issues of whether celibacy, and an all-male priesthood for that matter, are sustainable. For their part, liberals in the media had a conversation that they were avoiding as well: why do the vast majority of these priest molestation cases involve boys or male teenagers? To admit this was, in some quarters of the press, tantamount to giving ammunition to homophobes.

Well, the sheer magnitude of the scandal has overwhelmed both of those taboos: the bishops are now having 'The Conversation', like it or not. It is being led by none other than Jason Berry, who confronted both sacred cows – the bishops and the gays – in a 3 April *New York Times* op-ed headlined 'Secrets, Celibacy, and the Church'. ❏

Carl M Cannon *covers the White House for* National Journal. *A longer version of this article appeared in* American Journalism Review (*May 2002*)

THE EPIC THAT WILL NOT DIE

IRENA MARYNIAK

IN ROMANIA, AS IN MUCH OF EAST AND
CENTRAL EUROPE, THE GHOSTS OF
COMMUNISM STALK THE CHANCELLERIES
AND HOLD ALL THE LEVERS OF POWER.
TRUTH COMPETES WITH SILENCE FOR THE
PUBLIC EAR AND RECONCILIATION IS A
LONG WAY DOWN THE ROAD

'It won't matter what you write, really,' the NGO consultant said. 'Nobody will know.' He had been in Bucharest throughout the 1990s and was in the know. But he didn't want to be named. 'Think of this as background. Ceauşescu's secret service people are an elite – like the aristocracy back in the UK. After 1990, they were well placed to get round the bureaucracy and act as entrepreneurs. And they're better operatives. It may be crony capitalism but you can see it pragmatically.'

My Romanian interlocutors seemed less inclined towards pragmatism, and their narratives were bolder, more colourful: tales of malevolent ghosts, corruption, revolution, and a dotty dictator summarily executed on Christmas Day who laid waste his country's heritage and demolished a third of its capital to rebuild it as Europe's Pyongyang.

Thirteen years on, the boulevards of Bucharest are choked with rattling traffic and desolate or cheerful poverty, while people fish in the thick, mossy river. And here in a cloistered courtyard, with birches and poplars tall as the Orthodox church next door and a complex of creaking staircases reminiscent of Maurits Escher's, you can sit drinking beer or tepid tea and hear tales of the great and powerful, of secret agendas and opaque intentions. With weary dogs sniffing at your feet, you can participate in the informal wars of narrative that drive the Romanian body politic.

But out there in the rigid geometry of the Piata Unirii or the echoing spaces of the metro the stories seem to be fewer. In Nicolae Ceauşescu's vast 'House of the People' (now Romania's parliament), or on national television, or in history books, narratives still hang on vestiges of tattered epics that legislate, reassure and warn. The ideological and national myths taught in schools in the Ceauşescu era are not quite buried, and there are new myths, too, about heroes of the 1989 revolution such as pro-Nazi dictator Marshal Ion Antonescu, or the leaders of the new Romania: Prime Minister Adrian Nastase (cosmopolitan, sophisticated, wealthy) and President Ion Iliescu (man of the people).

The assumption that Romania's voters don't need a multiplicity of credible narratives, but do need fantasy and myth, still obtains. There are narratives that legislate, and narratives that subvert: the first must be promoted and the second suppressed. Because, as one major journalist wrote in 1999 during a press campaign against the rewriting of the national-communist version of history, some myths 'are indispensable to the self-esteem of any nation'. They satisfy an affective longing for received Truth.

The discrepancy between experience and expression that characterised life under communist regimes lives on and communication, as ever, prefers the private domain. If there is inadequate discourse in the public space and only titles, functions or party cards actually matter, real stories – the puzzles and the speculations – thrive in kitchens, bedrooms, church enclosures and a few publications with limited circulation.

Stories about revolution, for example. In 1989, the world witnessed two summary executions, dancing crowds, unexplained gunfire, a military response and the deaths of 1,100 people. 'Terrorists' were arrested, but no one was formally charged. What happened? Did the former communists of the National Salvation Front (now the governing Social Democratic Party [PDSR]) 'steal' the revolution? Or was it not a revolution at all but a messy intervention manipulated by foreign security forces: the KGB, the Hungarians or the Americans?

Stories about World War II. Can it be true that in 1941 a 'death train' packed with Jews circulated between cities until everyone aboard had starved to death? Or that Marshal Antonescu, executed in 1946, was responsible for the deaths of over 300,000 Jews?

Or stories about Prime Minister Nastase's former career. Did you know that in the 1980s he was Ceauşescu's 'human rights ambassador' in Strasbourg, Norway or Brussels? That he now controls the main financial resources of his party, the PDSR? And that this summer he took a holiday in a Black Sea resort and had the area around his villa plunged into silence on pain of rigorous controls and hefty fines? Beach muzak was turned off, concerts cancelled at a few hours' notice, bars instructed to cooperate and 20,000 tourists had to make do.

More intriguing still are the personal connections mulled over in cafés or hinted at in broadsheets read by urban intellectuals: the pointers to who may be who in a country where no one really knows. The story that Nastase had ties with the former head of the parliamentary committee overseeing Romania's foreign intelligence, Ristea Priboi. That, years ago, Priboi trained Nastase to be a Securitate agent in the West. And that Nastase withdrew his backing after the publication of documents showing that Priboi had worked in the department that coordinated attacks on Radio Free Europe, including a bombing in 1981. Priboi resigned from the intelligence committee, but remained an MP.

Or the one about President Iliescu who did so well under Mikhail Gorbachev and must have been KGB-controlled in Moscow in the 1950s because he was president of the foreign students' association there. Extraordinary too that his Securitate file was reported to have been found almost empty. 'The documents just seemed to break off . . .' Or about Dan Voiculescu who collected tax from international deals to the tune of US$60 million in Cyprus, returned home after the revolution to build an empire in business and the media and is now in partnership with the government. Or hotel magnate George Paunescu who worked in the Romanian consulate in Italy in the 1980s and was expelled for spying but now owns a string of hotels, a football team and is one of the most prominent figures in Romanian business.

And so it goes on. Things get said (though scarcely ever on television) or occasionally published (though not in the tabloids most people read). Journalists face frequent lawsuits. In December 2001, the 'most deserving' reporters, those who had told the right stories, were reportedly offered money, gifts or holidays in the mountains.

'The Romanian present is haunted by *strigoi* – ghosts, monsters,' says Horia-Roman Patapievici, a prominent member of the National Council for the Study of Securitate Archives (CNSAS). 'Politicians elected by voters who are unaware of their background are virtually all from the *nomenklatura*: former Securitate agents, administrators, directors, inspectors. They've been rebaptised, but the internal rationality of old institutions has been preserved. This travesties social relationships, ownership and justice; it falsifies the culture institutionally, politically, economically.'

Those who had what it took to reinvent themselves after 1989 often worked abroad, people say – in foreign trade, for example. They travelled smoothly as Securitate agents, returned in the 1990s and, thanks to their

*'The Merry Cemetery', Sapanta, Romania 2002: laughing all the way to the grave. The
dead have no secrets here, their lives exposed in comic and curious carvings and verses
memorialising their faults and foibles. The 2,000-year-old tradition is continued by
woodcarver and versifier Dumitru Pop. Credit: Dan Comanescu / NYT*

experience and expertise, are now negotiating for Romanian entry into
NATO and the EU. Yet the idea that anyone might be prepared freely to
discuss these connections is unthinkable. Either the memory is associated
with intense shame or too much is at stake. 'No one is proud of what they
did under Ceauşescu,' journalist Dan Perjovschi of *Revista 22* says. Historians
are still reluctant to speculate on the number of people arrested but it is
widely accepted that 300,000 never returned from prisons and camps. The
Securitate tapped, intercepted, bugged, followed people and sat in cars
outside their homes. It employed or coerced up to 700,000 informers who
wrote reports on colleagues, family and friends. In a country of 20 million,
an estimated 1.2 million people were watched and a collection of about
2 million files was built up.

These days, the main concern of politicians is to build a future that will protect them from their past. Research on security matters is discouraged and, as biographies are hidden and lives rewritten, the fictions grow. 'We are prisoners of rumours and scenarios,' TV talk-show host and writer Stelian Tanase says. 'Facts are ignored. We exist in a second-hand reality unable to live fully, challenge things and change. The past is everywhere.'

Romania is not alone. Everyone over 30 in East Central Europe has a doppelgänger, a 'double' – the turncoat he or she was or might have been – that other, merged identity ready to come up and bite you in the night, compromise and expose you, or destroy any faith in loyalty and friendship. In 1998, Vaclav Havel had to revoke an award to former Vienna mayor Helmut Rilk amid claims that the Austrian had once had links with the Czech secret police. In Hungary and Poland, 'lustrations' or screening procedures are being reviewed and revived. Hungarian Prime Minister Peter Medgessy has admitted that he was a counterintelligence agent between 1977 and 1982. The names of a further ten former government ministers who appear to have been involved in the secret services have been leaked. The choice, according to Peter Gyorgy of Budapest University (ELTE), is between de-stabilisation if too many MPs are compromised and a paralysis of public suspicion if names are not formally released. In Poland, a former aide of President Lech Walesa, Tadeusz Kwiatkowski, was found recently to have been registered with the security service in the 1970s, and an MP in the new socialist government has come under investigation.

But the Romanian case stands out because of the tightness with which things were bound, the sheer numbers of informers and the fact that those recruited were not, generally speaking, party members. Ceauşescu pursued a policy of keeping the Securitate and the party separate. Many political prisoners were terrorised into collaboration or released on condition that they wrote reports on their friends. Known informers have argued – outrageously, victims might feel – that they did the job to protect their surveyees from others who might have been more ruthless or inventive. In any case, after the 1989 revolution, the anti-communist opposition absorbed many people who must have collaborated. 'It wasn't us and them,' Perjovschi says, '"we" were also "them". "We" were part of it. In the early 1990s everything seemed black and white. When it turned out that all these great anti-communists were informers all the moral arguments collapsed.'

This crisis of identity and personal narrative has left Romanians with little to hang on to except the hope that materially, at least, things might improve. Incomes average US$100 a month, there is rising unemployment and 30% inflation. The West represents a house, a car and liberation from an economy in which people have to smuggle clothes out of Turkey or work in Italy, say, and send their earnings home by informal shuttle bus from Rome. Though Romania is rated twelfth in the queue for EU accession, 76% of those questioned in a July opinion poll said Europe is what they want. 'We have to belong to something to preserve ourselves,' Perjovschi says. 'I was East Central European after 1990, East European after 1996 and now I'm South European or Balkan. Better belong to Europe than not know who you are.'

Romania's *strigoi*, its present leaders, have not been blind to the necessity of improving Romania's credibility abroad. A law giving access to Securitate files, fragile and full of loopholes as it is, has been one of a series of measures introduced in anticipation of the November NATO summit in Prague at which Romania hopes to be invited to join the alliance. Others include a property restitution law, a strategy for the better integration of Romania's 2 million gypsies, a law giving minorities the right to use their own language in dealings with the authorities, the banning of fascist symbols and the intro-duction of Holocaust teaching in schools. President Iliescu has been recon-ciled with Romania's exiled King Michael after decades of animosity. And following a report in the *Wall Street Journal* that NATO may be reluctant to share its classified information with ex-Securitate officials, it was hurriedly announced that anyone likely to have access to NATO secrets will be screened. But the defence minister also warned newspapers that had reprinted the *WSJ* article that life is short and health too valuable to endanger it by launching 'stressful debates'. The ministry later explained that the comments were meant to be 'satirical'.

It took six years of debate to pass a law stipulating that people running for public office must submit to verification – enough time, critics say, for political parties to jettison Securitate collaborators quietly or destroy the evidence. Since March 2001, everyone has had the right, in theory, to see his file. But only after it has been examined and cleared for breaches of national security by a joint commission of the current intelligence service (SRI) and the CNSAS. According to Patapievici, parliament is now pushing to subordi-nate this commission to another one that controls the SRI.

The CNSAS is a nominally independent body that should, by law, control all Securitate archives. It represents a range of political views including those of a small, isolated group of radical former dissidents who have managed to attract media attention but aren't influential enough to bring much into the open. 'The problem is each time they've come close (they had files on the Church and media people) the documents weren't made public. Even though they know the truth,' says Alina Mungiu-Pippidi, director of the Romanian Academic Society. The files of the old Central Committee have been transferred to the army. Others are held by the interior ministry, the foreign ministry and the SRI. The existence of files that could be embarrassing is generally denied and the CNSAS has no appropriate budget for premises to store the miles of paperwork. 'There's a constant sense of doubt. People who get their files don't know if they're complete or touched up. We don't have the whole picture; it's like looking through a keyhole,' Patapievici says. Only the files of people who informed to get out of prison seem to be readily available.

Attempts by CNSAS 'radicals' Patapievici, Mircea Dinescu and Andrei Plesu to make public the names of Securitate officers, as well as informers, provoked an unprecedentedly sharp response from the SRI. 'They threatened us with prison,' Patapievici said. 'Now we're completely barred. They say it's classified information. The law prohibits the current secret service from employing people who were in the political police before 1989. So if they're in the service, they're there illegally. And of course they are. We have proof.' The names of small-time informers peripheral to the Securitate are being released while its former management is protected. Meanwhile, Prime Minister Nastase has accused the CNSAS of squeezing advantages from government-funded jobs.

But in comparison to former East Germany, where 3.4 million people asked to see Stasi files between 1992 and 1997, demand in Romania has been muted. 'Those who are sensitive to the past are the victims,' says Andrei Pippidi, director of the Romanian Institute for Recent History. 'Most people prefer to ignore a reality which was systematically concealed and distorted. They may have benefited from the former regime as peasants who moved into town and got jobs. There's also a feeling that it would be better for common wealth and public peace to forget. People learned to keep silent about their past – the Holocaust, the political crimes of the 1930s, the brutality after 1947 that blotted out much of what had gone before. Hardship, humiliation, even happier times were inconvenient to recall and memories weren't passed on down the generations. It was meant to protect the children, save them from the dangerous consequences of casual imprudence. Family history, when it was not suppressed, became secret. Private censorship was added to official surveillance.'

Now that files are beginning to be available there is also the question whether the narratives they contain can be treated as serious evidence. Should the tales of tell-tales serve as historical and legal interventions? Can the stories and documents of forgers, tricksters and mischievous masters of play be used as reliable sources of information? Can lustration or screening be politically neutral and avoid being a witch-hunt masquerading as a quest for truth? In Poland, President Lech Walesa was accused of working for the Sluzba Bezpieczenstwa (SB) until a 1985 interior ministry report was found detailing the use of professional forgers to fabricate documents which made it look as though Walesa was a paid agent. Prime Minister Aleksander Kwasniewski was similarly cleared. In September 2000, *Gazeta Wyborcza* editor Adam Michnik wrote in an open letter to Prime Minister Jerzy Buzek: 'You can't judge people or their behaviour under the dictatorship on the basis of SB archives or the reports of SB functionaries. They are not trustworthy. Both you and I remember these characters and their methods . . . the lies, the blackmail, the provocation. What makes you believe (as I cannot) that these people can be a source of real knowledge about you, me or our friends from the Solidarity underground?'

But if the files are no more than misleading curiosities, where does that leave Truth, Reconciliation, Historical Reckoning and Justice or, indeed, the sanity of those who were victimised? Documents are proof at least, as Patapievici says 'that it wasn't all hallucination, paranoia'. Gabriel Andreescu of the Romanian Helsinki Committee feels that any notion of a South African-style Truth and Reconciliation Commission is a non-starter. 'We need law, real justice in police courts. "Truth" and "reconciliation" have no practical meaning. What truth? Run by whom? We can't get at the truth because of continuous resistance from the Securitate and the Communist Party. That's how it's been with the CNSAS. Justice presupposes independent courts and the security of functioning institutions. We need political change to shape real institutions that would do a real job.'

At the moment, any idea of just reparation for victims and their families is notional, though one case in particular has attracted attention. It concerns Gheorghe Ursu, jailed in the 1980s for keeping a diary that fell into the hands of his factory colleagues who passed it on to the Securitate. Ursu was jailed and in 1985 beaten to death apparently on Securitate instructions. The case was later brought to trial by his son and remains unresolved. Here the more recent stories begin: the judges seem set against the victim, the defendants are said to be hugely wealthy, those involved have risen to the status of chiefs of tribunals in the ministry of justice. 'They feel secure enough to be offensive,' Andreescu says. 'There's no chance of touching them.'

Today, the professionalism of communist security service operatives is internationally recognised, their morality publicly abhorred and tacitly accepted. It is a state of things which makes people such as Patapievici very bitter. 'Jack Straw once said something like: "Before 1989 you spied on us. But we did the same to you. Discussion closed." This is astonishingly cynical. Europe condemned lustrations in the Czech republic in the early 1990s as "discriminatory". Imagine saying that of the Nazis. The West has failed to make any outright condemnation of communism as social practice and criminal ideology. This has prevented the economic, juridical and political development of Romania. The apparatchiks are still in charge.'

Hungary's socialist prime minister, Peter Medgessy, has made some political capital out of an open hearing on his former secret service job. His performance was confident, decisive and sophisticated. He emerged as a professional, a man who knows how things work, now leading a party with impeccable credentials on matters such as racism, anti-Semitism and tolerance to neighbouring countries. Earlier this year, he was the first Hungarian prime minister to attend Roma Holocaust Memorial Day. If he chooses to stay in office, there isn't much about him at the moment that's likely to raise eyebrows in Brussels. A more sensitive issue is his possible connection with the KGB, which he continues to deny, and the question of whether Russia's presumed possession of compromising data on him and other agents from Hungary and elsewhere could erode NATO's confidence in its new Central European allies.

However NATO chooses to deal with this issue, the old communist security network will remain a presence, a fact of life, a *fait accompli* like Ceauşescu's 'House of the People'. It may disperse in time as the world moves on and the *nomenklatura's* children – well travelled, western-educated, less stodgy – take on the burden. But for the moment its undeclared interests, prejudices, loyalties, suspicions and anxieties drive East Central European politics and make the ghosts of the past very present. ❏

Irena Maryniak

institute for war & peace reporting

Public Record of Afghanistan's Loya Jirga

In June, Afghanistan held its first open political event in more than 20 years when 1,600 delegates at the Emergency Loya Jirga elected Hamed Karzai president and endorsed a transitional government for the next two years.

IWPR has created a public record of the Loya Jirga. On the scene with seven Afghan reporters, we wrote over 15,000 words of news and analysis during the ten days, and recorded all 70 hours the Jirga was in session.

The Loya Jirga Public Archive, funded by the International Organisation of Migration and in cooperation with Bakhtar Information Agency, is a unique public record of the most important open public event in Afghanistan's modern history. The CD-ROM and book contains a full, searchable transcript of the proceedings in the original languages (Dari and Pashto) in Microsoft Word format, and selected highlights, a timeline and IWPR's own reports in English.

The book and CD are being distributed free in Afghanistan to local and international media organisations, government bodies and NGOs. They are also available from our London office. The full transcript of the proceedings is also viewable on the web at: http://www.iwpr.net/index.pl?afghan_index.html

Lancaster House
33 Islington High Street
London N1 9LH UK

Tel: (44 20) 7713 7130
Fax: (44 20) 7713 7140
Web: www.iwpr.net
E-mail: info@iwpr.net

THE UNQUIET GRAVE

VERA RICH

EVEN AFTER DEATH, THE BODY POLITIC MAY RISE AND DISPUTE THE RESTING PLACE OF THE FALLEN

Some 50km from Minsk, the capital of Belarus, lies the 'memorial complex' of Khatyn. Once a flourishing village, it was destroyed by the Nazis during World War II. All that remains of its houses are the chimney stacks; birch trees, planted at three corners of a square, the fourth being empty, commemorate the 'every fourth one' that Belarus lost during that war.

A touching memorial? Yes, but also a cynical piece of disinformation. For the Khatyn complex was created in the 1960s as the Kremlin's answer to inconvenient enquiries about Katyn in the Russian Federation where, in April 1940, several thousand Polish officers – taken prisoner after the Soviet invasion of Poland in September 1939 – were massacred on Stalin's orders. Not even the Soviet propaganda machine could deny that the officers were dead; instead, it maintained that the killings had taken place in 1942 under the Nazi occupation. And visiting Western politicians asking questions about Katyn on behalf of Polish-born constituents found themselves taken to *Khatyn*. No mention was made in Soviet histories of 'Khatyn' – until 'Katyn' began to prove embarrassing. Anglo-Saxon mispronunciation of the Cyrillic phonemes aided and abetted the Soviet deception.

Soviet responsibility for Katyn, and other massacres of Polish officers at sites in Russia and Ukraine, was acknowledged early on by the post-communist leaders of those countries, and the Poles were enabled to establish proper cemeteries, where memorial Masses could be said and relatives of the victims could come on pilgrimage.

Yet in Belarus Soviet atrocities continue to be denied. Back in 1988, it became public knowledge that the popular picnic site of Kurapaty on the outskirts of Minsk had served as an execution ground during the Stalinist terror of 1937–41. The site was duly excavated by archaeologists, and the objects found with the bodies (items of leather clothing, coins and other objects from pockets, and, above all, shoes) were classified. To everyone but diehard communists, the excavations irrefutably established that these were the victims of Stalin's purges and mass round-ups, taken in many cases

Katyn, USSR 1989: Polish woman mourns Polish officers massacred in 1940 on Stalin's orders.
Credit: AFP / Wojtek Druszcz

directly from their homes to the killing field. Trusting in Moscow's new policy of glasnost (openness), elderly witnesses came forward to talk of the fence around the site in the late 1930s and the shooting heard from behind that fence. But to the hardline officialdom of the then Belarusan SSR, the culprits were, once again, the Nazis.

As in most of the USSR at that time, new patriotic and pro-democracy 'informal associations' were springing up in Belarus. These pressed for further investigations at Kurapaty and a proper memorial. A ten-metre-high cross with a barbed-wire 'crown of thorns' was erected, pending a future, more substantial monument. However, since Alaksandr Lukashenka became president of Belarus in 1994, official 'doubts' about Kurapaty have become increasingly vocal – in line with Lukashenka's apparent ambition to recreate the Soviet Union with himself at the head, and the current rewriting of Belarusan history textbooks by presidential apparatchiks.

And so, in 1998, the Belarusan prosecutor-general Aleh Bazhelka declared officially that it was 'still unknown' who, in fact, was buried at Kurapaty. In his version of events, the original investigation had been carried out in an 'extremely unobjective manner', by 'specialists from the Institute of Archaeology [correctly History] of the Academy of Sciences, and the person leading it was Zianon Pazniak'. Partly as a result of his discoveries at Kurapaty, Pazniak later became leader of the pro-democracy, pro-independence Belarusan Popular Front and, in 1994, challenged Lukashenka for the presidency. He is now a political exile in Poland.

In 2001, plans to extend the Minsk ringroad were announced. This would, in effect, have driven through and destroyed the Kurapaty site. But the bulldozers were forestalled by young patriots who saw the defence of Kurapaty as part of the fight to retain their country's independence. In spite of repeated, forceful attempts by the police to eject them, the Kurapaty squatters stayed in occupation throughout the severity of the Belarusan winter. Eventually, the plans for the road were amended to bypass the site – at least for the moment.

Other 'successor states' are less squeamish about Soviet crimes. In September 1939, thousands of Polish civilians fell into Soviet hands and were deported to the Russian Arctic, Siberia and Central Asia (*Index* 3/2002). After Hitler's invasion of the Soviet Union, they were grudgingly allowed to leave and make their way via Iran to safety. Many thousands perished in the appalling conditions of this exodus and at the assembly point in Uzbekistan. In the early 1990s, the Uzbek government set up a provisional memorial, with a small Latin cross and inscriptions in Uzbek and English, and in 1999 it was reported that negotiations were under way with the Polish government for a more substantial monument with an inscription in Polish.

But political changes and new borders can leave survivors cut off from their dead on the wrong side of the line. When only ordinary citizens are affected, even the most stringent regime may make concessions: even under the communists, the Budapest–Bratislava morning bus on All Souls' Day was crowded with Hungarian pensioners taking candles and bunches of chrysanthemums to ancestral graves in (hardline) Slovakia.

But when the dead are 'heroes' who fought against what has become the ruling regime, the situation is more delicate. During the twentieth century, the city known – according to the regime in power – as Lemburg, L'vov, Lwów or L'viv has changed rulers at least eight times. In the inter-war years, it formed part of the Polish Second Republic and the Poles duly consecrated there a cemetery of the 'Eaglets', Polish students who, in the Polish–Ukrainian conflict of 1921, had died defending the city 'for Poland'. But when the Soviet Union annexed the area in 1939, all physical traces of the Austrian and Polish past were either destroyed or, in the case of institutions, renamed. The 'Eaglets' cemetery was laid waste and its memorial destroyed.

When Ukraine became independent, the surviving ethnic Polish inhabitants of what was now L'viv, supported by their compatriots in Poland and the worldwide Polish diaspora, petitioned for the 'Eaglets' cemetery to be restored. The city fathers agreed, the site of the graves was located and put in order, new plans for a memorial drawn up, and a provisional date fixed for the dedication. But then came the problem: what inscription should the monument bear? 'The same as before,' said the Poles. But for the Ukrainians, flushed with their regained independence and committed to their government's policy of 'state building', this was going too far. Recognising the bravery of former enemies was one thing; wording that implied a Polish claim to L'viv was something very different.

The local Ukrainian press vehemently attacked the proposed monument. Old scores and old grievances were refurbished on both sides. When Polish and Ukrainian prime ministers or presidents met, the cemetery inevitably appeared on their agenda. And, after every meeting, press releases from Kyiv and Warsaw would announce a new date – and in L'viv the rows and recriminations would burst out afresh. The latest such date, 21 July 2002, has now passed into oblivion. In mid-August, official Ukrainian condolences to Poland on the flood disaster included, almost routinely, a commitment to the dedication of the cemetery and monument. But when, and with what inscription, neither side knows. ❑

Vera Rich is a freelance journalist specialising in Russian and Central European affairs. She is the publisher of Manifold, *an independent poetry magazine*

THE HOUSE OF BURNED BOOKS

STACY MARKING

SEVENTY YEARS AFTER THE NOTORIOUS
BOOK BURNINGS BY THE NAZI REGIME
IN GERMANY, THE PHENOMENON IS STILL
ALIVE AND KICKING, MOST NOTABLY IN
THE UNITED STATES

The point of burning a book is visibility: the public display of a book in its death throes. Burning a book is qualitatively different from merely suppressing it. Where censorship is a means of social control, an attempt to impose order, book burning is essentially *disorderly*. It is populist and often out of control. It requires passion. Those who fling books on to flames often talk about purging, purification, exorcising, punishment, revenge. Redolent of witch burning, book burning involves something superstitious and magical: given its association with sorcery and magic, little wonder that JK Rowling's *Harry Potter* books are the most burned of this century so far.

One might suppose that the Nazi bonfires in 1933 caused such universal outrage and condemnation that book burning would have stopped for ever, if only in aid of better public relations. But 'the history of reading is lit by a seemingly endless line of censors' bonfires,' writes Albert Manguel in *The History of Reading*. In an era of mass communication, burning has become a gesture of theatre, to mark a protest or to invoke fear. But books are still burning well in 2002.

There have been examples in Tblisi (material by Jehovah's Witnesses), Cairo (eighth-century homoerotic poetry), Kashmir, Jakarta. Reports of regular burnings in the last year range from the religious right in the USA (work deemed 'scripturally unsound' or even 'liberal') to the Communist Party in Vietnam (western pornography and the diary of General Tran Do, their erstwhile hero).

On 10 May 2003, it will be 70 years since the Nazis burned books in Berlin. While 20,000 books were burning, Joseph Goebbels, the minister of propaganda and public enlightenment, addressed a crowd of over 100,000, emphasising the symbolic nature of the event: 'Tonight you do well to throw in the fire these obscenities from the past. This is a powerful, huge and symbolic action that will tell the entire world that the old spirit is dead. From these ashes will rise the phoenix of the new spirit.'

Munich 2002: Georg and his books. Georg Salzmann has dedicated his life to the collection of works by all the authors whose books were burned in May 1933. Many of his 10,000 volumes are now rare, their authors fallen into obscurity as successive German governments have failed to rehabilitate them. 'If these writers are forgotten,' says Salzmann, 'The Nazis will have won.' Credit: Stacy Marking

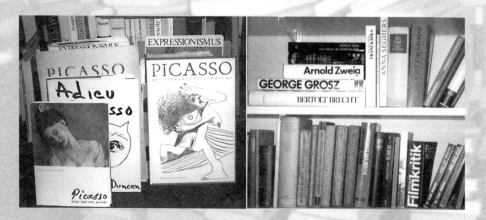

The list of books that Goebbels chose to burn is all too familiar: Catholic, Jewish, Marxist (500 tons of it) and 'un-German' authors – Albert Einstein, Sigmund Freud, Heinrich and Thomas Mann (classified as degenerate), Erich Maria Remarque, Bertolt Brecht, Maxim Gorky, VI Lenin, Karl Marx, Joseph Stalin, Leon Trotsky, Marcel Proust, Emil Zola, HG Wells, Arnold and Stefan Zweig, Jack London, Ernest Hemingway, Upton Sinclair, Sinclair Lewis, John Steinbeck, John Dos Passos and Helen Keller (who ironically had given in perpetuity all royalties from her books to German soldiers blinded in World War I).

There followed a conflagration of 'Degenerate Art', involving 1,004 paintings and sculptures, and 3,825 drawings and watercolours, many from museums and city galleries. They were burned 'as an exercise' in the courtyard of the Berlin Fire Department. The journalist Walter Lippmann noted that 'the ominous symbolism of these bonfires is that there is a government in Germany which means to teach its people that their salvation lies in violence'.

In Munich, there is an extraordinary private library of virtually all the titles that were burned in 1933. They have been collected by Georg Salzmann, the son of a dedicated Nazi who committed suicide when Germany lost the war, who has spent his life and most of his disposable income on this rather valuable collection, which he has now offered to Munich. There is an imaginative scheme for it to be housed beneath Königsplatz, the plaza that Hitler declared 'the ceremonial centre of his movement'. But the city, which has never fully come to terms with its Nazi past, and the Munich authorities, presumably embarrassed by the offer, seem incapable of recognising this opportunity for restitution, and the library may now go to Washington.

Not all cultures burn books. In the former Soviet Union, books and manuscripts were not burned but preserved. The books seized by OGPU (later the KGB) were carefully recorded, copied, filed and stored. After *glasnost*, the official censor boasted that it was thanks to him that, for instance, Solzhenitsyn's manuscripts were saved. That was certainly true of Mikhail Bulgakov's diaries. Seized by the OGPU in 1926, they were returned in 1929 and Bulgakov immediately burned them himself. Sixty years later, the KGB admitted it had made copies and the entire text was published (*Index* August/September 1991).

But there were exceptions. In *Crucifying the Orient*, Kalpana Sahni records that the Soviets publicly burned Arabic and Persian works as they forced ethnic minorities (Uzbeks, Kazakhs, Turkmen, Ossetians, Tajiks, Kurds) to adopt the Russian script. 'The mere fact of being in possession of a book in the Arabic [and Persian] script was sufficient grounds for imprisonment and death. Fear drove many to the destruction of priceless libraries . . . There were bonfires of books in the Arabic script in the main city squares of Bokhara, Kiva, Baku.' In the 1990s, the Serbs, too, burned valuable collections of Islamic manuscripts.

China has a history of denying its history. Mao's Cultural Revolution was in fact part of a long and ardent tradition. The rewriting of China's history began with the Emperor Tsin-Shih-Hwang, builder of the Great Wall. Wishing to be the First Emperor of China, in 213 BCE he ordered that on pain of death every existing document should be burned: 'Destroy the written records and the past ceases to exist.'

Another 60-year period on, fragments of the old records were found and history reconstructed. But the story does not turn out happily. The new Emperor ordered that the Five Confucian Classics should be carved in their entirety on huge tablets of non-flammable stone, but mobs infuriated by the cost of the project smashed them into fragments. In *Wild Swans*, Yung Chan describes an identical riot smashing identical rock inscriptions (*Index* 6/1999).

Sincerely believing Mao's maxim 'the destruction of the old is a way of creating something better', the young Red Guards began to burn books by the million. Books were major targets of Mao's order to destroy. Because they had not been written within the last few months, and therefore did not quote Mao on every page, some Red Guards declared that they were 'poisonous weeds'. 'Books were burning all across China. The country lost most of its written heritage,' writes Jung Chang.

Other Maoist regimes, such as Pol Pot's in Cambodia and Sendero Luminoso's in Peru, also followed Lin Piao's exhortation that everything representing the old culture should be destroyed, and there is no doubting the sincerity and fervour of these young burners.

Though there are often more protesters than burners, bonfires in the USA are mainly inspired by the morality of the religious right. They have become a Sunday evening ritual for many congregations. Material for a recent bonfire near Pittsburgh included the 'Bible' of the Jehovah's Witnesses, *The Book of Mormon*, Bruce Springsteen CDs and a video of Disney's *Pinocchio*. With no detectable irony, the pastor declared that *Harry Potter* was 'the big flashpoint'. When a Christian group in Maine proposed last November to burn JK Rowling's books for 'encouraging witchcraft, occult practices, and even rebelliousness among children', the fire department refused them a permit on the grounds that public book burning constituted a fire hazard. Instead, they held a 'book cutting' ceremony, a somewhat comical exercise lacking both the symbolism and power of burning.

The US has quite a tradition of burning books. The US Post Office was responsible for the burning of James Joyce's *Ulysses*, published in serial form in *The Little Review* between 1919 and 1920. Its publisher and editor, Margaret Anderson, says: 'It was like a burning at the stake as far as I was concerned . . . the tears, prayers, hysterics and rages we used on printer, binder, paper houses; the addressing, wrapping, stamping, mailing; the excitement of anticipating the world's response to the literary masterpiece of our generation . . . And then the notice from the Post Office: BURNED.' Anderson moved to Paris, and Joyce came to believe that his work would never be published. When at last *The Dubliners* was printed, he described how 'some very kind person bought out the entire edition and had it burned in Dublin – a new and private *auto-da-fé*'.

These moral bonfires persist through the decades: Kathleen Winsor's bodice-ripper *Forever Amber*, which sold 100,000 copies in its first week, banned and then burned in the streets of Boston in 1944; Irving Wallace's *The Man* in Michigan in 1949; six tons of William Reich's work on sexual matters burned by the US Food and Drug Administration in the 1950s. And in 1966, George Martin described the burning of Beatles' records being broadcast on live radio after John Lennon had claimed to be 'more popular than Jesus now'.

It is all in the tradition of Anthony Comstock, founder of the New York Society for the Suppression of Vice in 1872. Before his death he boasted he had 'convicted persons enough to fill a passenger train of 61 coaches . . . and destroyed 160 tons of obscene literature'. His definition of obscene literature included the work of Balzac, Whitman, Tolstoy and Shaw. The annual list of 'The Most Challenged Books' in the US invariably includes Twain, Huxley, Salinger, Steinbeck and a disproportionate number of classic black writers – Angelou, Morrison, Walker, Wright. The American Library Association, ardent opponents of political and religious censorship, collates and publishes this list.

In a culture where belief in God can no longer be taken for granted, it is hard for the English to credit the passion involved in burning books. It's not that we have not burned books – most notoriously William Tyndale's

English translation of the Bible. Although copies had to be smuggled from Belgium, at the high price of three shillings, Tyndale became the most published writer in England. The Queen herself – Anne Boleyn at the time – had a copy. But the burnings, ferociously encouraged by Sir Thomas More, were so thorough that only one complete copy survives, now in the British Library. Thorough but ineffective: 84% of the Authorised Version of the New Testament is taken word for word from his translation, and it is to Tyndale that we owe the familiar cadences of the King James Bible.

The most extraordinary, and unrepentant, of modern burners was Allen Lane, founder of Penguin Books – the same Allen Lane who risked publishing *Lady Chatterley's Lover*, for which he went on trial in 1960. Only six years later, he staged his own spectacular bonfire. Penguin was producing an edition of the sometimes scatalogical French cartoonist Siné, whose work was published in the satirical *Canard Enchainé*. Lane ceremonially burned every copy (15,000–20,000) at his farm in Berkshire and the book was never reprinted. His objections were not to Siné's many explicitly sexual cartoons, but his few savagely anti-clerical ones.

Comparatively recently, the *Observer* review section, a Channel Four book programme and the booksellers Waterstone's have all used the image of burning books for commercial purposes with complete disregard for its terrible history. They might argue that they were paying homage to the power of the word, but it is dangerous to blunt reaction so frivolously. It matters. Books are not to be silenced. It takes vigilance and care to ensure that books 'stand intransigent, shoulder to shoulder, always ready to offer resistance.' ❏

Stacy Marking was writing for the Guardian *from Latin America when she was arrested and detained in Paraguay for possessing a book called* Revolución en Arquitectura; *she has been interested in censorship ever since. She is a writer and film-maker living in London*

HOLDING ON TO BABEL

HELENA DRYSDALE

OUR LANGUAGES ARE THE GREATEST
ACHIEVEMENT OF OUR INTELLIGENCE,
AN INTELLIGENCE BOTH HUMAN AND YET
MYSTERIOUS. WHEN A LANGUAGE DIES, A WAY OF
LIFE DISAPPEARS AND WE ARE ALL THE POORER

In the tiny church at Plogoff, perched on a headland in Brittany, the Pardon festival Mass was over. Most people had gone home for lunch, carrying traditional Pardon cakes, but I stayed on, awaiting the afternoon's events. A bar had been set up in a field. I asked the middle-aged barman why Mass had been in French.

'Because nobody speaks Breton now,' he grunted, without looking up. 'We all speak French.' He was rinsing glasses.

'Are you Breton?' I persisted.

He planted his hands on the bar top. 'Me, I'm Breton, I live here in Plogoff, but I speak French. My wife is not Breton. Our children don't speak Breton. They don't understand a word.'

'The one Breton hymn this morning was the only one sung with enthusiasm,' I pointed out.

He shrugged. 'Oh, a few songs, that's all they know. Breton – it's gone. *C'est du folklore.*' He turned back to his glasses. I walked away, near to tears with disappointment at his indifference.

Is Breton now merely *du folklore*, dragged out for tourists and festivals? Perhaps the barman was over-pessimistic, but it is certainly endangered. According to recent figures, of the 1.5 million inhabitants of Basse Bretagne, the traditional heartland of Breton, only 18,000 speakers use the language every day. The speed of its decline is frightening. In 1905, Breton was spoken by an estimated 1.4 million people; in a couple of generations it has gone from being the mother tongue of almost everyone in the region to one no longer spoken at home or school (apart from in a handful of private Breton primary schools), and barely featuring in the media. Despite the efforts of activists, the future for Breton is grim.

Breton is one of some 40 languages spoken within the EU that are not that of the state. All of them are endangered. Through the Charter for

Regional and Minority Languages, the EU pays lip service to its indigenous minorities, but in reality many EU states, including France, have refused to ratify the charter, arguing that it contradicts their own constitutions. Meanwhile, funding for the Brussels- and Dublin-based European Bureau for Lesser Used Languages has been cut.

THE COMING CENTURY WILL SEE EITHER THE DEATH OR THE DOOM OF 90% OF MANKIND'S LANGUAGES

According to linguist Michael Krauss: 'At the rate things are going, the coming century will see either the death or the doom of 90% of mankind's languages.' It is estimated that a language dies somewhere in the world every two weeks.

Eighteen thousand Breton speakers sounds a fairly reasonable number, safe in the short term, but not enough to sustain it indefinitely. Even a language with several hundred thousand speakers can be endangered, at least in the medium term. Frisian, for example, is spoken by some 400,000 people in The Netherlands, but with little schooling, media or political and financial support, it is at risk. Even some national languages such as Danish feel threatened, Denmark having lost its overseas territories plus a chunk of Schleswig-Holstein, then seen Germans settle on its southern border, then been culturally swamped by English. French defensiveness towards their language is one reason why France is so intolerant of linguistic minorities such as Breton.

All languages change, but it is important to establish when 'change' becomes 'decline'. Linguists believe the difference is one of extent, range, quality and speed. Languages do not die uniformly. Different aspects of languages change as they decline. They often begin by borrowing extensively in both grammar and vocabulary from dominant languages. Just as Welsh has incorporated numerous English words, so Breton borrows from French. (During the nineteenth-century revival, a Breton dictionary was published with French words expunged, but in the absence of Breton replacements, Welsh had to be substituted. Likewise Romanian, a Latin language that feels threatened by its Slavic neighbours, has been through a long process of excising non-Latin words.)

It is hard to estimate precisely when a language dies, because it is hard to say precisely when a language is a separate language and not a dialect. It is generally accepted that if two speech systems are mutually unintelligible, they are separate languages. Sometimes dialects can turn into languages, either because they drift further apart, or because of politics, as in Macedonia. Here, the nineteenth-century Slavs spoke dialects of Bulgarian, but it was considered necessary to create a distinct national language, so Macedonia adopted as its standard the most westerly dialect of Bulgarian, and Bulgaria the most easterly dialect. They became two separate languages because the people wanted it so.

When does a language die? At the last count, Akkala Sami was spoken in Russia by a mere eight people. Does that mean Akkala is not yet dead? A language dies with its last speakers, but it can be said to have died before that if speakers are so widely scattered that they have no one to communicate with. Language is a tool for communication; if it cannot be used it is dead. It can continue in written or recorded form, so long as someone can read or understand it, and it can even be revived, as Cornish has been. But Cornish can hardly be described as a living language, more an exhumation.

The common classification of language endangerment is: safe; endangered; moribund (a fruity term borrowed from the medical profession, meaning doomed), and extinct. Those distinctions can be subdivided into: small; nearly extinct; potentially endangered, seriously endangered and so on. But for all these terms, there is no hard-and-fast rule to enable language watchers to announce which stage a language has reached. Breton may have only 18,000 speakers, but since many of them live in towns such as Quimper (Kemper in Breton) where the Breton language has become a radical badge of identity, it may be used more than, say, North Sami, whose speakers are often scattered in isolated groups among Finnish, Norwegian or Swedish speakers (*Index* 1/2002).

Symptoms of language death also vary. A language can be used less and less, or be confined to a particular use, much as Coptic was confined to church liturgy before it eventually petered out. A language is intrinsically bound up with a culture. In a school near St David's, Welsh is the language of instruction and is the mother tongue of almost all the pupils, but in the playground the children speak English, something they attribute to the power of pop music. In the Arctic, the Sami language is entwined with the traditions of nomadic reindeer-herding. If reindeer-herding dwindles, much of the vocabulary will disappear, and soon the language will be seen to serve no purpose. Alternatively, Sami will be confined more and more to reindeer-herding, until it becomes exclusively a language of the open fells. It becomes too narrow and loses its prestige. No one wants to put money in it. It dies.

Why are these languages dwindling? Like most European languages, Breton had a great revival during the nineteenth century when popular nationalisms were spread by liberal intelligentsias who inspired – and were inspired by – lexicographical revolutions: the gathering-up of language, folklore and myth. There were the *Flibrige* of Provence, the Basque *Berpizkundea*, Catalan *Renaixena*, North Frisia's 'National Awakening', and the collecting of folk tales to create Finland's national text, the *Kalevala*. Breton was part of the Celtic Twilight that saw a revival of Welsh and Gaelic. Then, during World War I, Breton soldiers suddenly discovered the outside world, and found that their language was despised as the language of peasants. Progress socially and politically was seen to be French. A further blow was dealt during World War II when the Vichy regime supported Breton language study and financed private Breton schools. By the time the war was over, Breton had become tarnished by association with the Occupation. There followed vigorous French attempts at assimilation, with children punished in school for speaking their mother tongue. Their grandchildren, who may have spoken Breton at home in infancy, lost it as they grew up, through peer pressure or schooling; because they left home; through a general process of globalisation, expanding transport and other communications; or, like the barman in Plogoff, because they married non-Bretons. Now, in a final blow, the last speakers are dying off, taking with them living Breton encyclopaedias, living dictionaries.

Some people do not care. To them, an ideal world would be one in which communication was aided by a reduction in the Babel of languages that only serves to alienate us from each other. But they are wrong. Single languages do not create peace; there are a thousand other forces that conspire to divide us. We only have to look at Northern Ireland. And if the world was reduced to one single language group, which language would that be? All speakers would choose their own language, naturally. It is often supposed that Belgium would benefit politically if everyone spoke the same language – but which one? No one can decide. Flemish speakers do not want to surrender to French speakers, and vice versa, not to mention the third official language group, German. The failure of Esperanto to catch on is one proof that we don't really want to speak a lingua franca – or, if we do, we want to hang on to our own language as well.

Not all community or tribal feeling depends on language. Many Bretons feel Breton without it. But a young Breton activist I met near Plogoff insisted that no one could be a convincing Breton without knowledge of the language. It is the same in Wales. Many people feel Welsh even though they have never spoken a word; however, the Welsh poet and Anglican priest

Plozevet, Brittany 1997: speaking in tongues.
Credit: Richard Pomeroy

RS Thomas argued that those who have forgotten their ancient tongue have no right to claim to be Welsh and accused them of betraying the land of their fathers. 'I imagine Wales,' he wrote in 1992, a few years before his death, 'beautiful at all times, deserted and betrayed by so many who should have remained faithful to her.' He could have been talking about the barman at Plogoff.

Thomas warned of the subtle assimilations, and the impending loss of some of the world's great literature. A language is dead – just a mass of squiggles – if no one can read it. And alongside comes the death of a way of communicating, a repository of collective memory. The Plogoff barman has lost part of his identity; his community has lost much of its vitality and cohesion, its pride in its culture, its self-confidence. His society has been impoverished and has lost touch with its own history. It matters to all of us because the loss of Breton is as bad as the loss of the threatened plant and animal species that we hear so much more about. It is part of the same loss, the loss of diversity in all things.

It also matters because Breton is interesting for its own sake. It looks blunt and humorous, and sounds not sophisticated like French but ancient and peasant-like. It wears sabots. Languages can be excluding and divisive, but we can also take pleasure in their strangeness, in the sounds of them, their grammatical foibles, the aesthetic sensations they create, what Orwell called 'the joy of mere words'. Our languages are the greatest achievement of our intelligence, an intelligence both human and yet mysterious. What they cannot survive is indifference.

'IT'S NOT ONLY THE LANGUAGE THAT'S DYING. IT'S OUR WHOLE WAY OF LIFE'

At Plogoff, the last remnants during the lunchtime lull were a man in a lemon-coloured jacket and his lady friend. We picnicked together on crêpes and Pardon cakes. The man came from Kemper and, unlike the barman, was passionately pro-Breton. He also had been disappointed by the lack of Breton in the Mass.

'It's not only the language that's dying,' he mourned, 'It's our whole way of life.'

'Do you two speak Breton?' I asked.

'We do,' they chorused.

'Yet you were speaking French among yourselves.'

They looked almost shamefaced. It was, they confessed, what they'd got used to. ❏

Helena Drysdale is the author of Mother Tongues: travels through tribal Europe *(Picador, 2001)*

DEATH OF A NATION

AMINATTA FORNA

SIERRA LEONE'S LONG-TERM DICTATOR SIAKA
STEVENS MAY BE DEAD, BUT THE PEOPLE LIVE
WITH THE DEVASTATING LEGACY OF HIS REIGN.
HE KILLED DEMOCRACY AND TRANSFORMED THE
COUNTRY INTO A ONE-PARTY STATE; HIS ARMY OF
PAID INFORMANTS AND CRIMINAL THUGS PAVED
THE WAY FOR THE BRUTAL DEPREDATIONS THAT
STRIPPED THE COUNTRY OF ALL CLAIMS TO BE A
FUNCTIONING STATE

I have never been here before and yet the sight is somehow intensely familiar. It has the air of impersonal grandiosity of a hotel or conference centre. The building is a modern design of interconnecting hexagons, the public spaces cavernous, the grounds terraced. To my right are the staff quarters – four floors of them. The covered walkway leads to double doors of solid, dark wood. Inside, twin staircases curve from the vestibule leading me, the first-time visitor, towards the focal point of the house. I sense the architect's vision as I climb the remaining stairs and stop before the wide stretch of window. There is the city far below, lines of traffic and crowds constantly forming and reforming like creatures under a microscope. Up here it is quiet. Ahead of me the coastline is drawn in narrow bands of gold and of white surf, beyond that lies the immensity of the Atlantic Ocean.

From where I stand I can see the blue-and-white UN helicopters lift and land on the dark tarmac: the same helipad once used by the mercenary helicopter hired by the government to quell the growing rebel onslaught. I can see the lines of tents of the troops. I can see the SOS Children's Village where some of the child soldiers are temporarily housed. I lift up my camera to take a photograph. A man in camouflage trousers and a blue T-shirt comes to stand in front of me, one hand raised palm flat to the camera. He is polite, but he doesn't smile. No photographs.

Back inside, black mould bubbles under the flaking paintwork. Bare wires protrude from the walls, all the light fittings have gone. A solitary chandelier hangs askew over the well of the stairs – just out of reach. Thirty feet below it are rows of bunk beds, neatly made: the sleeping quarters of Kenyan soldiers, some of the 17,000 UN peacekeepers posted to this theatre of war. Some are off duty. They write letters. Play cards. Dream of home.

Every failed state has one. The place that one day becomes an icon of past greed, where journalists and television cameras pilgrimage. In the Congo it is Gbadolite, Mobutu's weekend retreat. In Romania it is Ceauşescu's palace. In my country this place is called Kabassa Lodge, the home of Sierra Leone's long-term dictator Siaka Stevens. Stevens ruled for 20 years. He killed democracy in post-colonial Sierra Leone, transforming the country into a one-party state and securing his supremacy with an army of paid informers and criminal thugs. Stevens is dead, far from the reach of those who live with the legacy of his reign.

Later that afternoon, in the vaporous heat of Freetown, I pass the old PZ department store. It is closed up. Refugees from the war have occupied some of the floors.

On Siaka Stevens Street, in the centre of town, stands the mighty Cotton Tree, branches soaring above the city – symbol of the free state, once called the Athens of Africa, founded at the end of the eighteenth century by former slaves and British philanthropists. Beggars stretch amputated limbs towards the passengers of the cars circling the massive trunk. In his bid for absolute power, Stevens strangled the country's nascent sense of nationhood, encouraging instead a cult of personality, referring to himself as the 'Father of the Nation', changing Independence Day to the anniversary of his own election into power.

Nearby are the Law Courts built by the British in the era of colonial rule. The white-and-blue façades are intact; the insides are hollowed ruins. A painted sign announces the proposed rebuilding, paid for with international aid.

At the top of Independence Avenue, State House lies ransacked and abandoned – the president and his cabinet had decamped to a temporary site. A short way further up the hill is the old Ministry of Finance, burned by the rebels of the Revolutionary United Front when they invaded the capital in 1999, wreaking their revenge on the people and the government alike – burning homes, hacking at limbs, destroying this building, the emblem of a corrupt regime. Nearby in the marketplace there is no meat; rice, which we once exported to the rest of the region, is now imported from Asia at exorbitant prices; a young woman sits behind her stall and a pyramid of three tomatoes.

Sierra Leone: sisters mutilated by rebels.
Credit: Jenny Matthews

Down by Government Wharf, a ship is unloading the latest consignment of second-hand clothing shipped from the USA. It is a long time since anyone in Sierra Leone bought new clothes. Here, a few months ago, I encountered an old acquaintance, Jacob, a young man who had once dreamed of running a tour business. He had escorted me on a hike to the waterfalls at Number Two River. I remembered the day had been marred by the behaviour of his partner Eric, who had been drunk and uncouth. A few days later, Eric, red-eyed and faintly aggressive, had hassled me for money. I gave him some so he would go away. Privately, I had let Jacob know that if he wanted his venture to succeed he'd have to drop Eric. Jacob was working as a cook at the UN HQ. 'And Eric?' I asked.

'Ah,' replied Jacob. 'When the war started he went to Kono [the diamond area] to join the fighting.'

This is what Robert Kaplan called 'the coming anarchy'. In 1994, his essay, published in *Atlantic Monthly*, caused a sensation and an outcry. He predicted a future for significant parts of the world characterised by the end of democracy, the onslaught of chaos, the implosion of the state into a swelter of tribalism and disease. He started with Sierra Leone. Back then, I remember, war raged across the border in Liberia. Our country was peaceful. There were reports of isolated pockets of fighting upcountry. The government assured the populace that the army had it all under control. We weren't worried. Liberians were not the same as us. They were, well, almost American. It could never happen here, we said.

Sierra Leone became independent in 1961. The state is just three years my senior. By the time I turned 35, Sierra Leone was on her deathbed, classified a collapsed state. Government was moribund; there existed no functioning police force or army, thousands had lost their lives to roving bands of murderous bandit warriors from the RUF. The RUF were not so much the cause of the country's fate as the final symptom of a slowly spreading necrosis.

For me, it began in my teens one morning when our car came to an abrupt stop on the road where we lived. The driver had never seen a traffic light before. The traffic in Freetown found its own route, like water trickling down the sand at low tide. At peak times police officers in white armbands mounted blocks in the middle of busy junctions to direct the traffic. We waited there, watching: red, amber, green, amber, red. There was no junction, no school, no pedestrian crossing, no apparent reason why a traffic light should be there at all.

It was 1980, the year Sierra Leone hosted the OAU conference. Determined to put on a display for his peers, Stevens built luxury villas for the delegates and flew in a fleet of limousines. Zebra crossings were hurriedly painted across streets and traffic lights put up all over the city with no regard whatever to road planning. PZ was filled with luxury imported goods, and yet the country was in hock, hopelessly in debt for generations to come – the money used to finance Stevens's growing power. When the head of the national bank denounced the vast expenditure, Stevens had the man dragged from his bed at night and thrown out of the window.

In 1991, the first RUF forces, trained by Liberia's Charles Taylor and funded by Libya's Colonel Gaddafi, entered the country from Liberia. The first units included disaffected former students who had fled Stevens's clampdown on the university. That year I returned home for a visit after a decade of living in London. I stepped back into the city of my childhood. Where were the spreading suburbs, the office blocks, the altered cityscapes that seem to appear inevitably with the passage of time? I experienced the eerie feeling of time stopped, time shifting into reverse.

At home, my parents contemplated the purchase of a generator. The electricity supply was intermittent, increasingly more off than on. People in the know built their houses close to those of government ministers, where you could be assured of a constant supply. From the crest of the hill, Kabassa Lodge glowed like a beacon. Stevens had ostensibly retired, handing the country to one of his own. He had the government buy Kabassa Lodge and then return it to him as a gift.

Some evenings we went to the beach to eat kebabs and drink beer, stuffing a backpack with wads of notes, like a police agent off to negotiate with a kidnapper. The leone was virtually worthless.

Two coups later in 1996, the country was briefly returned to democracy. The elections were hailed as a triumph of civil society. On polling day, women's groups who had organised and lobbied for elections faced down armed soldiers on the streets. The combined force of the citizenry and the IMF – which made new loans conditional on democratic elections – swept a new president into power. But democracy was as effective as a sticking plaster on a gaping head wound. By then all formal structures of government had eroded or been dismantled. Fighting that had begun around the diamond regions now spread through the remainder of the country.

The new government denied the existence of an emergency. In 1997, when I was in the USA, the president was overthrown by the army and fled to Guinea. The new junta joined forces with the RUF. They embarked on a spree of theft, rape and murder throughout the country, including the capital. This was not warfare and ultimately finite, but rather lucrative crime under the cover of warfare and therefore infinite in its potential for destruction. This was anarchy in its purest form.

Whatever ideology the RUF had once peddled had vanished. The RUF leadership swelled the ranks with a lumpenproletariat: Sierra Leonians, Burkinabes, Guineans, Liberians. The fighters were mainly young men who had left their villages and thus the authority of the extended family and their chief to go to the city where they inevitably failed to find work. These youths, who massed in the slums of cities, were neither subjects under Africa's long-standing systems of social control nor citizens in a modern state. Kaplan blamed the death of the nation state in Africa on her own cultural weakness. But Kaplan was wrong. The weakening of Africa's own systems, the failure of the departing colonial powers to replace them with anything more solid, the subsequent social and political vacuum engineered by opportunistic rulers in their endeavour to subvert the mechanisms of the state: these are the patterns that emerge when African states collapse.

By 1998, the RUF controlled all the diamond districts and the north of the country, where they made their headquarters and where my father's family lived. My aunts and uncles fled back to the old village, deep in the forest. For months we heard nothing more. A year later, during the brief ceasefire that followed the intervention of Nigerian troops sponsored by the Economic Community of West African States (ECOWAS), my father's sister Memuna appeared in Freetown. She had lost a third of her body weight and was suffering from malnutrition, her feet were a mass of ulcers – aged 60, she had walked most of the 100 miles to the capital.

In the years following the millennium, I have returned several times, to a country propped up by the combined efforts of ECOWAS, the United Nations and the British. People claim to be positive about the future, and yet the exodus continues. All but one of my friends from childhood now live in the United States or Europe. Africa loses 60,000 professionals a year, and countless more skilled workers. Sierra Leone is ranked by the UN as the worst place in the world to live, with a life expectancy that has dropped to just 38.

On my last trip I attended open day at the primary school of my seven-year-old ward. The class sang the national anthem to the assembled adults, who sat on chairs at the front of the class. Afterwards, the children recited the history of Sierra Leone. The teacher prompted and the class mouthed the replies they had learned by rote in singsong voices. After the national pledge she asked: 'Who is the father of the nation and the first president of Sierra Leone?' The children did not hesitate: 'President Siaka Probyn Stevens.' ❏

Aminatta Forna is a writer and broadcaster. She is the author of The Devil that Danced on the Water *(HarperCollins), an African memoir*

WOMEN AND WAR

VICTORIA BRITTAIN

> WOMEN HAVE BECOME, AS NEVER
> BEFORE, THE PRIMARY VICTIMS IN
> THE WARS OF OUR TIMES

Sexual violence, sexual slavery, trafficking of women and girls in wartime, are now happening on an unprecedented scale, threatening the future social fabric of societies where they have become the norm. For underlying social and physical reasons, economic and social breakdown during and after these wars, combined with the pandemic of HIV/Aids and the dominance of international criminal syndicates feeding on war conditions, have a disproportionately hard impact on women.

Today's wars have a different shape from the wars of our history books, even modern history books on the familiar stories of the twentieth century's World Wars, or the United States' war in Vietnam. These were wars where armies fought each other; front lines shifted inches or miles; civilian casualties were often unfortunate sideshows to the sacrifice of a nation's young men in uniform fighting for big ideas. Then came the liberation wars against colonialism, where Algerians, South Africans, Mozambicans, East Timorese — mostly men — fought vastly superior powers for an ideal: independence.

But many of the wars of the late twentieth century and the beginning of the current one have been of a different kind. Today, 90% of war casualties are civilians, compared with 65% in World War II, and 5% at the beginning of the twentieth century. Key protagonists in these wars are frequently shadowy non-state forces, though often these militias (as in Colombia or East Timor or Sierra Leone) are fighting as proxies for a state. Such groups are often funded by illegal trade, as in drugs, diamonds and timber, and are notoriously difficult to penetrate or influence. These are wars fought mainly with such weapons as AK47s, so light a child can carry them, or domestic implements such as machetes or hoes. This has contributed to a blurring of the line between civilians and combatants. And, increasingly, the parties to these combats see civilians as legitimate targets.

In Central and West Africa, in the Balkans, in Colombia, in the Occupied Palestinian Territories and in East Timor in the closing days of the Indonesian occupation, civilians, and specifically women, have been frontline targets. The myth that women are protected from violence by their sex is demolished by research on the ground in all these war zones. In eastern Democratic Republic of Congo, there are women who live naked in the forests, gang-raped and looted of everything by local militias; in Sierra Leone, women have lost their minds after being forced to dance and sing as their husbands were killed in front of them by the Revolutionary United Front; in Colombia, women activists have been driven from their homes by chillingly explicit death threats from right-wing paramilitaries; in newly independent East Timor, the Balkans and northern Uganda, there are families who must live with the knowledge that their girls have been taken away as sex slaves. What has happened in these societies as a result of this treatment of women has been the unravelling of social cohesion – with incalculable long-term results reaching into future generations.

These are wars where civilian lives and deaths are of no account, except where they can be used to destroy the will and morale of the other side, or prick an uneasy conscience in the international community into intervening – with food or arms – and change the natural balance of forces. In the Reagan years of the 1980s, the last Cold War confrontations were wars such as these: in Central America, Angola, East Timor. They were known then as low-intensity conflicts, a formula that distanced them from any mainstream interest. The thousands of women and girls who were kidnapped as sex slaves from villages across Angola by Jonas Savimbi's Unita, or by the occupation forces of the Indonesian army in East Timor, were a wholly invisible subtext to the war's ebb and flow announced in thousands of propaganda declarations. In the aftermath of those wars, the women's difficulty in re-integrating into their original families and communities with the children born from coercive relationships and, in many cases, years of attachment to their kidnappers, is a shadow over reconciliation and reconstruction.

A decade and more later, civil wars in the former Yugoslavia brought more international interest and a particular focus on women's experience after the revelations of mass rape as a tool of that war.

Meanwhile, the civil wars unravelling African states such as Sudan, Liberia, Sierra Leone, Democratic Republic of Congo (DRC), Somalia and Angola were invisible and usually explained away either as ethnic or religious wars, or as wars of resources – land, diamonds, oil, timber. But these African wars are a different phenomenon, best described as wars of under-development. They are both a product of underdevelopment and a cause of it, and they bode ill for their region's future. The primitive fascism of Unita in Angola, the Interahamwe and Mai-Mai in DRC, the Lord's Resistance Army in northern Uganda, and what the RUF in Sierra Leone became have been marked by extraordinary cruelty and violence towards women. Only by listening to women's experience will their real character be known, but the women's stories are not easily told, even when their personal ordeal is over.

The stigma of sexual violence means that often the family will encourage the victim to keep quiet, or the woman herself may not even tell the family for fear of repudiation. Sometimes a collective story is easier to tell. In a clinic in Kigali, I met several dozen widows, all infected with HIV/Aids during the 1994 genocide. They were young, middle-aged, elderly, country women and elegant town women. Asked who wanted to tell her story, they replied, 'There are no special stories, it is all one story, the same for all of us, rape, many rapes, and torture.' And in Goma, in eastern DRC, I met a large group of women displaced and homeless after their villages had been looted and burned by Interahamwe raids. They came to the meeting to talk about loss of husbands, children, livelihood; but several held up handwritten placards saying, 'We have been raped.'

The hidden war going on against women and girls in the forests of eastern DRC has been well documented by Human Rights Watch in *The War within the War* (June 2002). Abduction, rape, sexual slavery, torture and death have become an everyday reality that terrorises every woman. Three national armies, from DRC, Rwanda and Uganda, long-entrenched rebel groups of three neighbouring countries, Uganda, Rwanda and Burundi, and proliferating local militias have made this part of DRC the most militarised in Africa (*Index* 1/2001). And women are paying the price for a culture of violence that is completely out of control. A gynaecologist in the eastern town of Bukavu told HRW that he felt: 'If you are born a woman in this country, you are condemned at birth . . . why are we silent about this?' He added that in his many years of work he had never before seen women who had suffered atrocities like those committed against some of the women he had recently treated. One of his patients explained this by saying, 'It is just hatred.' But the hatred is inexplicable, irrational and against the rural culture of solidarity that was once the norm here despite waves of ethnic tension during the Mobutu period. 'There is real madness with all this sexual violence linked to the war – another kind of attack on the Congolese people,' said a counsellor in Bukavu. The HRW report documents dozens of appalling cases including women who had parts of their genitals sliced off with a razor blade, women shot in the vagina after rape, women who had their breasts cut off when they resisted rape, girls as young as five and women as old as eighty attacked. In Liberia and Sierra Leone, equally terrible stories of violence against women have been documented in *War-Related Sexual Violence in Sierra Leone* (Physicians for Human Rights, 2002).

Although the experience of Africa's women is extreme in its extent, women in conflict zones from Asia, Latin America and the Balkans are similarly caught in a vicious circle of constantly reinforcing negative factors triggered by violence against them.

The circle goes through displacement, psycho-social fragility, economic stress, loss of education, sexual exploitation, failing health and HIV/Aids. In every case, women's experience is dramatically different from that of men caught up in the same war zone and their vulnerability is increased by also having to take care of children.

Among the world's 34 million refugees and internally displaced people, 80% are women and children. Some, such as Palestinians, have been displaced for as long as 50 years; others, such as Angolans, for 25 years. And many, such as Angolans, Colombians and Congolese, have been displaced many times over.

Such experiences leave women psychologically deeply affected. After flight in terror, loss of collective identity in family or community, they are alone and have to create a new life for their children. The economic stress of being a refugee adds to their psychological burden. Women usually lose the family breadwinner to the war in one way or another, either when he becomes a soldier, flees into exile or, as in the particular case of the Occupied Palestinian Territories, is prevented from working by closures or imprisonment. Women must then take jobs they would never have considered before.

In Rwanda, for instance, tens of thousands of women were widowed in traumatic circumstances during the 1994 genocide. Women who tradition-ally had little practical information about money and property were suddenly responsible for large families of dependent children and forced to adapt to new skills and new roles just when they were at their most vulner-able. In all rural war zones, especially in Africa, though also in Colombia and in Cambodia, where women are the backbone of the rural economy, the loss

Opposite: Rwanda: widows work the land.
Credit: Jenny Matthews

of their land when they are displaced is the loss of their livelihood for the family. The acute drama of refugees' economic situation is exemplified by the reports from Afghanistan of families selling one of their children to get food to keep others alive. In eastern DRC, too, displaced women from the highland pastures and woodlands of Masisi and Walikali have sold little girls as maids for as little as US$5. As one social worker said of these children, 'They'll never see the inside of a school, they'll be malnourished, and vulnerable to every kind of exploitation.' In all these war zones, girls' education is among the first casualties.

But loss of schooling is catastrophic for the future of girls in these situations and makes it more likely that prostitution will be only valid economic option for them. Recently exposed scandals in West African refugee camps have brought to light the common practice of refugee women routinely selling sex for access to the food and other rations they have a right to. In such a situation of poverty and powerlessness, sex is the only currency women have. The climate is prepared for a high incidence of prostitution, sexual slavery, trafficking and general sexual violence including rape. The HIV/Aids epidemic thrives in just this context, and affects women worst.

The sexual violence and extreme cruelty towards women revealed in the Balkan wars produced a sea change in international attitudes to what had been a disregarded or little-known phenomenon. International humanitarian law to protect women has been extended by recent judgements at the International Tribunals for the former Yugoslavia and Rwanda, though the statutes for the International Criminal Court do not include all the most positive elements. In *Women facing War* by Charlotte Lindsay, the International Committee of the Red Cross concluded optimistically that sexual violence in warfare is not inevitable. It can be prevented by the application of existing international humanitarian law. It took 50 years for the so-called Comfort Women used by the Japanese army in World War II to have their day in court and some international recognition of the unacceptable fate they suffered (*Index* 3/1995). HIV/Aids and the nature of Africa's wars of underdevelopment make it unlikely that Africa's women victims will see a similar satisfaction. ❏

Victoria Brittain is a research associate at the London School of Economics

FUCKING SOLDIERS

ALEX DE WAAL

THE BLAME FOR AFRICA'S AIDS EPIDEMIC
FALLS ON WARS, SOLDIERS AND CULTURES
OF MILITARISATION. FIGHTING IT DEMANDS
BETTER RESOURCES AND LEADERSHIP
THAN AVAILABLE AT PRESENT

Aids activists and policymakers have a taste for military metaphors. They speak of 'fighting' Aids, 'mobilising as if for war' and, more optimistically, 'vanquishing' the disease. Some diseases – smallpox and cholera are cases in point – are amenable to military-style campaigns. But sexually transmitted infections are not. Measures such as the incarceration of sex workers by the US police during World War I haven't often been effective. Policing sex rarely works. In fact, it's simpler to wage a war than to 'fight' HIV. States are designed for war-making. They have emergency powers and mobilisation capacities, while their leaders adore taking a posture of stern command. Even liberation wars, fought against states, invoke stirring slogans, promises of Utopia and nationalist sentiment.

Speaking of the need for 'war' on Aids alarms people, and they should be alarmed. In some African countries, national survival is indeed at stake. For a country with 20–35% HIV prevalence among the adult population – that is, all southern African countries – the lifetime chance of contracting the virus for a teenager today ranges up to 70%. Statistically, a 16-year-old in Botswana can expect two decades of adult life, just half of her or his parents'. About 28 million Africans are estimated to be living with HIV and Aids. Not only is this an incalculable human tragedy, the loss of human resources stands as the single greatest impediment to social and economic development, and a huge threat to stability and security.

Wars demand exceptional measures and clear and courageous leadership. Africa's leaders should see Aids as their number-one priority, laying aside all other national plans while they focus on the disease. So far, with just a few exceptions (notably Botswana), this is just wishful thinking. The 'war' on Aids is being conducted in a business-as-usual manner. It's a series of incremental programmes run by health ministries and voluntary agencies, mostly worthy but lacking the levels of both funding and leadership that are warranted. In fact, there's very little strategic coordination at all: ministries, aid agencies and donors make relatively short-term, narrowly focused decisions about what to do. All 'fronts' in this war are important, but some are more fashionable than others. Mother-to-child transmission of HIV has gained a lot of (deserved) attention. Soldiers, policemen and prison officers living with HIV and Aids have not. There is something to be said for allowing each of those involved to decide where and how to expend their energies. It makes for innovation and voluntarism. That's how the deregulated market in aid to Africa operates. It is not, typically, how wars are fought and won.

MOTHER-TO-CHILD TRANSMISSION OF HIV HAS GAINED A LOT OF ATTENTION. SOLDIERS, POLICEMEN AND PRISON OFFICERS HAVE NOT

The war metaphor is also misleading. War is a realisation of militaristic and, characteristically, masculine values, including hierarchy, command and obedience. In wartime, these values also permeate the personal and sexual lives of citizens. 'Fighting' Aids demands a rather different kind of 'war': a patient, frank engagement with some of the most intimate and deeply held beliefs and practices of communities and individuals. In this 'combat', governments and institutions should surrender some of their power and instead listen to ordinary young women and men. And even more to the point, men should negotiate sex with women as equals.

Truth is also, of course, a casualty of war. Here we run into a major contradiction: the 'war' on Aids demands intelligence, especially good epidemiological data: who has the virus, how they got it and whether they're spreading it. It's a shocking fact that the first 20 years of the Aids pandemic has produced such rudimentary epidemiology of HIV. Billions of dollars have been spent searching for a cure, but comparatively minuscule amounts on the kind of public health data that are useful in changing behaviour to prevent transmission. And a survey of the epidemiology will turn up one huge chasm from which virtually no information has escaped: the military itself.

This black hole is disturbing. A compilation of anecdotes and snatches of data suggests that armies have played an important role in the Aids epidemic in Africa. Right at the beginning of the pandemic, the pattern of Aids in Uganda in the mid-1980s reproduced rather precisely the progress of the Tanzanian army that invaded the country in 1979. This army had earlier been encamped on the western shores of Lake Victoria, the very location where many of the earliest cases of Aids were retrospectively diagnosed. What better vector to transform an isolated cluster of HIV cases into an epidemic than an army of young men, regularly paid, posted far away from home?

Sexual violence is a statistical no man's land. Indisputably, the reported cases of rape are a tiny fraction of the real number. Most likely, even fewer rapes are reported

A SURVEY OF THE EPIDEMIOLOGY WILL TURN UP ONE HUGE CHASM FROM WHICH VIRTUALLY NO INFORMATION HAS ESCAPED: THE MILITARY ITSELF

when the rapist wears a uniform. Rape by soldiers and policemen has only rarely become a public scandal. An exceptional case was the shockingly high level of sexual violence against Somali refugees in Kenya ten years ago. While most of it was perpetrated by criminal gangs known as *shifta*, a substantial number of rapes were carried out by the soldiers and policemen who were supposed to be protecting the refugees. Exposure by human rights organisations and a special programme by the UN High Commissioner for Refugees to protect women from rape helped overcome the problem. But, in the meantime, how many women became infected with HIV?

Rape has been documented as a weapon of war in a number of countries. There are stories of 'special' units of HIV-positive militiamen systematically raping Tutsi women during the Rwandese genocide of 1994. Mass rape has been perpetrated on women and girls captured by the Sudanese army in operations to burn villages and relocate their inhabitants to what they call 'peace camps' (See Brittain, p81).

It is probable that most soldiers' sexual encounters are consensual. But that does not make the woman an equal 'partner' – the very word conceals the hierarchy inherent in most soldiers' sexual encounters. Army garrisons are typically surrounded by bars and brothels. Soldiers are paid well and regularly by the standards of rural Africa, where impoverished young women may be obliged to resort to 'survival sex': selling their bodies for the necessities of life. Officers' macho culture encourages multiple sexual 'conquests', and their status and pay make them attractive to young women seeking favours and security. The risk-embracing nature of military life makes a mockery of safe-sex messages. Why use a condom tonight when you may go into combat tomorrow?

The UN agency responsible for coordinating Aids information and programming, UNAids, coyly remarks that HIV levels among African

Mozambique 2001: army Aids educator.
Credit: Jenny Matthews

militaries are typically two to five times greater than in the general popula-
tion. There are anecdotes of army units being tested and coming up with
HIV-positivity rates of 50%, 70% or even 90%. A consistent anecdote is that
HIV rates increase with rank and that they are higher among high-status
units (especially air forces) than in the infantry. But we don't know much.
The only published survey, conducted by the UNAids' Civil–Military
Alliance, was carried out in 1995–96 and has not been repeated. Its data are
now mostly a decade old. They don't give any reason for complacency: rates
were typically 15–45%.

There are many reasons why governments want to keep Aids in the army
secret. The reflex of the securitised states that dominate the continent is
secrecy. Any indication that the officer corps, which is often the power base
of the government itself, is riddled with Aids, might give solace to adver-
saries. They fear it might tempt a neighbour to attack, or cause dissension or
mutiny in the army itself. More immediately, the civilians surrounding army
bases might become hostile to the garrisons in their midst. All African armies
face the dilemma that if they were to acknowledge the scale of the problem,
the costs for medication and care for soldiers living with HIV and Aids, and
their families, would consume the entire defence budget and more.

Some African militaries have taken the threat very seriously. The first and
most famous case is Uganda. Shortly after the guerrillas of the National
Resistance Army had taken power in 1986, President Yoweri Museveni sent
some soldiers to Cuba for training. He was quickly informed that a number
(not disclosed) had tested HIV-positive. Museveni was newly in power and
full of revolutionary energy, he had a very close personal bond to the young
fighters who had won his war and he also has a charismatic, frank and often
humorous way of communicating. Museveni's campaign against Aids quickly
became Africa's best-known success story. Not only has the country weath-
ered the ravages of a disease that at one time was infecting more than 20% of
the adult population, but it is the only case in Africa in which HIV levels
have actually fallen substantially.

But there are reasons to question just how deep and long-lasting
Uganda's success is. Recently, the chief of staff, General James Kazini, again
remarked that Aids was a major problem in the Ugandan army. At war in
Congo and Sudan, the army has lost its earlier discipline and dedication and
is now better known for corruption. Despite constant military operations
and attendant casualties, more than half the deaths in service are reported
to be Aids-related. Soldiers who have been tested HIV-positive have also

criticised the army for their treatment: medication has not been provided for them or their families and they have been victims of discrimination.

Another, less well-known, case of the military containing Aids is Ethiopia. In 1996, discovering that the army had an infection rate of 6% (higher among senior officers), the chief of staff, General Tsadkan Gebretinsae, designated fighting Aids as its number-one priority. Six years later, while Ethiopia's national HIV prevalence has risen to over 7% and the national Aids campaign has stagnated, the army still has a prevalence of just 6%. (In the interim it has recruited more than 250,000 men for a war with Eritrea, fought that war and demobilised many of them.) The key to the army's success seems to be a legacy from its years as a revolutionary guerrilla force in the 1970s and '80s which endowed it with some quasi-democratic institutions such as the 'council of commanders'. This, uniquely, allowed the Ethiopian army to have an open internal debate and adopt a set of anti-Aids policies by consensus. But, ironically, the same secretiveness that has concealed high military HIV rates in other countries has also meant that the army's success is not well known even in Ethiopia, let alone more widely.

These successes are too few, but there are signs of progress elsewhere. Senegal is an exemplary case for civil–military cooperation. The Tanzanian army has an open and enlightened policy, considering Aids in the military as an employment issue in which workers' rights should be respected.

Privately, African military commanders are expressing their fears more than ever. The Pentagon has become concerned, at first because US security strategies for Africa rely heavily on African peacekeepers. But the scale and nature of the HIV/Aids crisis in armies is still hidden. Shining a light into this dark corner is long overdue.

A big part of the blame for Africa's Aids epidemic must fall on wars, soldiers and cultures of militarisation. Declaring 'war' on the virus risks deluding leaders, both in Africa and globally, that the pandemic can be 'defeated' by further militarisation. Certainly, the campaign against HIV/Aids needs more resources and stronger leadership. But it will succeed if its 'weapons' are civilian and feminised, including gender equity, truly consensual sex, and frankness about all aspects of sexual behaviour. As Albert Camus remarked through Dr Rieux in the closing pages of *La Peste*: 'It's not a matter of heroism, it's a matter of honesty. It's an idea that may seem laughable, but the only way of fighting the plague is honesty.' ❏

Alex de Waal is founder and director of the London-based Justice Africa

PRICE OF A LIFE – OR DEATH
PETER PRINGLE

THE COST OF THE PRESENT INQUIRY
INTO THE BLOODY SUNDAY KILLINGS IN
NORTHERN IRELAND FAR EXCEEDS THAT
OF COMPENSATION PAID TO THE VICTIMS
30 YEARS AGO. AND FOR WHAT? ASKS A
JOURNALIST WHO WAS PRESENT IN 1972

The cost of the British government's second public inquiry into the killing of 13 unarmed civil rights marchers on Bloody Sunday on 30 January 1972 keeps going up – the latest is a staggering £80 million (US$124.5 million) – and people wince and wonder where it will all end and what will have been gained by the time the lawyers are finished.

Each time a new cost estimate appears, I can't help comparing it with another Bloody Sunday money calculation, made in 1974 two years after the killings, which received little public attention at the time and has rarely been mentioned since. This is the government's actuarial assessment of the worth of the dead at the time they were shot.

Two years after the march in Londonderry, the government formally acknowledged what the evidence showed – that all the 13 killed had been innocent – and withdrew unequivocally allegations made at the first public inquiry, under Lord Widgery, that some of the dead had been firing or carrying weapons. The government apologised to the next of kin and publicly expressed sympathy for their loss. In return, the families were awarded compensation, providing they didn't complain. The families of six teenagers received a miserable £250 each. The wife and six children of Barney McGuigan, who was shot in the back of the head as he went to the aid of a dying man, received £3,750. The wife and six children of Paddy Doherty, who was shot in the buttock as he was crawling away from the gunfire, received the top payment of £16,575.35. I have often wondered how these calculations were made.

Admittedly, the youths had little prospect of work in Derry where unemployment for those who lived in the Catholic Bogside was running at 40%, or higher. But some of them had been employed. One was a barman, another a tyre fitter and another an apprentice weaver as well as an amateur boxer and seemed to have good prospects. Barney McGuigan, who was 41, was admittedly out of work. He had been laid off as a maintenance man at a local electrical factory that had closed because of the Troubles. He was doing odd jobs, painting and fixing up neighbours' cars. But Paddy Doherty, who was 31, had a regular job. For the six years previous, he had been employed at the US-owned DuPont synthetic rubber factory, starting as a labourer and rising to be a plumber's mate.

Thirty years later, it is impossible to watch the new inquiry at work, with all its high-tech equipment and batteries of lawyers, and not compare the measly awards to these families with the compensation received by the barristers and solicitors delving again into the killings. A barrister for the new inquiry under Lord Saville earns £1,750 a day when appearing at the hearings in Derry's Guildhall. The law firm that was hired to interview all the available civilian eyewitnesses was paid £10 million. Before the Saville inquiry has finished its work, the overall cost is expected to be more than £100 million. And what will have been gained?

There is no dispute that the 13 who were shot dead (five of them in the back) and the 14 who were wounded in under 20 minutes of firing by the paratroopers were unarmed. When the soldiers take the stand, later this year, the overall picture of the Bogside killing field is unlikely to change. The soldiers (those who are still alive) who shot people will certainly repeat what they said at the first inquiry – namely, that they fired at IRA snipers. Which soldier is going to admit that he shot Barney McGuigan in the back of the head, or Paddy Doherty in the buttock? And which soldier is going to own up to firing the bullet that sliced through the thigh of Peggy Deery, a 38-year-old widow with 14 children, as she stood watching the soldiers storm into the Bogside? One paratrooper said in the 1972 inquiry that he fired 19 of the more than 100 rounds fired by the soldiers that day into a bathroom window that turned out not to have a mark on it. Clearly, the rounds went somewhere else, but where? Is that soldier likely to account for them, 30 years later, even under cross-examination fire from the most highly paid inquisitors?

The chances are that the soldier could not remember, even if he had the sudden inclination to do so. Which raises the issue of what all the taxpayer millions allotted to the Saville inquiry is *not* paying for. Many of the civilian witnesses who have appeared before the inquiry have, by their own admission, had trouble recalling what they saw after such a long time. Others have

Ulster, N Ireland: mural based on photographs of Bloody Sunday taken by
Gilles Peress and Gilles Caron. Credit: Abbas / Magnum Photos

recalled incidents that clash with their previous evidence at the time, or with the evidence of those who might have corroborated their new recollections.

One might have thought that the new inquiry would have employed a memory specialist, or historians who would have been able to advise on the problems of reconstructing traumatic events after such a long time. But such a panel of experts is not on the inquiry's generous payroll.

Historians would have looked at the problem and applied some well-worn guidelines for reconstructing history – for example, the nineteenth-century dictum of Leopold von Ranke, who basically said dip your bucket as near to the source as possible.

The Saville inquiry has some unique primary evidence taken by reporters from the *Sunday Times* Insight Team (of which I was a member) immediately after Bloody Sunday. Since 1981, the *Sunday Times* has been owned by Rupert Murdoch whose editors handed over to Saville our unique archive of personal notebooks, confidential interviews and memos. In my view, the surrender of this material was a shameful disregard of the sanctity of agreements between reporters and their sources. Witnesses who took us into their confidence, sometimes risking their personal safety, now understandably feel angry and betrayed; in a few cases they deny ever seeing us. The potential damage to the evidential record is enormous.

When we asked the Saville inquiry to keep such material confidential, our request was turned down. The inquiry's position was that the material had not been 'made subject to any reservation as to publication'. While the inquiry understood our position on confidentiality, it warned 'the Tribunal is not bound by any assurances that may have been given to those who supplied the information' [in the *Sunday Times* archive] and is 'unable to accept that such assurances constitute a compelling public interest reason for restricting [its] distribution'.

None of the reporters then on the Insight Team now works for the newspaper, but they have been called to the inquiry not only to authenticate their reports but also to defend themselves against a handful of eyewitnesses who have attacked the probity of the archive, even suggesting that some of the notes were concocted.

My notebooks and the archive memos are artefacts, transcribed from tapes made at the time (the tapes sadly did not survive). They are Rankean primary sources, immutable, inanimate, unaffected by fading memories. In such cases, historians would surely have advised the new inquiry to apply Occam's Razor – the principle of research that warns against 'multiplying entities without necessity'. In other words, in situations of doubt, prefer the simplest explanation, with the fewest number of assumptions. In the case of Bloody Sunday, what an eyewitness wrote down at the time, or told reporters, and had had no opportunity to alter later was, in fact, the best description of what he saw.

What seems clear to me is that if the *Sunday Times* had insisted that the 'Rankean' notes, the hard facts of what happened, be separated from the confidential assertions, conjectures, assumptions and inter-office memos that were added as our personal comment; if they had insisted that the journalistic bond of confidentiality between reporter and interviewee be respected, they might have lost their case but at least our eyewitnesses would have known they were not abandoned. Lord Saville would have been able to proceed more constructively towards the truth.

If a debate about methods of handling our material took place within the Saville inquiry, it was not made public. The new inquiry is run by lawyers not historians and, however inquisitorial they are urged to be, lawyers are in the end gladiators. A barrister representing the families of those killed will try to discredit a soldier's evidence; the army barrister will attempt to discredit civilian testimony that threatens his client. They will fight their corner.

Under questioning by the Saville inquiry, eyewitnesses were first asked to put down what they remembered. Those recollections were, of course, subject to memory lapses and embellished by the telling and retelling of the story over the years. Only after completion of this 30-year-old recollection was the witness confronted with interviews given at the time, and sometimes not until they reached the charged atmosphere of the open hearings.

Understandably, they were startled by such a confrontation. Some agreed they did recall seeing Insight reporters; even that our notes had jogged their memories. Others said they simply could not remember. As reporters, we sympathised. In some cases, we could not remember interviewing them; but we knew we had because of our typed memos and notes, many of them with additions and corrections in our own handwriting. We may have made mistakes, but we did not invent things.

In still other cases, the witnesses may have wanted to forget or not own up to the contents of an original statement, perhaps because it might land them in trouble. At this point, the witnesses made the only move still open: they denied everything. The barristers of the inquiry tear away at these inconsistencies, a destructive process in which the search for the truth can become compromised.

Tony Blair reopened the government's public inquiry into Bloody Sunday in 1998 as a tangent to the peace process – the first time a public inquiry had been revisited in the history of the 1921 Act. Blair's idea was that the Saville inquiry should take the form of the 'Truth and Reconciliation' hearings in South Africa, but there was an important difference. In South Africa, the apartheid government no longer existed; the past could be recollected in relative tranquillity. The political battle in Northern Ireland is not yet over, as the Saville inquiry is constantly being reminded. Each time the inquiry tries to penetrate the military, political and intelligence establishment of the British government, they are rebuffed. The soldiers' evidence will be anonymous. The political and intelligence evidence is still stamped SECRET, as far as we know.

This means that the bigger and still unanswered questions about Bloody Sunday are unlikely to be resolved, despite the millions spent. It seems we may never know the real background to the political decision to put civilians at risk, or about the military decision to use the paratroopers, the nations' elite fighting force, to arrest stone-throwing hooligans, or about covert intelligence sideshows that planted 'evidence' to put the soldiers' actions in a better light.

While no one expects to see a piece of paper detailing a military plan to 'get some kills in Derry', and no one expects the security forces to go back on their original stories that they were fired on, there are enough senior commanders, politicians and government officials who are still alive and due to give evidence who ought to be able to explain a lot better than any such witness has done thus far what really happened. For the sake of the 'closure' to this tragic day that everyone seeks, this line-up of officials should include the government actuary who made out the compensation cheques to the families of those who were killed. ❏

Peter Pringle *is co-author, with Philip Jacobson, of* Those Are Real Bullets Aren't They? Bloody Sunday, Derry, January 30, 1972 *(Fourth Estate, 2000)*

HOLDING ON TO A DREAM
CAROLINE MOOREHEAD

SOME 5 MILLION PALESTINIANS, DESCENDED
FROM THE 1.4 MILLION ARABS WHO LIVED IN
PALESTINE BEFORE 1948, WERE GUARANTEED
THE RIGHT TO RETURN AT 'THE EARLIEST
PRACTICABLE DATE'. OVER 50 YEARS LATER,
PALESTINIANS THROUGHOUT THE DIASPORA HANG
ON TO A DREAM THAT IS ALL BUT A DEAD LETTER

Above the door and a little to one side, hung high and conspicuous in the ochre-painted room, with its cracked walls and chairs packed closely around the sides, is a framed photograph of a man in his 30s. He has a neat moustache, round rimless glasses and the quiet and scholarly look of a schoolteacher. His hair is cut short, trimmed carefully around his ears; he wears his pale blue shirt open at the neck. Fadwa, the young man's mother, much of her face covered by her black scarf, says that it is a photograph of her son, Abdel. Abdel, she explains, is a martyr. Employed by President Arafat as one of his security men, Abdel was killed last year in Gaza when Arafat's headquarters received a direct hit from an Israeli missile. Fadwa was in Gaza when it happened and saw the damage from her doorway. Abdel was 36, the father of three children.

Abdel is Fadwa's only martyred son. But, sitting in her two-room flat in the derelict and dusty suburb of Cairo where she brought up her large family, she waits every day for news that one of his brothers may have become a martyr too. Fadwa has three other sons, all of them working for Arafat in Gaza, Ramallah and the West Bank. Her two daughters, with their young children, live not far away from her in Cairo; a daughter-in-law, new wife to the son in Gaza, is pregnant and shares Fadwa's two rooms. They have plenty of room now that there are just the two of them. For many years, while the children were small, the two rooms were home to the entire family and though she kept hoping to move somewhere she could hang out her washing and see the sun, they never believed they would be in Egypt for long enough to make a move worthwhile. Fadwa's husband, who left Palestine in the late 1960s to work for the PLO abroad, was killed while trying to mend a faulty electric socket some years ago.

There are about 70,000 Palestinians living in Egypt today. Neither residents nor refugees, they occupy the no man's land of permanent exile inflicted on Palestinians in the Arab world, perpetuated by Israel and the Arab governments alike. They came to Egypt from Palestine in 1948, when Palestinians fled the first Arab–Israeli war and nearly 1 million became refugees outside what had been their own country. More left after the 1967 war. More refugees again were created by the 1970–71 civil war in Jordan, by Israel's 1982 invasion of Lebanon and by the 1991 Gulf War. Palestinian refugees today are estimated at somewhere between 4.5m and 6.5m, the largest single body of refugees in the world, with the highest number in Jordan, the only Arab state to have granted them mass citizenship. Over half are without the right of citizenship in any country.

Fadwa, like her husband, was born in Gaza, when Palestine was a legitimate entity lived in by its Palestinian citizens. Five of her seven children were born there before she left to join her husband in Cairo in 1973. As her sons grew up and went to work for the PLO, so they were sent to other PLO bases throughout the Arab world, to Tunisia, Yemen and Libya, while her daughters took jobs with the PLO in Cairo, in offices dealing with pensions and health and relations with foreign states. The Palestinian diaspora has particular meaning for them.

As for so many Palestinians scattered around the Arab world, this meaning includes a very particular idea of home. Home is Palestine or, more exactly, for Fadwa and her family, Gaza, which is where they came from and where they intend to go back. Fadwa has visited Gaza once in just under 40 years, in the late 1990s, when she got permission to join the entire family for a reunion, the first time she had seen her sons in many years. She had not seen Abdel for 20 years; his two younger brothers for ten and six. She says her journey was 'as good as visiting the mausoleum of Prophet Mohammed'. Her daughters have never been to Gaza at all. Asked what they regard as home, none of them hesitates. Gaza is where they belong. It is not something that needs to be discussed.

No one has treated the Palestinian refugees well. Certainly not the Israeli settlers who occupied their lands in 1948, drove them from 531 towns and villages and stole their water. But nor have the countries that took them in and chose to keep them in permanent limbo, hovering between memory and an unknown future.

The 5 million or so Palestinians around the world are descended from the 1.4 million Arabs who lived in Palestine before 1948. With the proclamation of the new state of Israel, some 780,000 fled from the territory controlled by Israel, but they did not stray far: 86% are said to live today in historical Palestine or within a 100-mile radius around it. Another 120,000, who lived in border areas, were recognised as refugees by the United Nations because they had lost lands and livelihoods. Late in 1948, the UN General Assembly, pressed by the UN mediator in Palestine, Count Folke Bernadotte, declared that all the refugees wishing to return to their homes to 'live in peace with their neighbours' were to be permitted to do so at 'the

> LATE IN 1948, THE UN DECLARED THAT ALL THE REFUGEES WISHING TO RETURN TO THEIR HOMES WERE TO BE PERMITTED TO DO SO AT 'THE EARLIEST PRACTICABLE DATE'

earliest practicable date'. It would be an 'offence against the principles of elemental justice', said Bernadotte, not to allow them to do so. Under Resolution 194, only two solutions were envisaged at that stage for the Palestinian refugees: repatriation and compensation.

And there, 54 years later, the matter still largely rests. Resolution 194 continues to stand, and has been reaffirmed, year after year, by the UN General Assembly, surviving even the ill-fated Oslo process. Countless resolutions have upheld the right to return, and condemned Israeli human rights violations. But since 1948, except in special cases, and under a variety of visas and permits, the Palestinian refugees have not been allowed back.

Palestinian refugees suffer from a further difficulty. In 1949, the UN Relief and Works Agency for Palestine Refugees in the Near East was established, mainly to help the refugees in matters of health, education and aid. When, two years later, the UN Refugee Convention was drafted, a decision was taken to exclude all those already protected or assisted by a UN agency – effectively denying protection to Palestinians under UNRWA's sphere of operations. To this day, many of the rights accorded to Convention refugees do not apply to UNRWA ones.

With repeated flights of Palestinians since 1948, their status has become further complicated. Some countries have treated them considerably better than others. In Lebanon, for instance, they have no civil rights, can only rarely work in the public sector or the civil service, and should they leave Lebanon they have no right to return. Over half live in camps. Egypt has been relatively generous to its Palestinians, particularly under President

Palestine 2002: visions of home.
Credit: Robert Appleby

Abdel Gamal Nasser, who provided many with work permits and travel passes and allowed them to study. But under President Anwar Sadat, their position worsened. As Palestinians in Egyptian government service retired, they were not replaced. Renewal of the travel document that ensures residency has become harder to obtain and when, at the age of 21, young Palestinians are required to furnish proof either of residency or full-time education, many have no choice but to disappear into the black economy and to live illegally. Without residence, there is no work permit. According to social workers in Cairo today, well over half the Palestinian population, many of them there for many decades, live in hardship.

Fadwa's life has not been as hard as that of many others. As the widow of a PLO official she receives the equivalent of US$120 a month and when her sons were working in the different Arab states they were able to send her money. When her own children were young, Palestinians were still able to attend Egyptian schools free. In recent months, however, her life has become tougher. No money has been reaching her from abroad and she cannot contact her sons in Gaza and the West Bank because their mobile phones are now blocked. Even were it safe or practicable for her to do so, she cannot get back into Gaza, having no visa. She is not permitted to own anything in Egypt, and her landlord, who wants the two-room flat back, is doing nothing about the spreading cracks. He is unpleasant to her. Were she not the 'mother of a martyr' and entitled to health care from the Palestinian community, she would not have been able to afford a recent eye operation. 'We've been living here for 30 years,' she says, 'but we feel ourselves to be strangers.' Their friends in Egypt are all Palestinians. When Fadwa's two daughters married, there was no question but that they would take Palestinian husbands so that one day, as Fadwa puts it 'we can all go home together'.

For the rest of the world the right of return has become a bitter and painful subject, argued with passion by historians, statisticians, sociologists and, of course, politicians. The Israelis find the idea of absorbing 5 million Palestinians absurd and threatening. For the Palestinians, this right to go home remains as sacred and moral as it was over half a century ago. A writer on Palestinian affairs and member of the Palestine National Council, Salman Abu-Sitta, has produced a detailed plan, based on demographical studies, population figures and economic forecasts, to show how full repatriation is perfectly possible with minimum dislocation to the Israeli Jews. Others talk of pragmatism and advocate some balance between repatriation, resettlement in other countries and compensation. Edward Said, who has accused Yasser Arafat and the Palestinian leadership of selling out the Palestinian people, supports the idea of new leaders who will press for the rightful claims of return and compensation. And so the arguments go on, the bilateral talks and quadrilateral meetings, with passion but no agreement.

For Fadwa and her daughters, who represent the voice of the refugees themselves, missing from many of the debates, it is all extremely simple. They are not greatly concerned about what happens to the Israelis, beyond wishing to see them disappear from Palestine. They rise above the stories of hostility encountered by those who return to Gaza and the West Bank, already the most crowded land in the world. Hard facts and political realities shimmer away in the face of a dream of terrible simplicity, fed patiently over many years. Historical memory and a profound emotional commitment have sustained them in their years as second-class citizens in a foreign country, constantly overlooked, discriminated against, impoverished. Home, that enduring mental construct that can make the unendurable possible to bear, is Gaza. The question for the three women is not whether they will go back, but when. ❏

Caroline Moorehead is a writer and journalist. She has a biography of Martha Gellhorn coming out next year and is presently working on a book about refugees and asylum seekers, both for Chatto & Windus

JUST A LITTLE FAMILY TROUBLE

THE CLOSURE OF A TV NETWORK IN
SYRIA PROVOKES A CONVULSION OF
INTER-FAITH TENSION — AND TURNS
OUT TO HAVE MORE THAN A LITTLE TO
DO WITH THE US 'WAR ON TERRORISM'

'This is an infernal spiral that could take us to into a major new confrontation,' predicts the English-speaking *Daily Star* newspaper in Beirut, as calls from the country's Christian community for action in defence of public liberties sound off against the protests of the country's Muslims.

The dispute follows the 4 September decision by the country's press council review tribunal to uphold the closure of the *Murr TV* (MTV) satellite network and *Radio Mount Lebanon*, both owned by Gabriel Murr, a Lebanese Christian parliamentarian and critic of Syria's continuing army-backed intervention in Lebanon. By a quirk of family fate, Lebanon's interior minister, Elias Murr, is Gabriel's uncle, who has had to execute an order that thinly disguises its pro-Syrian purpose.

Apparently a simple family affair; at worst a domestic political spat. Yet tension remained high in Beirut for a week after the decision. The National Congress for the Defence of Press Freedoms criticised the closures, but the French-language daily *L'Orient-Le Jour*, while regarding the matter as 'a veritable circus', maintained that it was 'not just a simple issue of freedom of the media'.

Indeed. In Lebanon, even these small-town machinations have geopolitical ramifications. 'To the pro-Syrians, Gabriel Murr and MTV long ago crossed the red line, notably in the station's reports on exiled Lebanese army general Michel Aoun — still the principal focus of opposition to Syrian intervention in Lebanon — and his visit to the United States.' While such internal opposition may be tolerable, follows *L 'Orient-Le Jour*, the authorities cannot tolerate the broadcast of programmes that touch on the interests of Syria, Lebanon's 'Big Brother'.

'The crisis of information and free expression in Lebanon is a direct consequence of the current trial of strength between the US and Syria,' argues the daily *an-Nahar*. 'The crisis has escalated in the days since the introduction of the US Syria Accountability Bill [the US Congress bid to bring sanctions down on Syria for its support of groups such as Hezbollah].'

At the same time, the debate over the order to close the Murr networks and the issues of free expression that it raises is being expressed in terms of simple definitions of support, or opposition, to the continuing Syrian presence in Lebanon. 'Independent of the questions of basic freedoms, right to information or all the other internal issues facing Lebanon, the question of the Syrian presence is, and has been for some years, the principal axis around which Lebanese political actors must position themselves.'

But if at first sight the decision to close the networks appears to have been made without taking account of the likely consequences, it should not be forgotten that Lebanon remains Syria's 'choice of location for the settlement of its accounts with the United States'.

An-Nahar suggests that by kindling communal conflicts in Lebanon, Syria aims to send Washington this message: 'A minor political–familial dispute has split Lebanon down denominational lines and may yet risk the future of the country's democratic system and its respect for basic rights and freedom of information. What would happen if Syria was not present in Lebanon to watch over its stability?'

Echoing this thesis, the daily *as-Safir* notes that the bid to introduce the Syria Accountability Act triggered a series of letters from President George W Bush to the US Congress warning that disputes with Syria bear heavy costs elsewhere. The pro-Syrian daily quotes at length one letter from Bush noting that the management of the 'complicated relationship' with Syria at a time when the US is closing on Iraq – the country's neighbour and long-time foe – requires a 'meticulous study' of the different choices that must be made in order to serve US interests. Imposing new sanctions on Syria could curtail US margins of manoeuvre at a delicate moment.

The crisis may end up as more than just a pretext to force negotiations between Syria and the US. In the event of US strikes against Iraq it would be wise for Syria to restrain itself on the regional stage in exchange for confirmation of Damascus's pre-eminent role in Lebanon and an adjournment of the Syria Accountability Act. ❏

Courrier Internationale

A censorship chronicle incorporating information from Agence France-Press (AFP), Alliance of Independent Journalists (AJI), Amnesty International (AI), Article 19 (A19), Association of Independent Electronic Media (ANEM), the BBC Monitoring Service Summary of World Broadcasts (SWB), Centre for Human Rights and Democratic Studies (CEHURDES), Centre for Journalism in Extreme Situations (CJES), the Committee to Protect Journalists (CPJ), Canadian Journalists for Free Expression (CJFE), Democratic Journalists' League (JuHI), Glasnost Defence Foundation (GDF), Human Rights Watch (HRW), Information Centre of Human Rights & Democracy Movements in China (ICHR DMC), Instituto de Prensa y Sociedad (IPYS), the United Nations Integrated Regional Information Network (IRIN), the Inter-American Press Association (IAPA), the International Federation of Journalists (IFJ/ FIP), the Media Institute of Southern Africa (MISA), Network for the Defence of Independent Media in Africa (NDIMA), International PEN (PEN), Open Media Research Institute (OMRI), Pacific Islands News Association (PINA), Radio Free Europe/Radio Liberty (RFE/ RL), Reporters Sans Frontières (RSF), Transitions Online (TOL), the World Association of Community Broadcasters (AMARC), World Association of Newspapers (WAN), World Organisation Against Torture (OMCT), Writers in Prison Committee (WiPC) and other sources including members of the International Freedom of Expression eXchange (IFEX)

AFGHANISTAN

Representatives from Afghan civil society and foreign media NGOs met in Kabul on 30–31 July and again in early September to discuss key issues facing the Afghan media. The seminars, organised by the Afghan government and the UN, considered a policy document published by the Afghan Ministry of Information and Culture. Proposals included the development of public service broadcasting networks, relaxation of restrictions on publication and an end to harassment of the media. (Index Online)

Afghanistan's Supreme Court dropped a blasphemy charge against interim Women's Affairs Minister **Sima Samar** for 'lack of evidence', said Deputy Chief Justice Fazel Ahmad Manawi in July. She allegedly told a Canadian newspaper that she did not believe in Islamic sharia law. (BBC Online)

Professor **Chris Csikszentmihalyi** of the Massachusetts Institute of Technology unveiled a prototype robot war correspondent - designed to cover wars judged too physically or politically dangerous for human reporters. Set up to send its reports via the Internet, The Afghan Explorer made its debut in June, predictably in a luxury hotel, not far from the bar. (AP)

ALGERIA

On 1 July, former Algerian Defence Minister General Khaled Nezzer sued ex-army officer **Habib Souaidia**, author of *The Dirty War 1992–2000*, an eyewitness account of how soldiers disguised as Islamist rebels massacred civilians. French state prosecutors declined to support his suit in France, citing Souaidia's right to free expression. (Algeria-interface.com, El País)

On 3 July, police forcibly broke up a peaceful demonstration by relatives calling for an investigation into the 4,000 Algerians who have 'disappeared' in police custody since 1993. (AI)

Algerian Berber leaders seeking linguistic and regional representation called for a boycott of local elections set for 10 October. A similar boycott resulted in a 3% turnout in May elections in the Kabylia region (*Index* 3/2002). Over 60 Berbers arrested at protests last year (*Index* 3/2001) were released on 5 August by 'presidential amnesty' to promote 'peace in hearts and minds'. (AFP/BBC)

Cartoonist **Djamel Noun** of the daily *al-Youm* went into hiding for three days after being threatened by employees of state-owned EN TV on 7 August angered by his cartoons lampooning its recruitment policy. On 30 July, the paper was ordered to pay the equivalent of US$2,635 in libel damages over an article alleging financial improprieties at the station. (RSF)

ARGENTINA

In July, Graciela Sureda, director of culture in Escobar City tried to ban a production of *The Vagina Monologues* scheduled for the city at the request, said the producers later, of the city's mayor, a former police officer during the Junta years. The ban was lifted within days and the show went ahead.

Alberto Lamberti, a town councillor with the Justicialista Party in Comodoro Rivadavia in southern Argentina, threatened on 7 July to 'make a **José Luis Cabeza**' out of each of the town's local journalists. Cabeza, a photographer, was assassinated in January 1997. Lamberti declined to apologise, claiming that the threat 'was a joke that had been made flippantly'.

On 26 July, unknown gunmen shot up a car belonging to radio presenter **Alejandro Colussi** and then attacked his police guard. Colussi's producer, **Pablo Bosch**, made a link to his programme's support for armed police operations against a local gang conducted the day before the attack. (*Periodistas*, *Página 12*, WiPC, IFEX)

ARMENIA

Independent TV A1+, forced to close in April after losing a tender for its broadcast frequency, looks unlikely to resume broadcasting soon despite international criticism of the tender process. President Robert Kocharian told the Council of Europe in May that A1+ could seek a new tender in October 2002 but station owner **Mesrop Movsisian** said he thought the decision would depend on how Kocharian's viewed his re-election chances in 2003. (RFE/RL)

AZERBAIJAN

A new law on television and radio broadcasting passed by the Azerbaijani parliament came under fire in late June.

Its clauses allow the president to select members of a national regulatory body to oversee broadcasting and are vague on procedures for obtaining broadcasting licences. (RFE/RL)

BANGLADESH

The future of Ekushey TV (ETV), Bangladesh's only independent TV station, was again thrown into doubt after a 2 July ruling by the Supreme Court. ETV has been accused of securing a broadcast licence in 1998 through a deals with members of the then ruling Awami League party, many of whom are investors in ETV. (BBC Online)

The investigation into the attempted murder of journalist **Tipu Sultan** in January 2001 (*Index* 2/2001, 3/2001) has been reopened. So far only one suspect in the attack, Farooque Hossain Mridha, has been arrested and there has been no reported attempt to ask India to arrest and extradite Joynal Hazari, alleged to have given the order to attack Sultan. (RSF)

On 3 September, the authorities in Bangladesh banned the latest novel by exiled feminist writer **Taslima Nasreen**. Authorities say the book contains anti-Islamic remarks, and may foster religious tensions. Nasreen told the BBC: 'The political parties use religion for their own interests and whenever they find any criticism about religion, they can't tolerate it, so they ban the book.' *Wild Wind* is the sequel to *My Girlhood*, published in 1999, also banned in Bangladesh for blasphemy. Nasreen, a doctor turned writer, rose to prominence in 1993 after her

first book, *Shame*, ran into similar problems. She fled the country shortly afterwards. (BBC Online)

BELARUS

'Top government members are clearly under attack, and the aim [of this attack] is to discredit them,' said Belarusan President Aleksandr Lukashenka, calling for a crackdown on 'violations' of the country's media law. The response was prompt.

A district court in Minsk sentenced **Pavel Sevyarynets**, leader of the opposition Youth Front, to ten days in jail for organising a picket outside the presidential office on 29 July. At the protest demonstrators called for the release of jailed independent journalists **Mikola Markevich** and **Pavel Mazheyka**. The two were jailed on 24 June for defaming Lukashenka during his much-criticised re-election campaign in the weekly *Pahonya*, banned in November 2001. The two subsequently had their guilty verdicts upheld on appeal on 15 August, though their sentences of 'restriction of freedom' and corrective labour — 36 months for Markevich and 24 for Mazheyka — were each cut by 12 months. Markevich called the ruling 'a crime against freedom of speech, morality, and justice'. (RFE/RL)

Svyatlana Nekh, 22, was released on 16 August after ten days in jail in Hrodna for joining 'an unauthorised protest', called to mark the second anniversary of the disappearance of journalist **Dzmitry Zavadski**. Nekh was arrested along with nine other demonstrators. Most of them received warnings, but the judge said Nekh's special sentence was due to her record of unauthorised protest. A month earlier the country's supreme court had dismissed an appeal from Zavadski's family calling on the state to reopen his case. Four men were sentenced to terms ranging between 12 years and life in May for kidnapping or conspiracy, though the family say the truly guilty escaped prosecution. (RFE/RL)

Burglars who broke into the independent Belarusan newspaper *Zhoda* on the night of 4/5 August ignored the office cashbox and stripped out the hard disks and memory chips of the staff's computers instead. Editor **Alyaksey Karol** called the raid 'an act of intimidation' and implicated Belarusan secret services. There has been a spate of such raids on critics of the Lukashenka regime, including the Belarusan Helsinki Committee – burgled four times – and the papers *Den* and *Komsomolskaya Pravda v Belorussii*. (*Belorusskaya Delovaya Gazeta*)

Protestant churchmen in Belarus registered their concern in July at a new law that gives the Russian Orthodox Church the lead role in the country's religious affairs. But Mufti Ismail Alyaksandrovich, head of the Muslim Religious Association in Belarus, said he understood the 'historical circumstances', even if the law was 'not completely positive'. The Mufti conceded: 'We are strangers here. Islam came here with us 600 years ago. We account for a paltry 0.3% of the population . . .'(RFE/RL, Belapan)

BELGIUM

On 29 May, a Brussels court ordered **Douglas de Coninck** and **Marc Vendermeir** of the Belgian daily *De Morgen* to reveal their sources for an 11 May article reporting that a new railway station in Liège was over budget. They were fined €25 for every hour that they refused to do so. Reporters sans Frontières said the decision flew in the face of journalists' right to protect their sources, a right guaranteed by the European Court of Human Rights. (RSF)

BOSNIA

On 6 August, a British court vindicated a US policewoman investigating the sex trade in Bosnia, who was sacked by her employers when she reported the scale of the problem. A 'damning dossier' sent by **Kathryn Bolkovac** revealed links between UN personnel, international aid workers and prostitution rings in the Balkans. After a two-year court battle, an employment tribunal ruled that she had been unfairly dismissed by her employers, Dyncorp, which had been contracted to investigate the trade, (*The Times*, Index Online)

BRAZIL

TV journalist **Tim Lopes** was reported tortured and killed by drug dealers in Rio de Janeiro on 2 June after going missing for a week. Police blamed fugitive drug lord Elias Maluco for the killing of Lopes, who was investigating drug trafficking and sexual abuse of young girls in Rio's slums. President Fernando Henrique Cardoso called it 'an attempt to silence

press reports about drugs'. (CPJ, IFEX, Periodistas)

BURKINA FASO

Four plainclothes policemen arrested **Christophe Koffi**, an Agence France-Presse and Reporters Sans Frontières correspondent, on 7 August. They confiscated documents and computers, and quizzed him in connection with the investigation into the murder on 1 August of **Balla Keita**, a former Côte d'Ivoire minister who had joined the opposition and subsequently sought asylum in Burkina Faso. (RSF)

BURMA

Burmese photographer **Khin Aye Kyu** was reported released from prison in June after serving a four-year sentence for distributing unauthorised videotapes and illegally possessing video equipment. She told RSF that she was trying to resume her career as a photographer, but that she had to look after her brother, **Ko Sein Ohn**, a cameraman, who remains in prison in Mandalay. Another photographer **Khin Maung Win**, also known as Sunny, is also still imprisoned. (Burma Media Online)

Attacks against Muslims were highlighted in a 12-page briefing paper, *Crackdown on Burmese Muslims*, released by Human Rights Watch on 18 July. The Burmese government 'has imposed restrictions on Muslim religious activities and taken no action to punish those responsible for destroying Muslim homes and mosques,' said HRW's Mike Jendrzejczyk. (HRW)

CANADA

The Royal Canadian Mounted Police (RCMP) refused press passes to certain journalists trying to cover the 26–27 June G8 Summit in Alberta. The assumption was that they aimed to ban publications associated with anti-globalisation protestors but the RCMP refused to explain the policy. Instead, the barred reporters were advised to make applications under the country's Access to Information Act – a process that takes weeks or months. (CJFE)

Criticism of CanWest Global's editorial interference in newspapers it owns peaked with reports that it had fired **Russell Mills**, publisher of the *Ottawa Citizen*, apparently for publishing material critical of the government without clearing it with it first. CanWest, which has gained control of a third of the country's national and regional press, has been condemned by the Canadian Journalists for Free Expression group for abusing its managerial rights 'by dismissing or disciplining not just a publisher but reporters and columnists who dare to challenge its corporate views in public'. PEN Canada has warned of the dangers of concentration of media ownership in Canada, which it says causes journalists to 'fear for their jobs simply for doing what they're supposed to do'. (CJFE, PEN Canada)

CHILE

Chile's parliament voted in July to bar journalists from the Chamber of Deputies' cafeteria and corridors after they reported how deputies were spending their time there instead of in the chamber itself – resulting in the failure of at least one government bill for lack of house votes. These and other restrictions are being challenged in the courts by the parliamentary press lobby. (IPYS, IFEX)

CHINA

The 'appalling behaviour' of the Chinese press corps covering the 2002 World Cup triggered an unprecedented row over the ethics of its new commercial media. The *China Daily* declared frankly that if 'the Chinese press used to bore their readers with political diatribes, they are now turning them off with bad taste and low ethical standards'. The state agency Xinhua said the Chinese commercial media in Korea offered bribes to team members for exclusive interviews. (*The Times*)

British-based Chinese author **Hong Ying**, author of the romance *K: The Art of Love*, published in English in June, was taken to court in China by the real-life daughter of one of his book's central characters. She wants the book banned for the next three generations or 100 years. The book deals with the relationship between an English teacher and a Chinese woman called 'K' or 'Lin', allegedly based on the real-life Chinese writer Ling Shuhua, who died in 1990. Ling's daughter, Chen Xiaoying, who lives in London, alleges that the novel's 'unbearably pornographic descriptions' slander her mother. Western legal codes halt such actions with the death of the defamed, but Chinese law allows people to seek redress for defamation of long-dead relatives' reputations. (*Asia Times*)

On 4 June, **Wang Wanxing**, 52, began his tenth year of custody in a secure Beijing psychiatric hospital where he is being treated for a 'political abnormality disease'. Wang unfurled a banner in Tiananmen Square on 3 June 1992 protesting against the 1989 crackdown on student demonstrators. He was reported to have been transferred to a ward for violent criminals in August, and there are concerns for his safety. (Index Online)

Radio Free Asia (RFA), quoting a letter received from Zhang Liang – a pseudonym for the Chinese civil servant who compiled the official documents used in The Tiananmen Papers (*Index 2/2001*) – reported on 4 June that 23 people had been detained in China by a specially formed task force to find the source of the leaks. While no one has been charged with compiling the documents, 'several people' have been arrested for possessing a copy of the book. (Radio Free Asia)

The US-based exiled poet **Bei Ling** (*Index 5/2000*) was refused entry into China from Hong Kong on 6 June. Bei had read a poem at a commemorative rally in Hong Kong on 4 June, and was told by border guards that officials in Beijing therefore declared him 'anti-government'. (AP, BBC, ICHR, Kyodo, RFA, *South China Morning Post*)

RFA reported on 5 June that in mid-May a government publishing house in Xinjiang Province burned 128 copies of *A Brief History of the Huns and Ancient Uyghur Literature* and 32,320 copies of *Ancient Uyghur Craftsmanship*. Both titles were deemed to promote 'separatist religious beliefs' among Xinjiang's Muslim population. The official *Kashgar Daily* reported that 330 'problematic' books had been censored. Xinhua reported on 7 June that Xinjiang University would teach all major courses in Chinese from 1 September, although some courses such as 'minority languages and literature' would still be taught in Uyghur. (RFA, Xinhua)

Li Lan, from Hunan Province, was arrested on 9 June and charged with 'malicious slander' of local officials whom she had accused of corruption. Her campaign against corruption, which included travelling to Beijing with 17 others to submit a petition, began in 1999 when her daughter was killed in crossfire between rival gangs supported by different police and official factions. Her arrest followed publication on 29 May of an account of the feud in the *New York Times*. (AP, NYT)

Harry Wu, who chronicled his 19 years as a political prisoner in China's labour camps, was refused entry into Hong Kong on 24 June. Wu and Perry Link, co-editor of *The Tiananmen Papers*, were to speak on press freedom at a conference held by the International Federation of Newspaper Publishers. Official sensitivities were high ahead of the arrival of President Jiang Zemin for 29 June celebrations to mark the fifth anniversary of Hong Kong's handover.

On 28 June, Qiao Xiaoyang, vice-chair of China's Legislative Affairs Commission, repeated a February request that Hong Kong enact an anti-subversion law, as required by the region's post-handover constitution. Hong Kong's Secretary for Justice, Elsie Leung, said the law, expected within the next five years, would not be aimed at 'imposing sanctions on any group' such as Falun Gong, but refused to be drawn on whether shouting 'Down with Jiang Zemin' would violate the law.

Asia Television (ATV), the second largest broadcaster in Hong Kong, is to be bought by a media conglomerate headed by Liu Changle, a former senior propaganda official in China's People's Liberation Army. Media analyst Stephen Vines said: 'People who are more outspoken as critics of the Chinese government are finding it more and more difficult to achieve the kind of outlets that they had in the past.' (AP, BBC, *South China Morning Post*, Xinhua)

The 15 June edition of *The Economist* was banned from distribution in China because of a feature article on the need for political reform and an editorial entitled 'Set China's politics free'. Previous issues have had contentious articles ripped out, but this is the first time that an entire issue has been banned. (*South China Morning Post*)

A 32-clause circular was distributed to the Chinese media in late June banning reporting of sensitive political issues such as class division and President Jiang Zemin's decision to invite entrepreneurs to join

the Chinese Communist Party (CCP). The stated aim was 'to create a suitable atmosphere' ahead of the November CCP Congress where party factions will vie for leadership positions. (*South China Morning Post*)

A fire on 15 June that killed 25 students in an unlicensed Beijing Internet café triggered renewed efforts to control the Internet in China (*Index* passim). The day after the tragedy, Beijing officials closed all 2,400 web cafés in the city for 'rectification', with other cities following suit.

As well as registering with four separate ministries, web café owners are now required, unusually for China, to pass fire safety examinations. On 28 June, it was reported that the cafés had two weeks to install software to block 500,000 banned sites, read all usernames and passwords and automatically report to police if a user tries to access a proscribed site.

The heaviest sentence yet recorded for a web crime was handed down on 24 July to **Li Dawei**, an ex-policeman from Gansu Province, 11 years in prison on charges of 'subversion'. He was said to have printed out 500 'reactionary articles' from foreign-based pro-democracy websites and emailed Chinese dissidents abroad.

Thirty Internet cafés reopened in Beijing on 17 July under strict operating rules, including a ban on under-18s. Fewer than 46,000 of China's 200,000 Internet cafés were expected to be still in business by 1 October after compulsory re-registration. Meanwhile, Chinese internet service providers (ISPs) and search engine sites were told to sign up to a March 'self-discipline' pact barring signatories from producing or spreading material 'harmful to national security and social stability'. The Committee to Protect Journalists (CPJ) estimated on 15 July that 130 ISPs had signed the pact, including US-based Yahoo Inc. Eighteen prominent academics – including Mao Yushi (*Index* 3/2000) – issued an open letter to government on 29 July questioning the legality of restricting public access to the Internet under China's constitution and two UN covenants ratified by China. *The People's Daily* reports that as of end June, there were 45.8m registered Internet users in China – up over 70% on last year. (AP, BBC, CPJ, ICHR, Reuters, RSF, SCMP, Xinhua)

COLOMBIA

The Foundation for Press Freedom (FLIP) reported three media workers killed, three kidnapped, four attacked, four forced into exile and two threatened in Colombia in July alone. Among them were **Mario Prada Díaz**, of the weekly *El Semanario Sabanero* in Santander department in northeastern Colombia, kidnapped from his home on 11 July and found shot dead the following day nearby, and radio journalist **Dennis Segundo Sánchez** of Radio 95.5 Estero in El Carmen de Bolivar, murdered on 17 July while at home with his wife. **Elizabeth Obando**, distribution manager for the regional newspaper *El Nuevo Día* in the municipality of Roncesvalles, died on 13 July

from wounds sustained at a roadblock two days earlier. **Angela Yesenia Bríñez**, the municipality's spokesperson, died in the same attack, which was blamed on members of the Revolutionary Armed Forces of Colombia (FARC). Obando had been threatened by the local FARC commander in March.

Rebeca Jaramillo and **Breitner Bravo**, news presenters on local TV station Notimar in Buenaventura, in eastern Valle del Cauca province, were wounded on 15 July by gunmen on a motorcycle. Jaramillo, three months pregnant, was hit by five bullets and Bravo by three. Bravo had earlier been threatened by the paramilitary United Self-Defence Forces of Colombia. (AUC)

On 28 June, **Efraín Varela Noriega**, owner of Radio Meridiano-70 in the northeastern town of Arauca, was shot dead by gunmen apparently in retribution for hosting programmes that had criticised paramilitary violence on both sides of Colombia's 38-year civil conflict. (FLIP, RSF)

CZECH REPUBLIC

Four people were arrested for plotting to murder one of the Czech Republic's best-known journalists, **Sabina Slonkova**, the Czech Interior Ministry announced on 22 July. Slonkova, who works for the daily newspaper *Mlada fronta Dnes*, was to have been targeted on 17 July. Two years ago the Czech Prosecutor-General's Office charged Slonkova and **Jiri Kubik**, also from *Mlada fronta Dnes*, with obstruction of justice after

they refused to reveal their sources for an article on a plot to discredit former Social Democrat Party deputy chairwoman Petra Buzkova. Charges were dropped in March 2001. (RFE/RL)

DEMOCRATIC REPUBLIC OF CONGO

On 7 August, **Eugène Ngimbi Mabedo**, publisher of the Kinshasa-based weekly *L'Intermédiaire*, became the fourth journalist to be detained in a three-week wave of police harassment. Three other journalists – **Delly Bonsange**, publisher of the Kinshasa-based daily *Alerte Plus*, his publication director **Raymond Kabala** and **Achille Ekele N'golyma** – were held with him in Kinshasa's Makala Prison. Ngimbi was questioned about a 2 August article on a campaign by Congolese human rights organisations to force the country's Court of Military Order to release **N'Sii Luanda** and **Willy Wenga**, two human rights activists also in detention. (RSF)

The Congolese Journalists in Danger (JED) group also reported that the country's National Intelligence Agency (ANR) had ordered Radio Fraternité Buena Muntu, Radio Télévision Débout Kasaï and Radio Télé Inter Viens et Vois to stop broadcasting news about principal opposition leader Etienne Tshisekedi and his supporters. On 7 June, **Nyemabo Kalenga**, publisher of the independent biweekly *La Tribune* was detained and questioned about an article on a financial scandal, and 12 days later **Felix Kabuizi**, publication director of the independent

La *Référence Plus* was quizzed about a story that reported the disappearance of seven rebel leaders at a sensitive moment in the country's peace process. Publisher **Raymond Luala** and reporter **Bamporiki Chamira** and three other employees of the paper *La Tempête des Tropiques* were detained on 11 June after reporting a clash between troops and civilians in Kinshasa that left four dead. (RSF)

CUBA

Bernardo Arévalo Padrón, director of the publishing house Línea Sur Press, jailed since 1997, was threatened with solitary confinement and his fellow prisoners with loss of visitation rights if he continued to send information to outside groups. The Inter American Press Association warned that such threats laid Padrón open to violence from other prisoners. (IAPA)

DOMINICAN REPUBLIC

The Minister of Higher Education, Andres Reyes Rodriguez, is demanding that all professionals be legally registered along with doctors, pharmacists, accountants, etc. Local media believe the true objective is to force the licensing of journalists so they can be banned later. (dr1.com)

EAST TIMOR

East Timorese prime minister Mari Alkatiri has demanded that newspapers provide the government with space to air their views. *The Timor Post* reported that since her nomination, Minister of Finance Madalena Boavida has refused to speak to the media, alleging bias against her. (*Timor Post*)

EGYPT

The number arrested as suspected members of the Islamic movement Hizb al-Tahrir has risen to 118, according to a statement on 20 June by a lawyer representing some of the detained, four of whom are British passport-holders. On 4 August 26 people, including three of the Britons, were charged with membership of an illegal Islamist group. (*Cairo Times*)

Female pilot **Nerin Salem** successfully sued her employers at Shorouk Airlines for loss of salary but failed to win back her job on 21 May. She had been dismissed for 'altering her uniform' by wearing a hijab veil under her pilot's cap. (*Cairo Times*)

On 27 May, the weekly tabloid *al-Midan* published what it said was the first picture ever published of the corpse of President Anwar Sadat after his assassination. The Higher Press Council judged its publication a crime and editor-in-chief **Saeed Abdel Khaliq** was fired the same day. Sadat's nephew is suing the country's intelligence service for releasing the image. (*Cairo Times*)

Film director **Inas al-Deghaidi** was reported on 2 June to have been reprimanded by a court for a line in one of her productions, *Diary of a Teenager*, that opined that 'most young Egyptian women get pregnant after engaging in sex outside marriage'. (*Cairo Times*)

On 8 June, a **19-year old student** was sentenced to three years in detention and fined US$65 for alleged homosexual behaviour. He was arrested after arranging a meeting with a police informer he had met on the Internet through a gay website. The use of undercover operations to trap suspected homosexuals is increasingly common in Egypt (*Index* 2/2002). Vice squad chief General Abdel Wahab al-Adly said in May that he had made at least 19 arrests of alleged homosexuals through such Internet entrapments. (OMCT)

Web designer **Shohdy Surur** (*Index* 1/2002, 3/2002) was sentenced to one year's imprisonment on 30 June for posting a poem on the Internet written by his late father, Naguib Surur, more than 30 years ago. According to the court, the publication of the well-known, politically critical poem, known as the 'Ummiyyat', violated publication laws aimed at protecting 'public morality'. Shohdy has been ordered to pay US$45 in bail, pending his appeal. (*al-Ahram*)

Playwright **Ali Salem** will be reinstated as a member of Egypt's Writers' Syndicate after a court ruling reported on 1 July. He was expelled in May 2001 for 'normalisation activities within the Zionist entity', having visited Israel several times and written articles in favour of normalisation. (*Cairo Times*)

On 2 July, the British film *East is East* was banned for being insulting to Islam. According to the censor, the Anglo-Pakistani comedy-drama depicted the Muslim family patriarch as ignorant, fanatical, backward and violent. (*Cairo Times*)

The seven-year jail sentence of Professor **Saad Eddin Ibrahim** (*Index* 3/2001, 1/2002) was upheld on 29 July in a retrial by the Supreme State Security Court, as were the guilty verdicts against three co-defendants. The director of the Ibn Khaldun Centre for Development Studies was accused of defaming Egypt's reputation after a documentary, monitoring elections two years ago, suggested voter participation was a good way of preventing fraud. Other charges included embezzlement and receiving foreign funds without authorisation. He has served eight months of the sentence, but said he would appeal again. (BBC/AI)

ERITREA

In August, the Committee to Protect Journalists (CPJ) confirmed that Eritrean journalist **Simret Seyoum**, a writer and general manager at the banned private weekly *Setit*, had been in Eritrean government custody since early January. This puts the total of jailed Eritrean journalists at 14, although government sources had acknowledged holding only 'about eight' media professionals. Seyoum, a hero of Eritrea's 30-year independence war against Ethiopia, was arrested on 6 January and is being held in solitary confinement near the town of Gyrmayka on the border with Sudan. All 14 journalists are being held incommunicado, and government officials refused to tell a CPJ delegation visiting

Asmara in July where the 13 other journalists are jailed. (CPJ)

ETHIOPIA

On 10 July, **Tewodros Kassa**, former editor-in-chief of the weekly newspaper *Ethop*, was sentenced to two years in jail for 'fabricating information that could incite people to political violence'. The charges relate to three *Ethop* articles published in 2001. Kassa was first imprisoned for a year in June 2000, on identical charges. (RSF)

FRANCE

A French minister rejected calls for a government inquiry into allegations that Algerian militants were tortured by French soldiers during Algeria's war of independence. Army Veterans' Affairs Minister Hamlaoui Mekachera, himself one of the so-called 'harki' – Algerians who fought for France during the 1954–62 war – rejected accounts that torture was widespread and committed with impunity. 'Let us not re-open wounds that have not yet healed over,' he told French Catholic daily *La Croix*. Earlier this year, retired army general **Paul Aussaresses** was fined €7,500 ($7,400) for condoning war crimes and defending torture by French forces in his memoirs. French veterans of the Algerian war are protected from war crimes prosecution by a 1968 amnesty. (*La Croix*)

The French government is seeking to ban the **Radical Unity group** – a far-right organisation linked to a man arrested for trying to shoot French president Jacques

Chirac. The group would be broken up by a 1936 law prohibiting groups that provoke racial discrimination or ethnic hatred. Radical Unity said that it was not a militia of the kind targeted by the law. (*Washington Post*)

Laïd Sammari, of *l'Est Républicain* newspaper, became the seventh journalist to have his telephone tapped over the last three years in conjunction with a French National Anti-Terrorist Service investigation targeting the Corsican nationalist leader François Santoni. Despite the legality of telephone tapping, the fact that judges are brushing off the principle of confidentiality of journalistic sources has become a significant press freedom issue in France, says Reporters sans Frontières. (RSF)

GAMBIA

The Gambian parliament has passed a new and tougher media bill, two months after President Yahya Jammeh vetoed it. The bill was passed by 53 votes to three, with ruling party members castigating the independent media for being 'unpatriotic' and always reporting 'the bad side' of the government. The Gambia Press Union is opposed to the bill, which provides for the establishment of a media commission with authority equivalent to that of a high court. 'The commission would register all reporters, be authorised to enforce the disclosure of sources and have the power to impose heavy fines for the publication of 'unauthorised government stories,' said the Union. It would also be able to sentence journalists to jail terms for contempt, close down media houses for non-compliance with its orders and admit evidence not admissible in ordinary courts. (AllAfrica.com, IPI)

On 2 August, **Pa Ousman Darboe**, a reporter for the Banjul biweekly *The Independent*, was arrested and detained by the National Intelligence Agency (NIA) in connection with the publication of an article about the financial affairs of the late husband of the country's vice-president. The managing editor of *The Independent*, **Alhaji Yoro Jallow**, was arrested on 3 July but was released the same day. (Amnesty International, RSF, Afrol.com)

GEORGIA

Georgia's justice ministry circulated a draft act on religious observance among all-faith communities and interested NGOs in July, marking the first attempt by the government to straighten out the legal framework on religion since Georgia declared independence in 1991. Jehovah's Witnesses, Pentecostal groups, Baptists and other denominations have all suffered at the hands of Orthodox Christian militants. But Giorgy Chkheidze, of the Association of Young Lawyers, argued that existing laws that could protect the minorities were not being enforced in spite of copious evidence of abuses. (IWPR)

GHANA

In late July, **Kweko Baako**, editor-in-chief of *Crusading Guide*, received death threats from two separate groups who claimed to be supporters of former Ghanaian president Jerry Rawlings. Baako recently published a controversial report linking the financial affairs of the former first lady, Nana Agyeman Rawlings, to a Swiss bank account. This is the second time this year that Baako has received death threats. (IFJ)

GUATEMALA

Anthropologist **Victoria Stanford** and journalists **David González** and **Wesley Boxed** have received death threats for beginning an investigation into mass graves exhumed in the Rabinal region of Baja Verapaz. The trio recently published evidence of crimes against humanity committed during the Guatemalan civil war in the *New York Times*. They were threatened by Kaibil, a leader of the Valentin Chen Gómez Army, said the Guatemalan Journalists Association. (APG)

On 14 July, the Jutiapa department offices of the Information Centre for Reports on Guatemala (CERIGUA) were broken into and a computer hard drive containing key information stolen. (IFEX, APG)

GUINEA-BISSAU

João de Barros, publisher of the independent daily *Correio de Bissau*, was arrested on 17 June after appearing on a chat show on independent Radio Bombolom in which he derided rumours of a coup plot against President Kumba Yala as attempts to divert attention from government corruption. He also dismissed Yala's military threats against neighbouring Gambia as 'pathetic'. De Barros was released on 19 June after going on hunger strike in detention. The next day **Nilson Mendonca**, editor of state-run Rádio Difusão Nacional, was also briefly detained after his station reported that Yala was to apologise to Gambian authorities for accusing them of supporting Guinabe insurgents. (CPJ)

HAITI

Haitian broadcast journalist **Israel Jacky Cantave** and his cousin **Frantz Ambroise** were kidnapped on 15 July and beaten and abused for two days before being released. Cantave's assailants made him listen to his mother plead for her son on a local radio station, telling him that it would 'the last time you're going to hear your mother's voice'. Cantave blamed forces angered by his reports for Radio Caraïbes and has since gone into hiding. (RSF)

Reporters **Darwin Saint Julien** of the weekly paper *Haïti Progrès* and **Allan Deshommes** of Radio Atlantik were seriously injured by police on 27 May while covering a demonstration organised by the Batay Ouvriyè (Workers' Struggle) group in the northern town of Saint Raphael. Armed men and local officials attacked the protesters, killing two. Despite serious injuries, the journalists were then briefly detained in the capital's National Penitentiary. The mayor of Saint Raphael, Adonija Sévère, claimed the demonstrators and the journalists were 'terrorists'. (RSF)

HUNGARY

The editor of Hungarian opposition daily *Magyar Nemzet*, **Gabor Liszkay**, used the front page of the 2 August edition to make a direct appeal to the daily's readers, accusing 'the powers that be' of trying to eliminate the newspaper. As a result of government pressure, the newspaper's contracts are being cancelled, a new printing press must be sought and advertisements have virtually disappeared from the daily. (RSF/RL)

INDIA

Indian police arrested **Kumar Badal** from the investigative website tehelka.com on 3 July after they claimed he had failed to give 'satisfactory' answers about his reports on the illegal poaching of leopards. The website's exposé last year of political and military corruption stunned India, and its editor says the arrest was politically motivated. 'It is pressure tactics of the government to force Tehelka to close down,' claimed Badal's colleague **Aniruddha Bahal**. On 7 August, Bahal was also arrested, on charges of assaulting a federal investigator. (tehelka.com)

Shahid Rashid, editor of the Urdu-language daily *State Reporter*, was shot in the neck and arm on 10 July by masked gunmen on his way to work in Srinagar, in India-controlled Jammu and Kashmir. (CPJ)

On 21 August, the Allahabad High Court banned news coverage of hearings on a proposed excavation at the disputed temple-mosque site at Ayodhya. Rival Hindu and Muslim groups are contesting proposals to excavate the disputed site to find whether a temple really existed there before a mosque was built on the spot in the sixteenth century. Militant Hindus demolished the sixteenth-century Babri mosque in 1992, vowing to replace it with a Hindu temple to Rama. The destruction prompted one of India's worst bouts of nationwide religious rioting between Hindus and the country's Muslim minority, which left 2,000 people dead.

On 6 June, Indian film censors demanded that director **Anand Patwardhan** make several cuts to his award-winning anti-nuclear documentary *Jang aur Aman* (*War and Peace*) before it could be released. Patwardhan claimed the censors had acted according to 'their own particular ideologies'. (*Times of India*)

Iftikhar Gilani, the New Delhi bureau chief for the Jammu-based newspaper *Kashmir Times* and a regular contributor to *Deutsche Welle* and the Pakistani *Friday Times* and *The Nation*, was arrested in the early hours of 9 June at his Delhi home. Police accused Gilani of possessing classified documents and arrested him under the Official Secrets Act but only cited a public document covering alleged human rights abuses by Indian troops in Kashmir, released in 1995 by Pakistan's Foreign Ministry. Gilani's father-in-law, **Syed Ali Shah Geelani**, a senior separatist leader in Kashmir, was arrested the same day. (CPJ)

Alex Parry, *Time* magazine's New Delhi bureau chief, sparked controversy with an unflattering profile of Prime Minister Atal Behari Vajpayee in the 17 June edition of *Time Asia*. Headed 'Asleep at the Wheel?' it was widely criticised by government officials for questioning Vajpayee's health and his ability to exercise proper control over the country's nuclear weapons. Government officials called Parry in twice for questioning about his British passport before 27 June when the Press Trust of India reported that *Time* had apologised to the government 'for the manner in which certain portions [of the article] were constructed and phrased'. (Press Trust India, *Times of India*, India Abroad News Service, Associated Press)

P Nedumaran, president of the Tamil Nationalist Movement, was arrested in Chennai on 1 August under the new Prevention of Terrorism Act (POTA) for making a speech in support of the Liberation Tigers of Tamil Eelam (LTTE) last April. Less than three weeks earlier, **Vaiko**, MP and leader of the Marumalarchi Dravida Munnetra Kazhagam, was also arrested in Chennai under POTA because of his public support for the LTTE in Sri Lanka. While local political rivalries have driven the charges, the BJP-led central government found its attempts to back its MDMK ally blocked by its earlier decision to add the LTTE to a list of 25 groups proscribed under the act. (Rediff.com)

The Madras High Court decided on 19 July to allow the first World Tamil Conference to take place in Chennai, despite police claims that the two-day meeting would feature speeches in support of the banned LTTE and sell books supporting its separatist war against the Sri Lankan government. The court overruled police once the organisers promised to ensure that the LTTE would not be mentioned at the conference. (Gulf News Online, *Frontline*, *The Hindu*, UNI)

On 22 July, **Amnesty International** (AI) expressed its 'deep regret' at the central government's de facto refusal to allow it access to Gujarat to investigate recent ethnic violence there (*Index* 2/2002, 3/2002). AI teams applied for visas but the government had failed to respond by a mutually agreed deadline of 12 July. (AI)

On 3 September, special Prosecutor SK Saxena admitted to the Delhi High Court that Ravi Kant Sharma, a much-decorated police officer and prime suspect in the 23 January 1999 murder of *Indian Express* journalist **Shivani Bhatnagar**, had 'fled the country to escape arrest and avoid investigation'. Sharma, who has been on the run since 1 August this year, had allegedly been having an adulterous affair with Shivani around the time of the murder, and may have stolen official documents from the prime minister's office. Shivani had apparently threatened to ruin his career by disclosing this information. (*The Hindu*)

INDONESIA

Two demonstrators have been prosecuted for defilement of the president's image by painting an 'X' on photos of President Megawati Soekarnoputri and Vice-President Hamzah Haz, according to the Indonesia Legal Aid and Human Rights Association (PBHI). Chief prosecutor Luhut Sianturi charged the defendants **Muzakkir**, alias Aceh, and **Nanang Mamija**, alias Junet, with violation of Article 134 of the Criminal Code on premeditated insults to the president or vice-president, which carries a maximum penalty of six years in prison. (PBHi)

IRAN

Siamak Pourzand, the renowned Iranian journalist and film critic who is serving 11 years in prison at the age of 72, has reportedly confessed to 'treason' before Iranian news agencies. The Writers in Prison Committee of International PEN fears that he may have been ill-treated or otherwise coerced into making the 'confession' and is concerned for his wellbeing. He was said to have been in apparent distress as he asked for a pardon. The Tehran Press Court sentenced Pourzand to 11 years' imprisonment in May on charges of 'undermining state security through his links with monarchists and counter-revolutionaries'. (PEN)

Iran's official Association of Muslim Journalists has given its backing to police operations to counter 'manifestations of immorality and corruption in society'. It welcomed the police strategy, which it said made it possible for individuals and families to pursue social activities in 'an atmosphere dominated by comfort, confidence and encouragement'. Other 'social disorder cases to be dealt with by police' include 'loud noise in passing cars' and 'transporting pets in vehicles'. Hojatoleslam Abdolhussein Ramazani, head of the police intelligence service, said police officers had been ordered to prevent certain public gatherings to promote and guarantee society's security. (IRNA)

On 16 July, Iranian political activist **Arman Nouri** was attacked at his own dental surgery in Paris. He was stabbed several times in the back, chest and stomach before the assailant escaped. (Private source)

The Supreme National Security Council (SNSC) ordered newspaper editors not to publish comment on the resignation letter of **Ayatollah Jalaluddin Taheri**, the eminent Friday prayer leader of Isfahan. In a major act of dissent from within the clergy, Taheri, a highly respected veteran of the 1979 revolution, attacked the authorities for their corruption, exploitation of religion and links with 'fascist' gangs. The SNSC's order was widely ignored and Taheri's statement was published in the reformist press on 10 July. (MEI)

IRAQ

Authorities in Iraq barred **Diar al-Umari**, Baghdad correspondent of the Qatar-based satellite TV station al-Jazeera, from working in the country for ten days 'as a punishment for certain words used in his dispatches'. The authorities did not specify the words in question, despite al-Jazeera's requests. (RSF)

Iraqi authorities barred travellers from bringing newspapers or letters – even Iraqi official publications – in or out of the country, Iraqi media reported in July. Each driver is now required to submit a written report on each trip made to either Amman or Damascus, the Iraqis' main gateways to the outside world. (Middle East Online)

ISRAEL

In August, Prime Minister Ariel Sharon ordered an investigation into the peace group **Gush Shalom** after it warned 15 senior Israeli army officers that their actions in the West Bank constituted war. Communications Minister Reuven Rivlin said Gush Shalom asked if such actions were not tantamount to treason. In 15 letters, Gush Shalom warned that the actions of one officer violated international law and that the movement might take him to court, either in Israel or at the International Criminal Court in The Hague. The previous month it was announced that in the light of the establishment of the new Hague court, the Israeli military has banned the use of soldiers' surnames, places of residence and military activities in reports from the Occupied Territories. (*Haaretz*, Index Online)

On 25 July, the Supreme Court refused a petition from **Mordechai Vanunu** (*Index* 1/1987 to 5/1997 passim) to meet British lawyers with regard to bringing a case against the British government for its failure to give him better protection while resident there. Vanunu was imprisoned for 18 years for whistle-blowing on Israel's secret nuclear weapons programme, after being lured away from Britain by Israeli intelligence operatives. (Campaign to Free Vanunu)

Yosef Barel, incoming news director of the Israeli Broadcasting Association, issued orders on 30 May prohibiting the use of the term 'settlers' on radio and TV broadcasts. The instructions came after Environmental Affairs Minister Tzachi Hanegbi told Barel he should 'put an end to the frequent use of the term "settler" by the IBA'. (*Haaretz*)

On 15 July, the High Court rejected a petition from the family of **an Israeli soldier killed in the 1982 invasion of Lebanon** seeking public access to classified information relating to the 1982 Sabra and Shatila massacre. The judges ruled that it was for the government to decide whether the public's right to know outweighed security needs. The issue will be re-examined in five years. (*Haaretz*)

ITALY

Italian public broadcasters announced plans to axe two programmes hosted by **Enzo Biagi** and **Michele Santoro**, known for being critical of Prime Minister Silvio Berlusconi (given the 2002 *Index on Censorship* award for 'Services to Censorship' in recognition of his baleful grip on Italy's public and private broadcast media). In April, he accused the journalists of making 'criminal use of public television' after Sciuscia investigated alleged links between the Mafia and one of Berlusconi's top associates. Actor Roberto Benigni said on Biagi's show that he would vote against Berlusconi. (IPI)

On 23 July, 23 Italian president Carlo Azeglio Ciampi used his authority to demand that the country's parliament take steps to tackle media regulation and break up monopolies, without citing Berlusconi by name. (ilmanifesto.it)

JAPAN

Four draft laws 'threaten to compromise press freedom and the rights of reporters' in Japan, say free expression campaigners. They are the clauses in the new Human Rights Protection Bill, the Personal Data Protection Bill, the Emergency Security Bill and a bill to protect young people from sexually harmful and violent images. 'Taken together they constitute a menacing package of regulations that could threaten free media,' said International Federation of Journalists General Secretary Aidan White. (IFJ)

JORDAN

A lawsuit was filed by the Jordan Press Association (JPA) and the editors-in-chief and owners of three weekly newspapers – al-Liwa, al-Sabeel and al-Ittijah – to contest new and harsher penalties for journalists who breach media law clauses in the new revised national Penal Code. The court rejected the suit on 16 July, claiming that the four 'could not prove that harm has been inflicted on them due to the application of the Penal Code'. JPA President **Tareq Momani** noted that the disputed clauses had already been used against two of its journalist members. (*Jordan Times*)

On 14 May, the country's first woman MP, **Tujan Faisal**, was jailed for 18 months for 'spreading information harming the reputation of the state' and defamation. She was arrested in March after sending an email message to King Abdullah II accusing Prime Minister Ali Abu Ragheb of having 'benefited financially' from a government decision to double car insurance costs. Abu Ragheb is a shareholder in an insurance firm, but according to the government only a 'very minor' one. No appeal is allowed against the verdict of the state security court. (AFP)

KAZAKHSTAN

The death of **Leyla Baysetova**, daughter of Lira Baysetova, editor of the opposition weekly *Respublika*, has been blamed on criminal factions angered by the paper's coverage. Leyla disappeared on 23 May. On 16 June, an interior ministry official told Lira Baysetova that her daughter had been arrested for possession of heroin but she was denied access to her. She was finally told of her daughter's death on 21 June. Baysetova said her body showed signs of torture. Pressure had increased on Baysetova after she interviewed Geneva general prosecutor Bernard Bertossa about the Swiss bank accounts of top Kazakh officials, including President Nursultan Nazarbayev. (RSF)

KENYA

The publisher of *Finance* magazine and Kenyan MP **Njehu Gatabaki** was released by presidential decree five days after being sentenced to six months' imprisonment over an article linking President Daniel arap Moi with the deaths of 200 people in ethnic bloodshed in 1992. On 9 August, a court in Nairobi had found Gatabaki guilty of 'publishing an alarming publication'. Gatabaki told the court that he had suffered for publishing the truth. 'The articles were true,' he said. 'I'm ready to bear that burden of bringing the message to Kenyans.' The same month **Safani Asena Muyoma** and **Andrew David Matende** were ordered to pay a fine of Sh110,000 ($1,400) or serve 36 months' imprisonment on the same charge, in connection with a July 2001 article in the *Kenyan Monitor Weekly* linking Police Commissioner Philemon Abongo and Education Minister Orwa Ojode with an alleged plot to kill political rivals. (*East African Standard*, Index Online)

LIBERIA

On 24 June, **Hassan Bility**, editor of the Liberian newspaper *The Analyst*, and two others were arrested and held incommunicado. On 26 July, Information Minister Reginald Goodridge, admitting publicly that Bility and the others were in detention, accused them of running a rebel 'terrorist cell' in Monrovia. Despite repeated demands and a writ of habeas corpus, the government has refused to reveal Bility's whereabouts. Amnesty International said it is 'seriously concerned that the failure to produce the bodies of Hassan Bility and the two others could mean that they have been severely tortured or killed'. Bility had been detained twice this year and his paper shut down twice, most recently in May 2002 for its coverage of the case of human rights lawyer **Tiawan Gongloe**, unlawfully detained and tortured before being released without charge. (CPJ, RSF, Human Rights Watch)

Journalists **Bobby Tapson**, **Sherrif Adams** and **George Bardue** and editor **Jerome Dalieh** of *The News* were arrested and detained on 4 July by security forces in connection with a report that day on a number of corpses found in the streets of the capital. The men were kept in police custody for up to two hours before being released. (IPI)

LIBYA

On 19 August, Human Rights Watch criticised the choice of Libya to chair the United Nations Commission on Human Rights. The organisation called on the African Union to abandon the proposed nomination, citing widespread human rights abuses by the state, including summary executions, long-term detention without trial and numerous restrictions on the freedom of expression. (HRW)

MALDIVES

Haveeru newspaper reported that five men were arrested on 15 June for attempting to spread Christianity in the capital Male by dropping pamphlets on the street. The men are **Mohamed Fauzi**, **Mohamed Shaz Valeed**, **Abdullah Fayaz**, **Mohamed Suwaiz** and **Mohamed Amir**. (maldivesculture.com)

In late June, political activist and former MP **Mohamed Nasheed** (*Index* 2/2002, 3/2002) was returned to Male after several months' exile in the Raa atoll. Nasheed will serve out the rest of his two-and-a-half-year sentence for theft under house arrest. (maldivesculture.com)

In July, **Ibrahim Luthfee**, **Mohamed Zaki** and **Ahmed Didi** were each sentenced to 25 years' imprisonment and 12 months' banishment for attempting to 'assassinate the character' of President Maumoon Abdul Gayoom in the pages of the Dhivehi-language *Sandhannu* (*Index* 2/2002). **Fathimath Nisreen** received a ten-year sentence for writing 'baseless articles' against the government and for expressing support for *Sandhannu*. In early June, Amnesty International reported the release of **Ismail Zaki** and **Naushad Waheed**, who had also been arrested in the *Sandhannu* case. Maldivesculture.com claims, however, that Waheed is still being detained without charge. (maldivesculture.com, AI)

MAURITANIA

Officals banned the 2 July issue of the French-language weekly *La Tribune*, apparently in connection with a critical report on the government's efforts to prevent the re-election of **Mahfoudh Ould Bettah** as president of the country's Bar Association. Copies of the independent magazine *Le Rénovateur* were also seized on 24 July, apparently in connection with an article about foreign exchange and the increase in the cost of living in Mauritania.

And on 22 August, the Arabic-language weekly *Le Calame* was banned for reporting demonstrations during President Maaouya ould Sid'Ahmed Taya's recent visit to France. The Mauritanian media is subject to Article 11 of the 1991 Law on Press Freedom banning publications likely to undermine the principles of Islam or the image of the state, or compromise public order and security. (All Africa News, RSF)

On 5 June, two human rights organisations backed Mauritanian-born Frenchman **Mohammed Baba** in bringing a court action in France against the Mauritanian police, the interior minister and senior ruling party officials. Baba alleges that he was tortured while detained for nine days in April while in the country to visit his family. (allafrica.com)

MEXICO

The Acapulco Public Prosecutor has ordered journalist **Maribel Gutiérrez** of the daily *El Sur* to identify her sources for articles on the assassination of human rights activist **Digna Ochoa**. On 24 June, **Irving Leftor Magaña**, a cameraman with Telemundo cable TV news, had his leg broken by officers from the city of Pachuca Municipal Police as he covered the violent dispersal of a demonstration by the Agricultural Workers' Union. (RSF)

MOLDOVA

Parliament passed a law setting up Teleradio Moldova as a public broadcaster, local media reported on 15 August, despite a boycott by opposition deputies who say the bill did not take account of Council of Europe guidelines. The law will set up a supervisory board with 15 members appointed for a five-year term by the country's president, the parliament and the government. The board will also appoint the general director of Teleradio Moldova, who must also be approved by parliament. All current employees will be dismissed and must reapply for their jobs to a new administrative council. (RSF/RL)

MONTENEGRO

The free expression campaign group **Article 19** has expressed concern at plans to amend the existing 1998 law on public information in place of the expected adoption of far wider-ranging and liberal media laws. The group warned that the amendments would be at the expense of 'three rather progressive draft media laws' prepared over the past year by a working group established by the government and including representatives of civil society. (A19)

MOROCCO

The territorial dispute between Spain and Morocco spread to the web during the recent military stand-off over Perejil (Parsley) Island. A Spanish website hacker attacked the Moroccan National Tourism Office, replacing the home page with a Spanish flag and a patriotic message. The attack followed threats from a Moroccan hacker called BreakIce against some 15 Spanish websites. BreakIce claimed that 'cyber-war has been declared' and that 'it will only be the start of a long series of actions that will ridicule Spain'. (*El Mundo*)

Demain magazine reported on 1 July that the government had opened a 'secret file' on suspected Moroccan Islamists living abroad, particularly in Europe. It said security services from several European counties helped in the compilation of a list of some 500 names, 40 of whom are classified as 'dangerous'. (*El País*)

NEPAL

Nepali journalists **Kishor Shrestha**, editor of the *Janaastha* weekly, and **Bishnu Ghimire**, editor of the *Janaprahar* daily, were detained for a day on 5 August for publishing accusations of police corruption and alleged extortion. The two were released after **Taranath Dahal**, president of the Federation of Nepalese Journalists, met senior police officers. Police have been given sweeping powers to limit media freedoms and detain anyone without warrants for 24 days as part of the government's fight against Maoist insurgents. (CPJ)

Ramhari Paudvai, a journalist with the daily *Samacharpatra*, was arrested by security forces on 13 June in Parphing, south of Kathmandu. On 23 June, **Bishnu Khanel, Liladhar Gautam** and **Khadananda Lamichanne**, respectively editor, executive editor and journalist for the daily *Surkhet Post*, were released by security forces after seven months' detention. On 26 June, the weekly paper *Jana Astha* reported that **Krishna Sen**, editor of the

pro-Maoist daily *Jadisha* and former editor of the pro-Maoist weekly *Janadesh*, had been tortured and murdered in custody. The paper also alleged that the government had tried to cover up the murder by passing it off as a routine 'encounter' between Maoist rebels and the security forces. Sen was arrested by security forces in a Kathmandu suburb on 20 May. Prime Minister Sher Bahadur Deuba said only that the government would 'reveal the facts in time'. (*Kathmandu Post*, CPJ, RSF)

The *Kathmandu Post* reported on 7 August that **Dhan Bahadur Roka Magar**, newsreader of the local Magar-language *Kham* news bulletin on Radio Nepal, had been taken hostage by Maoist rebels while travelling in a public bus to Surkhet on 1 August. (*Kathmandu Post*)

THE NETHERLANDS

Dutch legislators have declared digitally created false images of child pornography illegal. Offenders could get up to four years' imprisonment, while habitual offenders who make money from the practice could serve six years. The ruling means that the physical involvement of a child is no longer needed for a child sex crime to be committed. (Index Online)

NICARAGUA

On 18 July, **Luis Felipe Palacios** of the daily *La Prensa* was questioned by the Criminal Investigation Unit over an article linking a high-ranking military officer to alleged money laundering and arms trafficking. Chief of

Police Edwin Cordero said that on drug trafficking matters the police can act 'as a matter of course'. Photographer **Manuel Esquivel**, who took pictures of Palacios's interrogation, was forced to hand over his film. (RSF)

NIGER

Abdoulaye Tiémogo, publication director of the satirical weekly *Le Canard Déchaîné*, was sentenced to eight months' imprisonment without parole for 'defamation and insults'. He was arrested on 18 June 2002 on Prime Minister Hama Amadou's complaint to the court. He has been arrested three times since October 2001 and had spent almost two months behind bars before the latest charge. On each occasion, a member of the government was behind the legal action that led to his imprisonment. (RSF, Index Online)

President Mamadou Tandja declared a state of alert on 5 August after an army mutiny in the eastern region of Diffa. The Emergency Decree states that 'the dissemination by any media of reports or allegations liable to cast doubt on national defence operations is forbidden'. Media organisations may be closed and individual journalists face punishment for breaching the new ruling. After the mutiny of 31 July–9 August was suppressed, human rights activist **Elhadj Bagnou Bonkoukou**, head of the Niger Human Rights League, was remanded in custody on 16 August when he challenged the given official death tolls. The Niamey authorities claimed that only

two men died in the operation. If found guilty, he could
face up to five years in prison.
(RSF, All Africa News)

NIGERIA

The British organisers of the
'Miss World' competition
have been warned by hosting
nation Nigeria to avoid parts
of the country that practise
sharia law. Islamist groups
from northern Nigeria have
threatened to disrupt the contest; they particularly object to
the swimsuit competition.
The Jama'atul Muslimeen
Sokoto has called on the
Muslim community to offer
special prayers 'to thwart the
plans of this confederacy of
immorality that is aimed at
polluting the nation's moral
atmosphere'. The warning to
the organisers follows the
execution by stoning of at
least two women for 'illicit
sexual intercourse', and the
recent sentencing of **Amina
Lawal** for the same crime.
(*Guardian*, All Africa News)

PAKISTAN

Starting in August, Pakistani
cyber cafés will be required to
ask patrons for ID, keep
records of users and start registering with the government.
In March, US authorities –
after noting an increase in
email traffic out of Pakistan –
warned that al-Qaida might
be trying to reorganise
through the Internet. Pakistan
has blocked at least one al-
Qaida website, according to
local media. (*Dawn*)

The Bishop of the Roman
Catholic Church of Pakistan
has called for the repeal of the
death sentence for blasphemy
after a man was sentenced to
hang for claiming to be Jesus

Christ. Bishop **Samuel
Azariah** said he should be
given medical treatment.
Anwar Kenneth, a Pakistani
Christian, is alleged to have
written hundreds of letters
claiming to be a reincarnation
of Jesus Christ and making
sacrilegious remarks about
Islam. He pleaded guilty to
the charges, and refused to
accept the help of a lawyer to
defend him. (BBC Online)

On 11 July, the Supreme
Court dismissed an attempt
to reverse a constitutional
amendment that would allow
only politicians with university degrees to contest forthcoming elections. Only a
small percentage of Pakistanis
are wealthy enough to have
gone to university, in a country where at least one-third of
the population cannot even
read and write. Other amendments to the constitution
include the right to sack the
prime minister, the cabinet
and parliament, and the banning of any politician who has
been prime minister or chief
minister of a province from
holding the job again, a measure clearly aimed at President
Pervez Musharraf's political
foes, former prime ministers
Nawaz Sharif and Benazir
Bhutto. (*Guardian*)

The remains of journalist
Daniel Pearl were flown
to the United States on
8 August. On 15 July, British-
born militant Ahmed Omar
Saeed Sheikh and three others
were convicted for being
involved in the *Wall Street
Journal* reporter's kidnap and
subsequent murder (*Index*
2/2002, 3/2002). Sheikh was
sentenced to death by hanging and the others received
life sentences. (*Dawn*)

PALESTINE

A delegation of the International Federation of Journalists, which visited Palestine
and Israel between 16 and 20
June, condemned a decision
by Israel to ban Palestinian
journalists from receiving
press cards issued by the Government Press Office in
Jerusalem. It said the policy
was 'humiliating and vindictive . . . and amounts to collective punishment of all
Palestinians working for local
and foreign media'. (IFJ)

Palestinian freelance photographer **Imad Abu Zahra**
died in Jenin on 12 July, a day
after being seriously wounded
by Israeli army gunfire. The
French media rights group
Reporters sans Frontières
added that Abu Zahra lost a
great deal of blood over more
than an hour because Israeli
troops refused to allow an
ambulance to reach him. Five
journalists have been killed
and more than 220 injured by
Israeli fire during the two-
year al-Aqsa intifada. (RSF)

On 15 July Israeli troops
attacked the Ramallah offices
of PalNet, the main Internet
service provider in the West
Bank. The troops used a Pal-
Net employee as a human
shield and interrogated all
staff members. The damage
resulted in several websites,
including those of universities
and government ministries,
being offline for the day. No
explanation was given by the
Israeli army. (*Palestine Monitor*,
Palestinian Human Rights
Monitoring Group)

On 26 August, the Palestinian
Journalists Syndicate banned
journalists from photographing Palestinian children carry-

INDEX ON CENSORSHIP 4 2002   123

ing weapons or taking part in activities by militant groups, saying that the pictures harm the Palestinian cause. The organisation also called on Palestinian factions and their military wings to stop using children in their activities. Reporters were also banned from photographing masked men. (AP)

PARAGUAY

On 3 July, National Telecommunications Commission officials and police shut down community radio station Ñemity FM in Capiibary, San Pedro department, citing a November 1999 court order to close the station. The radio station had supported rural organisations during recent protests in San Pedro and run a fund-raising campaign for impoverished villagers. It was this, say supporters, which provoked officials into reviving the long-forgotten court order. (AMARC, IFEX)

PERU

On 28 June, six female supporters of the Agrupación Arriba Loreto political movement threatened **Nancy Villacorta Pérez**, a news programme host at Radio 10 in Iquitos, Loreto department. The six cited her comments about former television presenter July Pinedo, the group's candidate for regional mayor, and said they would 'destroy' her if she continued to question Pinedo's ability to administer a provincial municipality. (IPYS, IFEX)

QATAR

The Qatar-based al-Jazeera satellite TV station's popular open discussion programmes continued to provoke diplomatic rancour between Gulf and Middle East states. 'Saudi Arabia is angry,' Daud al-Shrayan, Riyadh bureau chief of the Saudi-owned pan-Arab daily *al-Hayat*, told AP. Riyadh might even go further, he speculated, 'by, for example, obstructing a plan to supply Qatari gas to Kuwait via Saudi territory. The dispute is now with Qatar, not with al-Jazeera.' The dispute was ostensibly triggered by a 25 June live debate on al-Jazeera in which participants criticised Saudi Crown Prince Abdullah's Middle East peace initiative, accused Saudi Arabia of having 'betrayed the Palestinian cause', and made disparaging remarks about the kingdom's founder. A similar row blew up in Jordan, where Information Minister Mohammad Adwan condemned an al-Jazeera talk show on 6 August in which participants alleged that Jordan was covertly allowing its territory to be used as a base for US-led operations against Iraq. Ordering the closure of the station's Amman bureau, Adwan said the televised debate had gone beyond 'all limits, all ethics' of journalism. Jordan lodged a diplomatic protest with Qatar and then recalled its ambassador in Doha 'for consultations'. (BBC, MEI)

ROMANIA

Laurian Ieremeiov, deputy editor of the daily *Timişoara*, has appealed for international help to find investigative journalist **Iosif Costinas**, 62, last seen in his home town of Timişoara on 10 June. Costinas has published articles about sensitive subjects, such as the unsolved killings during the December 1989 anti-communist revolt and the continued presence in high positions of Securitate communist secret police officers. He was also completing a book about the shady business underworld in the city, located near the Yugoslav and Hungarian borders. (Index Online)

RUSSIA

Former Federal Security Service (FSB) Lieutenant Colonel Aleksandr Litvinenko has named the late FSB deputy director German Ugryumov as the instigator of two massive apartment block bombings in Moscow in 1999, reported websites lenta.ru and gazeta.ru. Litvinenko's representatives handed over copies of a handwritten document said to be the testimony of Achemez Gochiyaev, wanted by the FSB in connection with the bombings. Gochiyaev alleged that he was approached by an unidentified schoolfriend in 1999 to rent four basements in Moscow for use as storage. Only after the two explosions did he realise that the locations were the ones that he had rented. He claimed he anonymously called the authorities and warned them about the other two bombs. Litvinenko, who lives in the UK, said that based on his contacts with two other men wanted in connection with the incidents, Timur Batchaev and Yusuf Krymshamkhalov, he accused Ugryumov as the force behind the bombs. Ugryumov headed FSB operations in the North Caucasus from January 2001 until his death on 31 March 2001, officially from a heart attack, but according to some reports by suicide. The FSB denounced Litvinenko's information as 'a promotional exercise by dubious people', grani.ru reported on 25 July. (*Moscow Times*)

Firat Valeev, editor-in-chief of *Vechernii Neftekamsk*, one of the only opposition newspapers in Bashkortostan, a sovereign republic within the Russian Federation, has been found dead, the VolgaInform agency reported on 20 July. Valeev's paper was well known for its critical coverage of President Murtaza Rakhimov, who tried on several occasions through legal and economic pressure to close it. (CPJ)

Russian Deputy Media Minister Valerii Sirozhenko announced the development of special devices capable of detecting the illegal use of the so-called '25th frame' to send subliminal messages to television viewers. Sirozhenko said that stations found to be sending such messages will be fined or lose their licences. The theory of so-called 'subliminal advertising' has been widely derided in recent years, though the practice, effective or otherwise, is still illegal in Russia and the US. (*Moscow Times*)

Russia's Federal Security Service has opened a case against US FBI Special Agent **Michael Schuler**, who investigated the case of Russians Vasilii Gorshakov and Aleksei Ivanov, indicted by the FBI for hacking into the computer systems of US banks and stealing credit card numbers. However, the FSB office in the city of Chelyabinsk charges that Schuler illegally accessed Russian Internet servers to gather evidence against the two, later lured to the US and arrested. According to the FSB public relations centre, the case is a matter of principle. 'If FBI agents used hackers' methods against hackers, they might also use them on other occasions.' (*Moscow Times*)

Lawyers for jailed journalist **Grigorii Pasko** are looking for new ways to find justice following the failure of their appeal against his treason conviction on 25 June. They are planning to file a 'supervisory appeal' to the presidium of the Supreme Court. The European Parliament called on 4 July for Pasko's immediate release and an end to his repeated prosecution. They also urged the EU to put the item of media freedom at the top of the agenda for the next EU–Russia meeting. Pasko, an investigative journalist who worked for the Pacific Fleet's newspaper, was arrested on 20 November 1997 by the Russian secret police and charged with high treason for writing about the nuclear safety issues in the Russian Pacific Fleet. (CPJ, RSF, Bellona)

Despite a Moscow court order granting a media ministry request to close down the nationalist newspaper *Limonka*, the paper continues to publish. *Limonka* is the official organ of Limonov's far-right National Bolshevik Party, and it was ordered to be closed on 26 July after receiving two warnings for publishing materials that inflamed ethnic tension and called for the violent overthrow of the constitutional system. The paper will continue to come out legally as it pursues its case through the appeals process. (Index Online)

Public interest in the novels of avant-garde writer **Vladimir Sorokin** has soared since criminal pornography charges were filed against him on 11 July, said Natalya Tyurina, deputy commercial director for Moscow's Dom Knigi bookstore. 'In recent days we have been selling more than 120 copies of [Sorokin's] *Blue Lard* a day, while before we were lucky to sell 16.' The store has placed a large order for all of Sorokin's novels with his publisher Ad Marginem. Meanwhile, in an interview with *Komsomolskaya pravda* on 19 July, Prosecutor-General Vladimir Ustinov said that 'regardless of whether elements of pornography are found [in Sorokin's novels], to me it is clear that there is a problem. It is time to screen out second-rate "art".' Asked whether he had read *Blue Lard*, Ustinov said: 'No and, I must admit, I don't plan to. What I've heard about the novel hasn't made me want to take it up.' (Index Online)

RWANDA

Robert Sebufirira, **Elly MacDowell Kalisa** and **Emmanuel Munyaneza**, all journalists with the independent weekly *Umuseso*, were sentenced to 30 days of 'preventative detention' by a court in Kigali on 23 July. The charges stem from a 17 July brawl outside a Kigali bar, involving a member of the military and civilian police, witnessed by the three journalists. Though eyewitnesses say the three were not involved, they were still arrested by military police who broke up the brawl. As Rwanda's only independent Kinyarwanda-language publication, *Umuseso* has consistently criticised the president's regime and has written extensively about police misconduct, says the CPJ. (Index Online)

SAUDI ARABIA

A Harvard Law School report has found that the Saudi government has blocked approximately 2,000 websites, mostly sex or religion sites, but also conventional sites about women, health, drugs and pop culture. Unlike the other countries under review, Saudi Arabia allowed Harvard full access to the proxy servers that selectively bar access to specified proscribed sites. If a site is banned, the user is directed to a page that explicitly states the fact. (*Wired*)

SENEGAL

On 26 June, Jules François Bocandé, a trainer with the Senegalese national soccer team, angered by local sports reporters' coverage of the team's preparation for a key World Cup match against Turkey, called on the Senegalese people 'to take up their responsibilities' towards the journalists. Senegal lost, 1–0. Mohamadou Mahmoun Faye, coordinator of the Africa Bureau of the International Federation of Journalists (IFJ) in Dakar, complained that in light of the 'passion that followed the elimination of the Senegalese team' the remarks may have been understood 'as a call to physical violence against journalists'. (IFJ)

SERBIA

Dragoljub Milanovic, one of ex-President Slobodan Milosevic's closest associates and former head of Serbian state TV (RTS), began a nine-and-a-half-year jail sentence for failing to protect 16 employees who were killed during a NATO air raid on the station in 1999. The judge at the Belgrade court said: 'You were fully aware of the dangers your people faced and did nothing to protect them . . . However, this sentence does not absolve NATO from what it did.' Sixteen employees of RTS, mostly young people, died in the raid. (IFJ)

SLOVAKIA

Ivan Ceredejev was fired as general director of the state-run TASR news agency in June on the orders of Slovak Prime Minister Mikulas Dzurinda, who complained that he had bought a US$33,000 BMW car for company use, twice the value allowed by state rules. Dzurinda also cited Ceredejev's 'vulgar' replies to claims that he earned more than the prime minister; he reportedly told one interviewer that the claim was 'bullshit'. (RFE/AL)

SOMALIA

The authorities in the self-declared autonomous region of Puntland banned two local correspondents from supplying reports to the BBC's Somali service, IRIN reported on 19 August. Isma'il Warsame, chief of cabinet of the region's leader, Abdullahi Yusuf, alleged that the reporters, Ahmad Muhammad Kismayo and Muhammad Khalif Gir, 'have not been and are not objective in their reporting of events in the region'. Kismayo denied any partiality. 'I challenge the authorities to come up with a single piece that could be remotely construed as biased,' he said. (IRIN)

SOUTH AFRICA

South Africa's Internet professionals, led by Internet Service Providers and lawyers, have petitioned President Thabo Mbeki not to sign a new bill that would allow the government to take control of the registration and administration of Internet domains, and give it free access to information stored on the Web. 'We are opposed to creating a huge bureaucracy to control an industry that has been fine as it is,' said Edwin Thompson, co-chairman of South Africa's Internet Service Providers Association, 'and we have said that this amounts to hijacking the cyberspace.' (BBC Online)

SPAIN

Spain banned a Basque political party despite concerns for free expression raised by peaceful critics of Spanish policy in the disputed region. The government says the party, Batasuna, which won 10% of the vote last year in regional elections, is the political wing of the banned Basque nationalist group ETA. Catholic bishops from the region warned that banning Batasuna could have 'sombre consequences' by worsening the violence and putting innocent civilians in greater danger. The new Act empowers the Supreme Court to ban any party it considers guilty of supporting racist, xenophobic or terrorist attitudes. (Index Online)

SRI LANKA

The human rights group Inform reported that on 11 June the Liberation Tigers of Tamil Eelam (LTTE) prohibited newspaper vendors in the eastern town of Batticaloa from selling the pro-Eelam People's Democratic Party (EPDP) newspaper *Thinamurusu*. The LTTE had also 'banned' the newspaper in May, but the ban was lifted after interventions by the Norwegian-led Sri Lanka Monitoring Mission, in the country to monitor a ceasefire between the LTTE and the government (Inform).

As promised in January (*Index* 2/2002), Prime Minister Ranil Wickremesinghe's government repealed the 119-year-old law of criminal defamation on 18 June, and replaced it with a civil offence. Despite the fact that the previous law had been used twice in 2000 against newspaper editors by President Chandrika Kumaratunga's recent People's Alliance (PA) government, it voted unanimously for the law's repeal. (AP, Lanka Academic)

TamilNet reported on 11 August that the nine-millimetre pistol used to murder Tamil journalist **Mylvaganam Nimalarajan** (*Index* 1/2001, 3/2001, 1/2002) had been found in the Jaffna offices of the EPDP. On 4 July, *TamilNet* also said that ex-EPDP member **Ponnambalam Tharmalingam** had surrendered to police the previous day in Jaffna in connection with Nimalarajan's assassination in October 2000. (TamilNet)

SUDAN

The daily *al-Ayyam* was banned for a day on 28 August in punishment for publishing a reply by the paper's medical correspondent to a reader concerned about the physical effect of his wife's childhood circumcision on their married sex life. A court ruled that the 14 August article was 'indecent'. (Justice Africa)

Sudanese authorities confiscated the 4 September editions of pro-opposition newspaper *The Khartoum Monitor* and summoned the editor, **Albino Okeny**, to hear complaints about an article that touched on demands by residents of a town on the border between southern and northern Sudan to be part of a proposed referendum on whether southern Sudan should remain part of Sudan. Okeny said that he and managing editor **Nhial Bol** were allowed to go free after questioning. 'They accused us of encouraging secessionist tendencies and warned us against that,' said Okeny. (AP)

SYRIA

On 24 June, the National Security Court sentenced opposition dissident **Habib Saleh** to three years in jail for 'undermining national sentiment and opposing the aims of the revolution' that brought the ruling Ba'ath Party to power in 1963. The businessman was arrested last year after holding debates at which he voiced criticism of the government. Journalists and diplomats were banned from attending the trial. (BBC/MEI).

On 26 June, Communist leader **Riad al-Turk** (*Index* 3/2002), was sentenced to 30 months in prison for attacking the Constitution, insulting the state and undermining national consciousness. Al-Turk had previously served 18 years' solitary confinement before being released. Amnesty International regards al-Turk as a 'prisoner of conscience'. (MEI, AI)

On 31 July, the Supreme State Security Court sentenced **Aref Dalilah** (*Index* 6/2000) and **Walid al-Bunni** to ten and five years' imprisonment respectively on charges of 'attempting to change the constitution by illegal means'. Dalilah, al-Bunni and eight others were arbitrarily arrested and detained for their involvement with emerging civil society groups and discussion forums. There are concerns about the health of Dalilah, who is reported to be suffering from deep vein thrombosis and in need of urgent medical treatment. He was allegedly beaten and ill-treated while held in 'Adra Prison. (AI)

Syrian security authorities arrested two journalists, sisters **Aziza** and **Shirin Sibini,** at the beginning of May. Several Syrian citizens, officially allowed to return from exile, have been arrested at the border in this way, says the Syrian Human Rights Committee. Many political prisoners are being kept in isolation, denied access to a lawyer and not being told their charges. (SHRC).

TAIWAN

The Taiwanese government has promised to amend laws

to strengthen restrictions on locally rebroadcast imported TV programmes and increase controls on cable TV, reported Taipei media. The policy is in response to demands by protesting TV actors and would ban local television stations from broadcasting imported programmes during prime time and limit imported programmes on cable TV to no more than 30% of a channel's output. (*Taipei Times*)

TAJIKISTAN

Less than a month after it was refused a radio licence, the independent Tajik news agency *Asia Plus* was told on 29 July that Tajik President Imomali Rakhmonov would personally instruct regulators to issue it with the licence it has sought for four years. On 8 July, the regulators had said that a private alternative to state-run radio in Dushanbe was 'unnecessary'. At present, there are 15 independent television stations in northern Tajikistan, but only state-run television and radio in the capital. (RFE/RL)

The Tajik Prosecutor General's Office has dropped a criminal case first opened in 1993 against **Dododjon Atovulloev**, Tajik editor of the opposition newspaper *Tcharoghi Ruz*. The original charges were dropped in 1997, but were revived last year in connection with his criticism of the country's present leadership. He narrowly escaped deportation to Dushanbe last year when he was arrested on his way through Moscow airport by police acting on an old Tajik extradition request. (LPJ)

TOGO

Claude Améganvi, leader of the opposition, was arrested and detained on 6 August in connection with an article in the publication *Agoo Nam* about the financial activities of President Gnassingbé Eyadéma and his son Faure. Interior Minister General Sizing Akawilou Walla said that **Julien Ayi**, editor of another newspaper, *Nouvel Echo*, had named the opposition leader as the author of the article. Améganvi is a trade unionist, chairman of the country's Workers Party and editor of the trade union newspaper *Nyawo*. (All Africa News)

TUNISIA

The editor of the online political magazine *TUNe-ZINE*, **Zouhair Yahyaoui**, was sentenced to 28 months in prison after being found guilty of spreading 'false information' on 20 June. Using the pseudonym 'Ettounsi' (The Tunisian), Yahyaoui set up the website in July 2001 in order to circulate news about the fight for democracy and freedom in Tunisia. Yahyaoui refused to attend the trial in protest. It is the first time the Tunisian judiciary has taken action against dissident activities on the Internet in the country. (RSF, *El País*, BBC)

Lawyer and human rights activist **Radhia Nasraoui** began a hunger strike on 26 June to demand the release of her husband, Tunisian Workers' Communist Party member **Hamma Hammami** (*Index* 2/2002), sentenced to prison on 30 March. He has since lodged an appeal, but Ms

Nasraoui complains that as Hammami's lawyer she has not been allowed to see him since early April. After 23 days of fasting, Nasraoui was admitted to a private clinic suffering from a heart condition and muscular pains. She ended the strike after 38 days. (OMCT, maghreb-ddh.org).

On 19 August, journalist **Abdallah Zouari** of the banned weekly *al-Fajr* was re-arrested after release from a ten-year jail sentence on 6 June, reportedly for failing to comply with an interior ministry order banishing him to the south of the country. A contributor to *al-Fajr*, the unofficial publication of the Islamic movement Ennahda, Zouari was arrested on 12 April 1991 and sentenced to 11 years' imprisonment for 'belonging to an illegal organisation'. (RSF)

TURKEY

The death penalty is to be replaced by life imprisonment without parole, although it will remain on the statute books for use in wartime – a change that will save the life of jailed Kurdish leader Abdullah Ocalan. Parliament followed this landmark reform by legalising Kurdish radio and TV broadcasts – one of the most controversial elements of the reform package – ending years of severe state restrictions. The country's estimated 12 million Kurds will also be allowed to have private Kurdish-language education. 'We are doing a completely humanitarian thing here. Forget the European Union, we are doing the right thing here . . .The country will not be divided. This will be good for

'They that can give up essential liberty to obtain a little temporary safety deserve neither liberty nor safety' **Benjamin Franklin**

NOAM CHOMSKY ON
ROGUE STATES

EDWARD SAID ON
IRAQI SANCTIONS

LYNNE SEGAL ON
PORNOGRAPHY

... all in INDEX

SUBSCRIBE & SAVE

UK and overseas

○ **Yes! I want to subscribe to *Index*.**

❏ 1 year (4 issues)   £32   Save 16%

❏ 2 years (8 issues)   £60   Save 21%

❏ 3 years (12 issues)   £84   **You save 26%**

Name

Address

B0B5

£ _____ enclosed.   ❏ Cheque (£)   ❏ Visa/MC   ❏ Am Ex   ❏ Bill me
(Outside of the UK, add £10 a year for foreign postage)

Card No.

Expiry   Signature

❏ I do not wish to receive mail from other companies.

INDEX   ✉ Freepost: INDEX, 33 Islington High Street, London N1 9BR
☎ (44) 171 278 2313   Fax: (44) 171 278 1878
🄴 tony@indexoncensorship.org

SUBSCRIBE & SAVE

North America

○ **Yes! I want to subscribe to *Index*.**

❏ 1 year (4 issues) $48   Save 12%

❏ 2 years (8 issues) $88   Save 19%

❏ 3 years (12 issues) $120   **You save 26%**

Name

Address

B0B5

$ _____ enclosed.   ❏ Cheque ($)   ❏ Visa/MC   ❏ Am Ex   ❏ Bill me

Card No.

Expiry   Signature

❏ I do not wish to receive mail from other companies.

    ✉ Freepost: INDEX, 708 Third Avenue, 8th Floor, New York, NY 10017
☎ (44) 171 278 2313   Fax: (44) 171 278 1878
🄴 tony@indexoncensorship.org

us,' Islamist MP Mehmet Bekaroglu told the assembly. Up to this reversal of policy, Turkey had been strictly resisting change to its existing laws on Kurdish language, education and representation. Among the numerous incidents registered by Kurdish and Turkish human rights groups are the arrest of 11 teachers and engineers at a covert Kurdish-language class in the city of Mardin in May, with six later released on appeal, and the confiscation of the fortnightly pro-Kurdish publication *Dema Nu* in May over two articles in an earlier edition deemed 'media propaganda for a terrorist organisation', despite the fact that the banned Kurdish rebel force PKK had been heavily criticised in both articles. (BBC Online)

On 31 July, **Abdullah Keskin** was fined US$500 for publishing 'separatist propaganda' for producing a Turkish edition of *After Such Knowledge, What Forgiveness? My Encounters in Kurdistan*, a book about the Kurds written by retired *Washington Post* correspondent Jonathan Randal. Keskin, who was out of the country and did not attend the hearing, will appeal against the verdict. Prosecutors based the charges on passages from the book that contained references to 'Kurdistan', judged as separatist because it literally means 'land of the Kurds'.

On 11 June, Turkish prosecutors in Diyarbakir brought 27 children aged 11–18 to court for demanding the right to Kurdish language lessons. The children were accused of 'aiding a terrorist organisation' with their request, and prose-

cutors called on the court to jail them for between nine months and three years. (*Hürriyet*, IMK)

In the same month, the band **Koma Denge Asiti** were found guilty of aiding and abetting the PKK for performing in Kurdish and jailed for between three and nine years. Lead singer **Ibrahim Raci Ozcelik** and three band members were arrested in the city of Bursa after undercover police watched them perform at the wedding of an official of the People's Democracy Party (HADEP), Turkey's main Kurdish party. The non-Kurdish-speaking officers said they recognised words such as 'Biji Apo', a reference to Ocalan, and 'Kurdistan'. The case has been sent to the Supreme Court on appeal.

Turkish economist **Atilla Yesilada** appeared in court on 25 June charged with spreading separatist propaganda after he referred to 'sayin' ('Mr') Abullah Ocalan, a show of politeness regarded as illegal in Turkey. He faces up to three years in prison under anti-terrorism law for the reference. In court, Yesilada said that he refers to everyone as 'sayin'. Ironically, former premier Tansu Ciller later referred to Ocalan as 'sayin' during a press conference – but corrected herself immediately. (Kurdish Media, *Turkish Daily News*, *Özgür Politika*, *Dem Nu*)

On 27 June, the Supreme Court rejected a bid by opposition lawmakers to overturn parts of a law that may clear the way to a bid to censor the Internet in Turkey and reinforce media monopolies. The Constitutional Court

also rejected a petition by over 100 opposition deputies to suspend a clause that could subject websites to the harsh penalties already applied to Turkey's traditional media. The law was originally passed in defiance of a veto by President **Ahmet Necdet Sezer**, who said it was unconstitutional and would curb freedom of expression and media diversity. (BBC Online)

Turkey's Committee for the Coordination of the Struggle Against Baseless Genocide Claims plans to open a museum to house and display documents designed to 'counter' Armenian historical records of the 1915 genocide. The group plans to collate and translate 20,000 documents from the Ottoman State archives and put them on the web with state support, via the committee, chaired by Deputy Prime Minister Devlet Bahceli. (*Turkish Daily News*)

On 11 June, the European Court of Human Rights ruled that Turkey violated the right to free elections in the case of renowned Kurdish parliamentarian **Leyla Zana** and 12 other former DEP (Democracy Party) MPs whose party was dissolved by the Turkish Constitutional Court on 16 June 1994. In its ruling, the court declared that Turkey had violated 'the very essence of the right to stand for election and to hold parliamentary office' and 'had infringed the unfettered discretion of the electorate which had elected the applicants'. (*Milliyet*, AFP, IMK)

Kurdish author **Hasan Oztoprak** was found not guilty of incitement to race hatred by an Istanbul court on 21 June. Observers from the EU and International PEN monitored the trial. The case had been brought over Oztoprak's book about Kurdish, *The Creation of a Language*. (AP, IMK)

On 25 June, it was reported that **Gulay Yildiz**, former editor of the daily *Cinar*, had been jailed for ten months and fined about US$370 for writing a review of *Mehmet's Book*, a collection of interviews by journalist **Nadire Mater** with veterans of the war in south-east Turkey, thus 'insulting and despising the armed forces'. Though the Court of Appeal dismissed the sentence on procedural grounds, the charges were resubmitted and a sentence reapplied. Yildiz is to appeal to the Supreme Court. (*Kurdish Observer*)

Hulya Avsar, one of Turkey's most famous singers and actresses, was charged at the end of July with insulting the Turkish flag. Prosecutors cited a musical number on her top-rated TV show, which featured her playing with hundreds of balloons bearing the Turkish flag. The number was staged to celebrate the Turkish soccer team's first appearance in the World Cup since 1954, but under Turkish law the flag may not be depicted on clothing or objects and must never touch the ground. The show's producer, an assistant and the suppliers of the balloons were also charged and face prison sentences. (*Turkish Daily News*)

UKRAINE

Ukraine's Supreme Court has upheld the acquittal of Yuriy Veredyuk, who was accused of killing television journalist **Ihor Aleksandrov** in Slavyansk in eastern Ukraine in July 2001, and called for a new investigation into the slaying. Veredyuk was convicted last year for beating Aleksandrov to death but an appeals court overturned the conviction in May after the judge said the evidence presented was groundless. Veredyuk died from heart failure last week, just before the 25 July verdict. His death is seen as a major setback for Alexandrov's family, who believe Veredyuk was bribed to take responsibility for the killing and hoped that he would identify the real killer. (RFE/RL)

UNITED KINGDOM

North Wales police interviewed BBC director general Greg Dyke after a repeat of allegedly 'racist' comments about Welsh people made by journalist and quiz show host **Anne Robinson**, it was reported on 30 July. No charges were brought under British laws against incitement to racial hatred. London police also investigated comments about the Irish made by *Guardian* newspaper columnist **Julie Burchill** in August. John Twomey of the London Irish Centre complained to police about her claim that the Irish Catholic Church was engaged in 'almost compulsory child molestation'. No charges were brought in this case either. (*Guardian*)

Former top British civil servant Sir **Quentin Thomas** has been named as the new president of the British Board of Film Classification, charged with classifying levels of taste and decency in films distributed in the country, and requesting cuts if necessary. Sir Quentin said that while he shared the conventional view that screen violence could be harmful, he would not be pressed into action 'every time there is a fuss in parliament or the press'. (*Guardian*)

French cinema chain UGC banned an **anti-euro advert** from its British screens because of its 'political and offensive nature', it was reported on 16 July. The 90-second advert, financed by British campaigners against the single European currency, caused a storm among British Jewish groups and war veterans, angered at a scene featuring a comedian dressed as Adolf Hitler. (*Guardian*)

Nine foreign terrorist suspects arrested in the UK in the wake of the 11 September attacks won an appeal against their detention without trial. Held under emergency powers brought in in 2001 by Home Secretary David Blunkett, the nine men successfully argued before the Special Immigration Appeals Commission (SIAC) that their detention was unlawful. (*Guardian*)

London chef **Sulayman Balal Zainulabidin** finally went on trial under UK anti-terrorism laws, on charges of operating a website offering would-be terrorists information on guns. Zainulabidin was arrested last October after the 11 September attacks on the US. The prosecution says Zainulabidin offered two- to three-week courses in firearms in the US under the name of 'The Ultimate Jihad Challenge'. Zainulabidin, who has been held in custody awaiting trial since 5 October last year, has denied all charges and has told police that all he offered on the site was self-defence and security training for Muslims. (*Guardian*)

On 19 June, Blunkett was forced to withdraw plans to widen the power of his new Regulation of Investigatory Powers Act to access details of private emails and mobile phone calls. Plans to give municipalities and civil servants right of access to private data similar to that already granted to the police, intelligence services and tax officials would have left the supervisory body tasked to oversee the practice overwhelmed with work, argued its director. (*Guardian*)

US police officers investigating Internet child pornography identified more than 7,000 British men who used their credit cards to pay for online paedophilic images. The card details and email addresses were passed to British police who promptly arrested at least 30 suspected paedophiles, with more expected to follow. (Index Online)

Queen Elizabeth II expressed disapproval at appearing on a poster promoting a sex manual. Buckingham Palace said on 25 June that it had written to Ann Summers, a British chain store specialising in racy underwear and sex aids, complaining that its advert 'did not comply with the guidelines on the use of the Queen's image and clearly carries no endorsement'. (BBC Online)

On 2 July, a BBC radio editor defended giving a platform to **Nick Griffin**, leader of the far-right British National party, and **Sheikh Abu Hamza al-Masri**, a fundamentalist Muslim cleric, at a debate at the Royal Academy. The two much-criticised extremists argued that they have the right to express their views through the media. (*Guardian*)

Two years after stating it could not act as a censor, London's Camden Council agreed on 14 June to remove the books of **David Irving** from its libraries. The decision followed a campaign by councillor Brian Coleman to ban the works of the author, found by a British court in 2000 to be 'an active Holocaust denier', and an anti-Semitic racist. The decision follows the lead of neighbouring boroughs that have also banned Irving's books. (*Jewish Chronicle*)

On 26 July, Belgian brewer Interbrew dropped legal action aimed at forcing British media organisations to hand over forged takeover documents, four days before a case against **The Times**, **Guardian**, **Financial Times** and **Reuters** news agency had been due to go court. The company wanted journalists to hand over manipulated papers on Interbrew's planned bid for rival South African Breweries (SAB). Interbrew said it would now leave the matter to the official Financial Services Authority. The forged documents, sent anonymously to the media, drove Interbrew shares down and SAB stock higher. Interbrew won a court order to get hold of the papers, but the media groups refused to surrender them. 'The vital issue of protection of journalists' sources remains key to this case,' said Alan Rusbridger, editor of the *Guardian*. While the right to protect sources is enshrined in law in the US and other European countries, journalists in Britain are limited by contempt of court laws requiring that the source must be revealed when not to do so 'stands in the way of the interests of justice'. (*Guardian*)

Prime Minister Tony Blair introduced US-style briefings to his weekly routine in a bid to counter perceptions that his government was manipulating the news agenda through use of Parliament's traditionally secretive and selective 'off the record' lobby briefing system. Selected journalists 'outside the lobby', including specialist reporters and foreign correspondents, will also be invited. Cynics dismissed the initiative as merely increasing the size of the privileged media 'hack pack'. (*Guardian*)

UNITED STATES

The Simon Wiesenthal Center registered a significant increase in the number of websites promoting hate on the Internet since the 11 September attacks on the US. The centre, which tracks global racist activity against ethnic groups, identified 3,300 websites as 'problematic'. Racist groups that use the Internet are said to have changed online strategy, concentrating on trying to lure people with music and games rather than overt recruiting. (Yahoo! news)

A University of South Florida professor waiting to see if he will be fired for alleged terrorist ties has accused the university of buckling under '9/11 hysteria'. Professor **Sami al-Arian**, a Palestinian-born US citizen who moved to the US in 1975, told a meeting in St Petersburg, Florida: 'If I were any other nationality or any other colour, believe me, that would not have even been a consideration.' Al-Arian, a tenured computer science professor, has been on paid leave since 27 September. USF's board of trustees voted 12–1 in December to recommend firing him after his appearance on a TV show caused an uproar. Al-Arian has never been charged with a crime and denies any links to terrorists. (AP)

A White House plan to exempt selected businesses from freedom of information laws in exchange for support for its Homeland Security plans could allow corporate crooks to hide their business activities from the public in the name of national security, the US House of Representatives heard in August. But opponents say that by allowing corporations the right to refuse Freedom of Information Act requests, companies could justify shielding anything from public view, including the kinds of accounting and business practices that brought down Enron and WorldCom. (Index Online)

Students at the University of North Carolina were allowed to join course groups to read and discuss the book *Approaching the Qur'an: The Early Revelations*, by Michael Sells, after a judge ruled that the sessions did not threaten religious freedoms. US District Judge Carlton Tilley Jr refused to grant the temporary restraining order requested by the conservative Family Policy Network, three unidentified students and a taxpayer. University Chancellor James Moeser said the course was never a required subject at the university and was intended to stimulate critical thinking in freshmen. Lawyers for the network argued that the course ignored violent passages in the Quran and sought to indoctrinate students with the idea that Islam embraced only peace. (*Charlotte Observer*)

NASA experts are reportedly trying to develop an airport security screen that will adapt space technology to receive and analyse brainwave and heartbeat patterns, to detect airline passengers who might pose a threat. The IT Register, among others, mocked the suggestion, noting that the frustrations of normal airline service would trigger identical signals. (IT Register)

US District Judge Gladys Kessler ruled on 8 August that the US Justice Department has not proved the need for a blanket policy of secrecy about more than 1,000 people picked up since the 11 September attacks, and ordered the government to release the names within 15 days. Kessler argued that al-Qaida would already be aware of all those cell members who have been captured by the US. The government argued that many detained were not thought to be al-Qaida members but were illegal immigrants suspected of having knowledge of terrorist activities, therefore releasing the names would give al-Qaida significant information that it might not already have. The government seeks a temporary stay of the order, which would allow it to keep the names secret until after the appeal. (Freedom Forum)

US Congressman Howard Berman has introduced a bill that could legalise efforts by entertainment companies to hack into computers run by people they believe are illegally copying and distributing their movies and music. The 'Peer-to-Peer Piracy Prevention' Act, presented on 25 July, would permit the use of 'technological tools' to prevent the illegal distribution of copyrighted works over the Internet. (AP)

US tattoo artist **Ronald White**, who has spent three years trying to get South Carolina's ban on tattooing overturned, has enlisted the help of former special prosecutor Kenneth Starr, the lawyer who led the investigation into former president Bill Clinton's various activities. Starr filed an appeal petition with the US Supreme Court on behalf of the tattoo artist. 'This was a very important issue in terms of our system of free expression,' Starr said. 'Our country believes in liberty, the ability of individuals to express themselves.' White, 33, has been fighting the ban since 1999, when he was arrested and fined US$2,500 for giving an illegal tattoo on television. Oklahoma and South Carolina are the only US states to ban tattooing. (Freedom Forum)

A federal appeal court has ruled that city officials in the city of Ogden in the western US state of Utah cannot display the Ten Commandments in its Municipal Gardens while barring other religions from displaying their beliefs in the same park. A five-foot granite monument inscribed with the Commandments was donated to the city in 1966 but when Summum, a Salt Lake City-based religion that draws on ancient Egyptian philosophy, sought to place seven of its statements of principles next to the tablet, the city said no. Summum devotees appealed to the court citing First Amendment free speech rights and after a series of hearings on 19 July the court upheld their case. Ogden Mayor Matthew Godfrey has said he may appeal against the ruling. (Freedom Forum)

The American Civil Liberties Union (ACLU) called the deployment of high-speed broadband Internet services the 'key First Amendment issue of the 21st Century'. ACLU claims that such systems can be easily adapted to censorship, as their providers would have exclusive control over what websites their users could access. An ACLU study, jointly written with the Center for Digital Democracy (CDD) and the Consumer Federation of America (CFA), recommended that cable firms should share their lines with independent firms that would provide alternative connections to the Internet. (ACLU)

The FBI is visiting libraries nationwide and checking the reading records of people it suspects of having ties to terrorists or plotting an attack, US library officials say. Judith Krug, the American Library Association's director for intellectual freedom, said the FBI was treading on the rights it is supposed to be upholding. Such searches are now legal under the Patriot Act that President Bush signed last October. The same law that makes the searches legal also makes it a criminal offence for librarians to reveal the details or extent of the searches. (AP, Freedom Forum)

American political cartoonists are under 'immense pressure from readers and advertisers to toe the patriotic line', according to **Steve Benson**, who draws for the *Arizona Republic* and other major US newspapers. Benson claims he has been called a traitor and received death threats. **Mike Marland** had to destroy and publicly apologise for a cartoon published in the *Concord Patriot* which humorously compared the Bush administration's attack on social security to al-Qaida's attack on the World Trade Center. Ari Fleischer, the president's spokesman, has said all Americans 'need to watch what they say'. (*Independent*)

Talk-show host **Bill Maher** has not had his contract renewed by ABC. He was attacked last year for failing to call the World Trade Center terrorists 'cowardly' on his programme *Politically Incorrect*. (*Guardian*)

A group of leading Americans have signed a declaration of their opposition to the Bush

administration's 'war on terrorism'. The statement invokes a conscientious obligation to speak out against 'a new openly imperial policy towards the world and a domestic policy that manufactures and manipulates fear to curtail rights'. One signatory, Jeremy Pikser, who wrote the film *Bulworth*, has said a lot of people who agree with the declaration 'haven't signed it . . . because they think it might jeopardise other things they're involved in'. (*Guardian*).

Lieutenant-Colonel **Steve Butler**, a US air force veteran of 24 years, was threatened with a court-martial in June for writing a letter to the *Monterrey County Herald* in California which read: 'of course President Bush knew about the impending [11 September] attacks on America. He did nothing to warn the American people because he needed this war on terrorism' and went on to call the president a 'joke'. Butler, who served in the Gulf War, was threatened with a court martial under a 1776 military law forbidding 'contemptuous words against the president'. (*Guardian*).

David W Carson and **Ed Powers** of the *New Observer* in Kansas City were found guilty on 17 July of seven charges of criminal defamation. The paper had alleged that the mayor of Wyandotte County did not live in the county but in a more affluent area nearby. Media rights groups worldwide argue that there is no justification for libel cases of this kind to come under criminal law. (CPJ)

UZBEKISTAN

Uzbek human rights activist **Yuldash Rasulov**, a member of the Kashkadaria branch of the Human Rights Society of Uzbekistan (HRSU), is still being denied access to his lawyer and his family. 'We are fearful for Rasulov,' said Elizabeth Andersen, executive director of Human Rights Watch's Europe and Central Asia division. Rasulov was arrested on 24 May. Police claim that he was recruiting Islamic militants. (RFE/RL)

THE VATICAN

Five Internet sites have been shut in Italy after complaints by the Vatican newspaper *l'Osservatore Romano* that they carried 'blasphemies against God and the Virgin Mary'. A special police unit 'took over an Internet site due to the blasphemous nature of unrepeatable words which accompanied the name of the Madonna', the paper said in July. Web surfers who try to visit the site find instead the words: 'Site seized by the Head of Rome's Special Police Force on the orders of Rome's Chief Prosecutor.' (AFP)

VENEZUELA

Fabio Cortés, owner of the daily *La Nación*, published in San Cristóbal, was reported kidnapped on 29 June 2002. The masked assailants broke in while Cortés was having breakfast with his family. One individual grabbed the journalist before fleeing with him in Cortés's wife's car. In a similar incident on 15 July, **Ernesto José Branger**, 60, owner of the radio station 96.1 FM in the same city, was kidnapped by a gang who crashed into his car, then seized him. (IPYS, Index Online)

On 1 August, a photographer for the daily *El Universal*, **Paulo Perez Zambrano**, and several other photographers and camera operators were attacked by supporters of President Hugo Chávez. According to the daily *El Nacional*, a police officer reportedly seized the camera and three rolls of film belonging to photographer **Alejandro Delgado Cisneros**. The confrontations took place as government supporters and opponents demonstrated outside the Supreme Court as it began hearings into bringing possible rebellion charges against officers involved in the 11 April *coup d'état*. On 1 August, the court announced that the four officers should not be prosecuted, provoking anger among government supporters. (RSF/IFEX)

VIETNAM

Prominent former Communist Party journalist **Nguyen Vu Binh** was detained on 19 July as the country's newly elected parliament was meeting. The California-based Democracy Club of Vietnam says he is among a group of dissidents who wrote to the Communist leaders early in July calling for political reforms and the release of political prisoners. The New York-based Committee to Protect Journalists reported that he was believed to be in detention somewhere in the capital, Hanoi. (CPJ)

Vietnamese Internet essayist **Le Chi Quang** was reported in August to be ready to go on trial on national security charges, seven months after being jailed for an article criticising Vietnam's border agreements with China. The article, 'Beware of Imperialist China', had been widely distributed on the Internet. On 7 August, authorities shut down a domestic website (TTVNonline.com) where viewers had posted articles on sensitive political topics. On 5 August, the telecommunications ministry asked local authorities to punish severely those caught spreading dissent online, the daily *Tin Tuc* reported. (Index Online)

YEMEN

The trial of Yemeni journalists **Abdulraheem Mohsen** and **Ibraheem Hussein** reconvened on 6 July in Sana'a, with both defendants forced to wear chains in the dock. Mohsen and Hussein are accused of inciting sectarianism and regionalism, insulting the president of the republic and abusing the national unity of the country. (CPJ)

ZAMBIA

Four journalists from the privately owned weekly *The People* were arrested on 5 June after writing that President Levy Mwanawasa had Parkinson's disease. The president has ordered the arrest of anyone who says he is ill. The Zambian Supreme Court refused on 6 June to grant bail to the four – editor **Emmanuel Chilekwa**, his deputy **Shaderick Banda**, reporter **Kinsley Lwendo** and trainee journalist **Jean Chirwa**. (CPJ)

ZIMBABWE

Since March, 36 journalists have been arrested and 13 charged, eight for allegedly publishing 'false news'. Several have reportedly been beaten in custody. No journalist working for the state media has been arrested or charged. As of 1 July, all journalists must apply for registration with a government-controlled Media Commission and may be refused registration if they do not meet criteria to be set by the Minister of Information, Jonathan Moyo. In May, three journalists – **Geoff Nyarota**, editor of the *Daily News*, **Lloyd Mudiwa**, journalist with the same paper, and **Andrew Meldrum**, correspondent for the London *Guardian* – were charged with spreading rumours of false news, which carries a maximum two-year prison sentence. They had published allegations that government supporters hacked a mother to death in front of her children. **Pius Wakatama**, a *Daily News* columnist, has been charged for commenting on the story while **Fanuel Jongwe**, a freelance journalist, faces a criminal defamation charge. On 15 July, Meldrum was acquitted of 'publishing false information' and 'abusing journalistic privileges' but was ordered to leave the country within 24 hours. On 16 June, three other *Daily News* staffers – **Guthrie Munyuki**, photographer **Urgunia Mauluka** and driver **Shadreck Mukwecheni** – were arrested while covering a meeting of the opposition MDC Party and charged under the recently enacted Public Order and Security Act with 'behaving in a threatening, abusive

or insulting manner'. They were detained for 48 hours and all three were reportedly beaten in custody. False news charges have also been brought against **Dumasani Mulaya** and **Iden Wetherell** of the *Zimbabwean Independent* for reporting that Mugabe's wife had been asked for help in a labour dispute involving her brother. **Bornwell Chakaodza**, **Farai Matsuka** and **Fungayi Kanyuchi** of the *Standard* are also charged for stories on police harassment of journalists and 'sex for freedom' deals in which police officers forced prostitutes to have sex with them.
(Article 19/CPJ)

A bomb attack on 29 August gutted the office of a radio station critical of President Robert Mugabe's government. A security guard said at least two men, one carrying a firearm, threw the bombs into offices run by the Netherlands-based media rights NGO Voice of the People in Harare's Milton Park suburb. The blast and a subsequent fire destroyed computers, recording and editing equipment, files and furniture. Voice of the People has been criticised by the government for circumventing a ban on independent broadcasting by sending recorded material in Zimbabwe's local languages for transmission by shortwave from The Netherlands.
(Radio Netherlands)

Zimbabwe's Minister of Home Affairs John Nkomo has dismissed the impact of expanded EU sanctions on the country's ruling elite. Nkomo told the UN regional news service IRIN that the EU is only a part of a broader

world. He considered deepening sanctions to be proof that the regime's policies on land reform and other issues were effective, 'or else they wouldn't have bothered'.
(IRIN)

Compiled by: James Badcock (North Africa); Ben Carrdus (East Asia); Gully Cragg (Western Europe, Northern America, Pacific and Australasia); Avery Davis-Roberts (Western Africa); Hanna Gezelius (South East Asia); Canan Gündüz (Eastern Europe); Andrew Kendle (India and subcontinent); Agustina Lattanzi (South and Central America); Ramsey Nasser (Southern Africa); Gill Newsham (Turkey and Kurdish areas); Shifa Rahman (East Africa); Neil Sammonds (Gulf States and Middle East); Katy Sheppard (Russia, Poland, Ukraine, and Baltic States); Tom Tàbori (UK and Ireland); Mike Yeoman (Central America and Caribbean)

Edited by Rohan Jayasekera and co-ordinated by Natasha Schmidt

Pakistan/India border 2002: rival armies face off over Kashmir.
Credit: AP Photo / KM Chaudary

INDIA & PAKISTAN

FOR THE PAST 12 YEARS,
THE TRANQUILLITY OF THE
KASHMIR VALLEY AND THE
LIVES OF ITS PEOPLE HAVE
BEEN SHATTERED FROM
WITHIN BY AN ARMED
INSURGENCY AND FROM
WITHOUT BY THE RIVAL
CLAIMS OF INDIA AND
PAKISTAN THAT RECENTLY
THREATENED THE
SUBCONTINENT WITH
NUCLEAR WAR. INDEX
LOOKS AT THE STATE OF
THE TWO NATIONS THAT
WOULD GO TO WAR

PARADISE LOST

ISABEL HILTON

'IF THERE IS A PARADISE HERE ON
EARTH, IT IS THIS, IT IS THIS, IT IS
THIS,' SAID THE MOGHUL EMPEROR
JEHANGIR, ON FIRST SEEING THE
VALLEY OF KASHMIR

When the French doctor François Bernier first set eyes on the Kashmir
Valley in 1665, he was astounded by the beauty of the place. 'In truth,' he
wrote, 'the kingdom surpasses in beauty all that my warm imagination had
anticipated.' The sumptuously fertile valley some 90 miles long and 20 miles
wide lies between formidable mountain barriers. The lower slopes of the
mountains, wooded with sycamore, oak, pine and cedar, descend to a valley
floor planted with walnut, apricot, apple and almond trees, with vineyards,
rice paddies, hemp and saffron fields. So seductive was this landlocked valley
that, like a beautiful woman despoiled by jealous lovers, Kashmir attracted a
succession of invaders each anxious to possess her.

The Moghuls established their control in the sixteenth century as
Kashmir became the northern limit of their Indian empire as well as their
pleasure ground, a place to wait out the summer heat of the plains. They
built gardens in Srinagar, along the shores of Dal Lake, planted with chenar
trees, roses and jasmine and filled with fountains.

After the Moghuls came the Afghans and the Sikhs from the Punjab, each
in turn establishing their rule in Kashmir, until the British defeated the Sikhs
in the nineteenth century and sold the Valley, to the abiding shame of its
residents, to a notoriously brutal former vassal of the Sikhs, the Hindu ruler
of Jammu, Gulab Singh. Calculated one way, the new maharajah of Jammu
and Kashmir had bought the people of the Valley for approximately three
rupees each, a sum he was to recover many times over through taxation.

Kashmir was also a crossroads. The Silk Route with its great camel trains
that carried goods from China to the markets of Europe passed just to the
north, and mountain passes opened routes to the Punjab, Afghanistan and
Jammu. Through them, successive intruders brought different cultures and
faiths that added to Kashmir's multi-layered culture. The language was close
to Persian, the handicrafts for which the Valley was celebrated were Central

Kashmir 1948: dawn over Dal Lake.
Credit: Henri Cartier-Bresson

Asian and the religious faith of Kashmir's rulers had been variously Buddhist, Hindu, Sikh and Muslim. Sufi masters had left a legacy of music and tolerance in their Muslim teachings. A Sikh who had lived many years in Srinagar described it like an old cloth so covered in patches you can't see what the original was like.

Today, the Kashmir Valley is predominantly Muslim, but the state of Jammu and Kashmir included largely Hindu Jammu and Buddhist Ladakh as well as Gilgits and Baltis, Hunzas and Mirpuris. The Valley itself boasted a large Hindu community, the Pandits, who filled the teaching posts and the government jobs, as well as a substantial community of Sikhs. There had been conflicts between the communities in the past, but by the mid-twentieth century Kashmir boasted a unique, syncretic and, on the whole, mutually tolerant culture.

The state escaped the inter-communal violence that Partition brought to neighbouring Punjab when the British left the subcontinent in 1947. Kashmir's violence was to come later, as the two newly born states of India and Pakistan became the latest of Kashmir's neighbours to fight over the Valley. Today, Kashmir itself is partitioned – Pakistan rules one-third, India some 40% and the rest is controlled by China. Kashmir's 12 million people are divided roughly equally between the Indian- and Pakistani-held territories, and relations between its many communities are marked by mutual suspicion and mistrust.

For 12 years, a bewildering list of combatants have fought a savage, irregular war that, in a steady daily toll of killing, has cost, depending on whom you believe, up to 80,000 lives. On the Indian side, there are the local police with its Special Operations Groups, the Border Security Force, the Central Reserve Police Force and the army, supported by various intelligence organisations and an irregular force of turncoat former militants who have muddied the public understanding of who, over the years, has done what to whom. Opposing them are the militant groups that proliferated until at one time more than 100 different outfits claimed to be active. Now there are about a dozen left, some of them known only by the press releases they send to local media outlets. Others – like the Lashkar-e-Taiba and Jaish-e-Mohammed, two Pakistani-based organisations listed as terrorists by the United States and recently disowned by Pakistan's President Pervez Musharraf – are fundamentalist and deadly. The largest group is the Hizbul Mojaheddin, a Muslim but not, its supporters insist, a fundamentalist movement, most of whose 1,000 activists are Kashmiris.

Overarching the ground-level killing is a wider and even more implacable hostility: that between India and Pakistan, which had at its core the status of Kashmir and which, this year, threatened to plunge the subcontinent into a war that had the potential to become the world's first nuclear conflict. One million soldiers still face each other off in the stark and hostile terrain of the de facto border.

Last October, I was permitted to go into what Pakistan calls 'Azad [Free] Kashmir' on a heavily supervised group daytrip. India has called this territory 'Pakistan-occupied Kashmir' ever since Pakistan's army wrested this north-west third of the original state of Jammu and Kashmir from Indian control in the war that followed Partition. For Pakistan, that was the first step in a liberation plan that is still to be completed.

We drove for five hours along the sides of vertiginous valleys, through Muzaffarabad, the capital of Azad Kashmir, on into the mountains to Chakothi, on the Line of Control – the ceasefire line established in 1949 after the first of three wars India and Pakistan have fought over Kashmir. There, Brigadier Mohammed Yaqub, commander of that sector, briefed us, complete with flip charts and maps, on the Pakistani view of the history of the present conflict.

He warned us that tension was high. The US bombing of Afghanistan had begun and Indian air force manoeuvres and troop movements had been detected. Brigadier Yaqub's list of the casualties incurred in the last ten years of what he saw as the freedom struggle on the other side of the border – that of, as he would put it, the people of Kashmir against the Indian military occupation – was startling and no doubt contentious: 740,625 killed; 80,317 wounded; 492 adults burned alive, 875 schoolchildren ditto; 15,812 raped; 6,572 sexually incapacitated; 37,030 disabled; 96,752 missing.

We took a path that led from a clearing through dugouts and fortifica- tions to a bluff overlooking a tributary of the Jhelum River. There was a slender, and that day deserted, bridge to the other side where Indian army fortifications matched those on our side. A line of washing flapped in a light breeze above a series of bunkers. We peered through binoculars at men peering back through binoculars at us. They waved. We waved back. A Pakistani officer admitted that, in more relaxed times, they met their Indian counterparts on the bridge once a month and shared tea and sweets. 'We don't talk about the war,' he said.

In Pakistan, Kashmir was the unspoken subtext of the Afghan war. As Musharraf threw in his lot with the US, the question that hovered in the air was: what would that mean for Kashmir? The connection was obvious: Pakistan had been the hub of the US mission to arm and train Islamic warriors to fight the Soviet occupation of Afghanistan, and the men of Pakistan's Inter Service Intelligence agency, the secret service that ran that jihad, had seen the opportunity to ginger up existing discontent in Kashmir by infiltrating hardline Islamist guerrillas there too. Eventually, they hoped, India would be forced to negotiate.

For them, both wars were a religious and a patriotic cause. But if the president was now turning his back on the Taliban and the strategy of binding Afghanistan to Pakistan's sphere of influence, would he also be forced to abandon a dream that Pakistan has clung to since 1947 – that of uniting the Muslims of Kashmir with the state of Pakistan?

In Pakistan, I was told that the conflict in Kashmir was simply the unfinished business of Partition, the bloody separation of what became predominantly Muslim Pakistan from predominantly Hindu India with the end of British rule in 1947. Kashmir at the time was a princely state with a majority Muslim population but ruled by a Hindu maharajah, Hari Singh, descendant of the brutal Gulab Singh and one of the last of that lost line of fabulously rich, feudal monarchs whom the British had manipulated to maintain their grip on much of India. The maharajah had opted to join India and the people of Kashmir had been deprived of the opportunity to decide their own future.

The maharajah, in fact, had dithered for months, unable to decide between two options that were, to him, equally unattractive. But in October 1947 he was pushed into India's arms by an incursion into Kashmir by tribesmen from Pakistan's Northwest Frontier Province. It began as a raid of sponsored irregulars, but war between the two countries followed. By then, the maharajah was out of the picture. He had fled Srinagar with his family in the first days of the invasion.

In Pakistan, what was remembered from that time was a promise made by the then Indian prime minister, Jawaharlal Nehru, to hold a plebiscite in which the people of Kashmir could make their own preferences clear. That plebiscite was never held. India blames Pakistan for failing to withdraw from Azad Kashmir after a ceasefire was agreed under UN supervision in 1949, a betrayal that, India says, vitiates the commitment to the plebiscite. Pakistan blames India for the failure to allow the people to choose their future, a failure exacerbated by decades of misrule and abuse by Indian security forces. Two more inconclusive wars followed. The present phase of the conflict – a Muslim insurgency in Kashmir itself – began in 1988.

The role of Pakistan in training and infiltrating armed Islamic militants to fight in that insurgency did not, in the Pakistani view, diminish the legitimacy of what had begun as an indigenous freedom struggle. The natural end of that struggle, they insisted, was unity with Pakistan.

Later that week, I met a member of one of the biggest militant groups in Kashmir. He called himself Iqbal, though we both knew that was not his name. Iqbal had grown up in a Kashmir that was under Indian rule but that was supposed, under the act of accession that the maharajah signed, to enjoy internal autonomy, with Indian powers limited to foreign relations, currency and defence. But India had repeatedly interfered in Kashmir, deposing the state's leaders when they were suspected of wanting greater autonomy and imposing their own men.

Under India's repressive rule, young Kashmiris lost faith in India's proclaimed secularism and began to abandon their own traditions of tolerance as they searched for an ideology that would channel their growing frustration. One friend had described to me his own upbringing in the Valley in the late 1970s and early '80s. It was a time, he recalled, of fevered political discussion, stimulated by engaged teachers who fed him the texts of the Egyptian Muslim brotherhood or the writings of Mao Zedong, depending on their own political persuasions. Resentment of Indian rule was high and Kashmiris were impatient for change. Their hopes were focused on the elections of 1987.

Farouk Abdullah, the son of Sheikh Abdullah, the popular Muslim leader who had been the scourge of the maharajah, was in power. But he had formed an alliance with the Indian Congress Party and many saw him as a traitor to the cause of Kashmir. Against him was the Muslim United Front, an alliance of 11 Muslim political parties that were campaigning on a platform of Islamic unity and greater autonomy for Kashmir. 'The 1987 elections were our last hope,' said Iqbal. The record bears him out: voter turnout in the Valley was 80%. But the fraud had been crude and blatant, and was followed by the arrest of many of the opposition candidates and party members. The results provoked widespread street protests that were brutally suppressed. For young men like Iqbal, the election was a watershed. 'When the results were declared,' he said, 'people decided that we could not free our land through peaceful means.' The uprising began.

'If you want to talk about Kashmir,' said Iqbal, 'you must talk about the 80,000 innocent martyrs. It's a death rate of 15 innocent civilians to every one Indian soldier.'

A few weeks later, on the morning of 13 December, that balance was to shift, marginally but dramatically, in the other direction in an act of terror that took the Kashmiri conflict to the heart of the Indian state. At 11.30 that morning, five men dressed in olive-green fatigues and armed with automatic rifles, grenades and explosives drove a white Ambassador car, complete with flashing blue light and security passes, through the gates of the Indian parliament complex in Delhi.

The session had just ended and the politicians were beginning to disperse. It was only after the parliament's security guards noticed the car turn the wrong way that they became suspicious. A guard began to run after the car, calling to the driver to stop. Alarmed, the vice-president's security guard, waiting by his official vehicle in the car park, challenged the white Ambassador. A burst of fire came from inside as the car rammed into the vice-president's vehicle and the men inside ran towards the parliament building.

In the ensuing firefight, all five terrorists died along with seven security personnel. The car was found to be packed with explosives. It was a terrorist assault on the heart of the world's largest democracy and India was outraged. The identity of the terrorists was not established, but in Delhi two Pakistani-sponsored groups were swiftly named. The Indian press published calls to finish this long quarrel with Pakistan once and for all with an all-out war.

In Pakistan, President Musharraf swiftly condemned the outrage and declared a ban on the two groups, closing down their offices in Pakistan and arresting hundreds of their members. India remained suspicious and unconvinced. Both sides built up their forces on the border and India began to lay mines along the entire length of the border with Pakistan – some 2,880 kilometres. Diplomats and statesmen scrambled for Delhi and Islamabad to try to talk the tension down.

The future of Kashmir seemed once again to be reduced to the outcome of this poisonous contest between these rival nations. Both claimed to have the loyalty of the Kashmiri people and blamed the other for the conflict. In this deafening exchange of accusations, the voice of Kashmir was silent. What did Kashmiris themselves want, caught between the crushing hostilities of their larger neighbours?

Ramesh Mahanoori was once a teacher in the Kashmir Valley. Now in his 50s, he lives in a tiny one-room house in a camp on the outskirts of Jammu, the largely Hindu city that was summarily married to the Kashmir Valley under the maharajah. Mr Mahanoori is a Pandit, a Kashmiri Hindu who, like most of his 1 million-strong community, lived until 1990 in relative prosperity in the Kashmir Valley. The Pandits formed the backbone of the teaching profession and the administrative class. They lived side by side with their Muslim neighbours and the harmony between communities was part of a general culture – the so-called Kashmiryat – of which both Hindus and Muslims were proud. But within the space of a few months, between October 1989 and March 1990, 1 million Pandits fled the Kashmir Valley, driven out by murders, riots and death threats. The Pandits – and Kashmir's traditions of tolerance – had become early victims of Kashmir's new Muslim insurgency.

The story of the expulsion of the Pandits was told to me in many different guises, to prove several different points. Mr Mahanoori, though, tells it as a straightforward case of betrayal. It began, he believes, with the Islamist underground, financed by Pakistan, which he says began to organise in Kashmir in 1986. After the farce of the 1987 elections, that movement found fertile ground in the anger and disillusionment of Muslim Kashmiris. The Pandits were driven out, he maintains, to pave the way for the Valley to join Pakistan. Many imagined that they would return in a few months' time, when things had returned to normal. Twelve years later, most of them are still refugees, many in these sad camps, waiting out a dreary exile that they no longer believe will end.

In the early spring of this year, I flew to Srinagar. The airport looked like a makeshift fortress, grimly holding out in enemy territory. The road out was blocked by an eclectic selection of barriers: metal bars set with eight-inch spikes waited for a tyre to shred; oil drums filled with concrete forced cars to weave a slow slalom path between them; rolls of razor wire lay ready to be pulled across the road. Beside one of them, in a bizarre juxtaposition from an earlier, more innocent time, a poster advertised the seductive charms of Kashmir. 'Kashmir – an adventure,' it said. 'The land of forests.'

In Srinagar, the journalists – themselves constantly threatened and often attacked by both sides – have grown weary of looking for new angles on death. Only the larger outrages – such as the car bomb attack on Srinagar's assembly building on 1 October last year which claimed more than 30 lives – are reported internationally. When the confrontation between India and Pakistan threatens a major war on the subcontinent, Kashmir briefly takes its place on the front pages. The constant searches, the de facto curfew, the daily detentions, like the killings, now pass virtually unreported. Now it takes the death of a foreigner to remind the outside world of what Kashmiris know too well: that in Kashmir, truth – like history – is highly subjective.

India has maintained a heavy security presence in Kashmir since 1947, and for most of that time its reputation has not been benign. Now the security services – the regular army, the local police and paramilitary police forces drawn from elsewhere in India – are half a million strong.

To local Kashmiris, these forces feel, and behave, like an occupying army. With the exception of the local police – whom some of the other forces regard with a certain suspicion – few of them speak Kashmiri. The security forces, in turn, are far from home, surrounded by people whose language they cannot understand and threatened by an enemy they cannot identify. To the Indian forces, anyone they encounter could be a Kashmiri militant or a terrorist infiltrated from Pakistan. 'If a dog barks in the market,' one Kashmiri trader told me, 'the Indians call him a Pakistani.'

For as long as the Indian forces have been in Kashmir they have been accused of human rights abuses: they are paid a bounty when they kill a category A militant – someone against whom there is evidence of subversive activity. It is a practice, I was told, that leads to fabricated evidence and trigger-happy forces. They are routinely accused, too, of torture and disappearances and, in the eyes of the local population, are rarely called to account.

The men they are looking for belong to the hazardous collection of militant groups, many with competing objectives, which have operated in Kashmir since the popular protests following the 1987 elections. The groups proliferated, all fighting in the name of Islam, and some began to impose on the tolerant culture of the Valley a more severe version of the faith, one that insisted that women be veiled and that such unIslamic businesses as bars and beauty parlours close down. The more radical groups began to attack foreigners, too: in 1995, Harkat-ul-Mujahideen, a Pakistani-sponsored force, kidnapped six western trekkers. Four vanished without trace and one escaped. The sixth was decapitated. There were episodes that had international resonance: plane hijackings that sometimes led to the release of captured terrorist leaders.

In Kashmir itself, the guerrilla war began in earnest: in the mountains and villages, there were armed encounters between Indians and militants; in the cities, car bombs and grenade attacks that would provoke indiscriminate firing in response as security forces tried to kill their elusive enemy. There have been repeated massacres that each side has blamed on the other.

Shopkeepers and university professors, impoverished farmers and well-heeled businessmen continue to complain of routine cruelty during the security forces' constant cordon searches: entire districts are sealed off and the inhabitants turned out of their houses, made to squat in the cold for hours as the troops ransack their houses. The men and boys are often beaten, occasionally shot; valuables go missing; men who are arrested sometimes never come back. The security forces had always been accused of abuses, but in the mid-1990s, the militants, too, were blamed for murder and rape, forced marriages and extortion as young insurgents discovered the intoxicating power of the gun. Both sides carried out individual assassinations, the

Kashmir 2002: Kashmiri nomad.
Credit: Camera Press / Findlay Kember

militants targeting those they suspected of helping the Indian state, the
Indian security forces eliminating those they believed were aiding the insurgents or men who, they said, were active international terrorists.

Srinagar is a subdued and depressed city, but as darkness fell each day the
tension became almost palpable. My interlocutors would begin to fidget,
caught between the obligations of hospitality and their anxiety that I leave
before the streets became unsafe. Nobody, they told me, goes out after dark
except in an emergency. A tremulous sociology professor described to me
the social effects of the long war – migration, unemployment, a breakdown
of traditional parental authority, broken families, universal mistrust and a
startlingly elevated rate of suicide.

He urged me to walk around the old city, a district I had been warned
against, to discover how people really felt. It was a hotbed of militancy, I was
told, and subject to constant cordon searches. 'Talk to people,' said the

professor. 'No one will harm you.' After a pause, he seemed to think better of his assurances. 'Don't tell anyone in advance. Don't make an appointment in case, in their innocence, they tell someone you are coming. And don't stay more than half an hour in the same place.'

Both India and Pakistan see in the conflict in Kashmir what they believe are each other's worst aspects. For India, founded on a claim to secularism and tolerance between rival religious communities, Pakistan's insistence on a separate Muslim state represents both a failure and a threat. If the Muslims of Kashmir were to respond to Pakistan's siren call, what signal would that send to the more than 100 million Muslims elsewhere in India?

For Pakistan, India's refusal to allow Kashmiri Muslims to join the Pakistani state merely confirms the belief that India has never accepted Pakistan's existence or abandoned a long-term ambition to establish Hindu domination on the subcontinent.

But for the people of the Kashmir Valley, with their distant memories of independence, neither neighbour offers a solution. The Islam of Pakistan's militant Islamists is at odds with Kashmir's Sufi-inspired traditions. The culture and language that the Muslims and Pandits of the Valley share are distinct from both India and Pakistan. Each country has been felt as a threat. People seem weary and disillusioned with the armed struggle and many of the men who are engaged in it. Militants who had been bought off by the Indian government and changed sides were blamed for many of the excesses of the early 1990s. Others capitulated and now live in comfortable houses.

But if the gun offered no solution, neither, it seemed, did politics. Even the members of the All Party Hurriyat Conference, an umbrella organisation formed by 30 political parties in 1993 to act as the political voice of a people who felt themselves disenfranchised, were considered to be living too well. The Hurriyat itself was deeply divided about Kashmir's future. Its members called for tripartite negotiations – India, Pakistan and the Hurriyat itself. But when I asked different members of the Hurriyat what their agenda for such negotiations would be, some wanted union with Pakistan while others wanted independence. Others still would settle for real autonomy within the Indian state. One wanted an Islamic state; another wanted a secular government. Some had links to the militants, others did not. Each claimed to represent a general majority and all claimed that such differences could be argued out if the need arose.

With no hope of a solution in sight, the 12-year insurgency has created its own mythology as new generations grow up in the Kashmir Valley knowing nothing but the war. Even if few still believe any longer that the Kashmir Valley's freedom can be won by armed struggle, the daily oppression and injustices of the occupation still drive new recruits to the gun.

Many of the militants are buried in Srinagar's many Martyrs' Cemeteries, some of them large adjuncts to regular graveyards, others crammed into small corners across the city. They were crowded with almost identical small concrete gravestones, covered in green Arabic inscriptions. A few bore English place names – Birmingham was one I noted, a sign of the appeal Kashmir has for disaffected western-born Muslims looking for a cause worth dying for.

But exactly what that cause was beyond the single word *azad* – freedom – remained confused. As I looked at the gravestones in one of the smaller cemeteries near Dal Gate one day, a group of boys collected round me and laboriously translated the inscriptions. They called all the dead 'martyrs', but they could not tell me whether they were martyrs to Kashmiri independence, to union with Pakistan or simply to Islam. The idea of freedom had no geographical or political shape, but to them it did not seem to matter. For an older generation, though, this steady accumulation of deaths has become unbearable in a war that seems to have no end.

In Srinagar, the politicians of the Hurriyat Assembly had debated whether to contest the elections due to be held in Jammu and Kashmir this year. To do so would be to affirm India's vision of its own democracy – a happy community of peoples equally valued and united in their diversity. But Kashmir did not subscribe to this image, nor could the Hurriyat swear the required oath of loyalty to the Indian state, an oath that their separatist alliance could not honour.

Instead, on 12 February, the Hurriyat announced their own electoral process. They were forming a commission, they said, to prepare for elections that would choose Kashmiri representatives to sit at the negotiating table with India and Pakistan. In the last few weeks, strenuous efforts by India to persuade members of the *Hurriyat* to change their minds have failed.

One million men, the armies of both sides, remain on the Line of Control ready for war. The governor of Jammu and Kashmir told me there was absolutely no possibility of India ceding any territory or sovereignty in

Kashmir: if it did, he said, it could trigger Muslim discontent all over India – a country which, Indians never tired of telling me, had more Muslims than Pakistan. It only reinforced India's grip, even at such a high price, on the few million deeply disaffected Muslims of the Kashmir Valley. Pakistan was equally stubborn: for Pakistan it was also a national cause, the continuing need to insist on the founding reason for that troubled state – the Muslim faith of its people and the belief that Kashmiris longed to be liberated by their Muslim brothers.

The Kashmiris longed for peace, but the omens were not good. President Musharraf, speaking on Kashmiri Solidarity Day, called for international mediation. It drew a rebuff from New Delhi. The conflict would stop, Prime Minister Atal Behari Vajpayee responded, when Pakistan chose to stop it. 'Pakistan may celebrate their Kashmir Solidarity Day,' he said, 'but they will not get Kashmir.' ❑

Isabel Hilton *is a staff writer for the* New Yorker. *Her most recent book is* The Search for the Panchen Lama *(Penguin 1998)*

BEYOND THE GUN
SHEBA CHHACHHI

For over a decade, images from Kashmir have been dominated by men with guns – Indian soldiers, security forces and police; Islamic insurgents, their faces hidden behind masks and scarves toting AK47s; Islamist infiltrators from camps inside Pakistani-controlled Kashmir – and their victims. 'Dead men – mutilated bodies, charred flesh and unidentifiable human remains – occupy the space left over by armed men,' says Sheba Chhachhi, introducing the images that follow. Between the two, the image has become no more than evidence of violence and oppression.

There are, too, the photographer concedes, traces of the remembered lost paradise revealed in postcard images of the lakes, gardens and mountain scenery so quintessentially Kashmir, and government posters depicting the same to reassure potential tourists that 'normalcy' is returning. What is lacking in this visual narrative are the faces of ordinary Kashmiris: except as victims, the men, women and children of Jammu and Kashmir are the invisible actors in the long-running battle between Indian government forces and insurgents. The human being disappears behind the propaganda; the land is 'depopulated' and becomes merely the 'territory', ownership of which India and Pakistan have disputed since Partition.

The photographs and voices on the following pages seek to bring the human back into the Kashmir story. Or, as the photographer says: 'to give space to the women of Kashmir, whose voices have been obscured by the clamour of war and contention.'

JVH

'Today the talk of separation hurts me. But what can we do? Our voice was not heeded properly. Kashmir was not part of India before 1947. From 1947 onwards, a kind of cold war started. There was discontent which was not allowed outward expression. Those who wanted to speak were suppressed. We had started to participate in the election process, national games. We began to believe that India was our country. There was terrible rigging in the 1987 elections and once again everything shattered. Riggings, firings . . . how could we feel this country is ours? People who do not come out of their homes much cannot differentiate between the government and the people. They began to feel that the Indian people are our enemies. In the midst of this dilemma this war started. Some people started to use guns instead of their minds. And what do we want? What do we want and how – those questions were left behind with the gun. When the gun is raised, dialogue stops.'
Gulshafan, *PT instructor, Srinagar*

'The militants came in the middle of the night and demanded food and shelter. We have never been involved with any militant group nor with the *azadi* movement. But what could we do? They had guns. At dawn there was a raid. The *faujis* cordoned the place and as the two men ran out into the snow they were killed. Then the CO ordered all of us out of the house and started beating my teenage sons and husband until they bled. "Keep militants here, do you? I'll teach you a lesson," they said. They took my husband away, warning us, "If any of my men had been killed, this village would have burned like Pattan, remember that."'
Haleema, *Buthu*

'I faced the power of his gun with the power of my mind. I felt no fear. I had the axe. Had the axe not been there; there was a rolling pin, a ladle. If I had a gun, they would have seized it long ago. These are my own implements. No one can take them away from me.'
Jana, a carpet worker, who escaped molestation by a Border Security Force Soldier, Awanpora village

'I knew my husband was a militant. I knew that some day he would be killed. I grieve, but I do not complain. When you are a militant, you are ready to die. But why did they kill the other seven men? They were innocent, they had not killed anybody. I have to bring up my children. Where does a woman go? What can she do? If women become militants, what will happen to the children? Who will look after them? Who wants all this killing? A woman cannot become a militant.'
Jameela, Malangaon, Bandipora

'Will your son become a *mujahid*?' we asked, watching a ten-year-old child playing with his toy gun. 'The child of a freedom fighter will be a freedom fighter!' But then, caressing the cheek of her 17-year-old, she almost whispers, 'As soon as even a tiny bit of beard appears, I shave it off. I can't lose him as well.'
Saira, *Bandipora*

'I asked them: why have you come here in the middle of the night, is this how you do your duty? I told them to go away, my husband is not here. "Where have you kept the money?" they demanded. We have no money, we're *mazdoors*, day-wage labourers. When they couldn't find anything they locked my children into the other room and raped me, one by one. They were soldiers from the ITBP [Indo-Tibetan Border Police] camp. They were both drunk.'
Rubeena, *a Bengali woman who had come to Kashmir eight years before and married a Kashmiri; this testimony was given the day after the rape*

'Community makes nation. Silence the community and the nation dies. War takes place. In war, one side wins, the other loses. What neither wins nor loses, but simply dies as a result, is humanity. Human values, human relationships, faith, trust. I fear for the end of all of this. I fear that humanity will not survive.'
Schoolteacher, *Avanporgaon, Pulwama district*

'My father was so handsome and strong. He looked just like Rajesh Khanna. Everybody loved him because he was always laughing and he was a good person. He used to ride a motorcycle. The Hizbul Mujahideen had warned him about drinking, but when he didn't care they killed him.'
Benazir, *a teenager, Bandipora*

'My husband was abducted by militants seven years ago. We have no idea whether he is dead or alive. Every time the talk of my remarriage begins in the family, we get a whiff of a rumour about his being alive. And so the wait begins again.'
Hamida, a half-widow, Bandipora (Islamic law permits the remarriage of a widow only after the husband's death has been conclusively established)

'We always considered ourselves as first-class citizens of Kashmir, but now I'm so confused. What do you think will happen? Do you think it will be safe for us to raise our children here?'
Kanwal, a Sikh woman in Srinagar, after the Chittisinghpora massacre of 36 Sikhs

'Suddenly my students began to wear veils . . . such pretty girls. They said they were being pressurised by their brothers and the speeches from the mosques. Until then we had secular ways in the college – all the girls in uniform . . . During the exams when I scolded a girl she turned around and said, "Madam, my cousin is a militant. How can you scold me?"'
Jai Kishori Pandit, professor, Government College for Women, Srinagar

'I didn't decide to leave. We came here for a holiday. Everything was left behind. We had to start all over again . . . from a spoon. Is this any way to live? Five of us in a rented room, no privacy, the heat, sleepless nights – this, after what we had been used to in Kashmir.'
Prana, refugee camp, Delhi

'Men go to mosques. We go to the *ziarats*, the shrines. There we weep together and unburden the load that sits heavily on the chest. We cannot face God on our own, so we ask the *Pir* [holy man] buried there to intercede on our behalf. I find great peace there. What are these men thinking when they burn down our shrines? Where will we go if this carries on?'
Abida, *Srinagar*

'You must not believe everything that people tell you. You must not listen with your ears but with your heart.'
Parveen, *a doctor, Srinagar*

'My son never asked me, "Ammaji, can I go to Pakistan and become a militant?" He simply left. I wept. That is the fate of the mothers of Kashmir. When he crossed the border on his return he was caught and jailed for two years. When he was released, the tanzeem [militant group] got after him because they felt he'd broken under torture. So he joined the Ikhwan to protect himself. Either way he was trapped. I don't sleep at night because of the numerous attempts on his life. This is not life but hell.'
Lala, *Bandipora; her son, the Ikhwan Area Commander, was ambushed and killed a few months later*

'We were afraid, but we thought it would blow over. First BK Ganju, a junior engineer in the telecom department, was brutally murdered. The women of his family were not even allowed to mourn. Then several other prominent members of our community were killed. Terrified, we left en masse.'
Pandit *refugee in Delhi, name withheld*

'It was years since we had all got together at a wedding – all of us women – Hindus, Muslims, Sardarnis. It was almost like the old days. We laughed and danced late into the night. Then, as we prepared to go to sleep, I heard some of the Muslim women whispering among themselves in the next room: "It's been such a lovely evening. It is true, isn't it, that a garden is only a garden of any worth when there are many kinds of flowers gracing it."'
Ranji, *one of the 18,000 Pandits who chose to remain in the Kashmir Valley* ❑

Sheba Chhachhi *is a photographer and installation artist living in Delhi. These testimonies and images are from 'When the gun is raised, dialogue stops: women's voices from the Kashmir Valley', a photo installation by Sheba Chhachhi and Sonia Jabbar. They also appear in* Speaking Peace: women's voices from Kashmir, *edited by Urvashi Butalia (Kali for Women, India, 2002)*

THE END OF SECULARISM
SALIL TRIPATHI

HINDU MOBS IN AYODHYA, MUSLIMS
MASSACRED IN GUJERAT. INDIA'S
PROUD BOAST THAT ITS SECULARISM
HELD TOGETHER ITS MANY CREEDS
AND RACES IS IN TATTERS

Ten years ago this December, a mob of Hindus destroyed Babri Masjid, a medieval mosque in Ayodhya, to liberate the land on which, they claimed, their revered God Rama was born.

Nothing was spectacular about that mosque, which had stood for four centuries. India has grander, more beautiful mosques, and Ayodhya has many temples commemorating Rama. Yet they targeted that particular mosque because it was built precisely where they believed a temple marking Rama's birthplace had once stood, and which, they claimed, the Moghul emperor Babar's invading army had destroyed.

The dispute simmered for over four decades, but a court order prevented any disturbance of the site. Throughout the 1980s, the Vishwa Hindu Parishad (World Hindu Council) made progressively louder noises seeking to reclaim the site. Muslims formed the Babri Masjid Action Committee, and refused to surrender their claim. Angry Hindus formed the Rama Janambhoomi (birthplace) liberation movement.

The Bharatiya Janata Party (BJP), now the majority party in government, led a movement to rebuild the temple. On 6 December 1992, Lal Krishna Advani, who is today India's deputy prime minister, was in Ayodhya, sitting and watching as a frenzied mob he had encouraged first climbed atop the mosque and then razed it, all in little more than four hours. *'Ek dhakka aur do, masjid ko tod do'* ('One more push, and destroy the mosque'), screamed Sadhvi Ritambhara, a Hindu priestess, cheering the crowds. The crude rabble-rousing shocked many Indians, but there were enough Hindus who saw redemption in that destruction.

In the past ten years, the new temple hasn't been built. Hindu activists have periodically turned up in Ayodhya, threatening to start construction, only to retreat after a fresh court order. In February this year, when one such bunch of Hindu activists was returning from Ayodhya, their railway compartment was torched by a Muslim mob in the town of Godhra in Gujarat state, killing 58 people. What prompted that is not known. What is known all too well is the aftermath. Hindus in Gujarat, where the BJP controls the state government, retaliated swiftly, killing hundreds of Muslims, razing Muslim shrines, looting property and displacing thousands of Muslim families. Capitalising on the riots, Gujarat's chief minister dissolved the legislature, seeking fresh elections later this year. Progressive Indians feared that Gujarat was the laboratory of Hindu nationalists. The VHP agreed, promising a repeat of Gujarat if Muslims dared to misbehave elsewhere. Such talk, reminiscent of the violence of Partition in 1947, is once again part of Indian discourse and signifies the failure of India's secular model.

The rise of Hindutva, the Hindu nationalist ideology, is possible because India's governing consensus has disintegrated over the past quarter-century. In the 1980s, India underwent a mid-life crisis. The Emergency of 1975–77 had shown that an autocratic leader could mangle the constitution. Even though Indira Gandhi lost the elections that followed, internal bickering among her successors disillusioned the voters. The Punjab insurgency from 1978, the military assault on the Golden Temple and Indira Gandhi's assassination in 1984 threatened national unity.

Rajiv Gandhi came to power promising a clean administration. Instead, corruption increased and his government capitulated to fundamentalist demands. First Gandhi banned Salman Rushdie's novel *The Satanic Verses*. Then he surrendered to conservative Muslims and denied Muslim women the right to seek alimony, effectively making them second-class citizens. Insurgency worsened in Kashmir.

Internationally, India's pro-Soviet non-aligned foreign policy appeared increasingly meaningless as one Eastern European nation after another became free in 1989. The economy stagnated even as India's East Asian neighbours experienced rapid economic growth. By 1991, India was virtually bankrupt. The same Congress Party that had ruled India since 1947, promising to build 'a socialistic pattern of society', made an about-turn and liberalised the economy.

The only solace for Indians, it seemed, were the Hindu epics *Ramayana* and *Mahabharata*, telecast on Sunday mornings and harking back to a golden age. These schmaltzy made-in-Bollywood TV programmes filled an ideological vacuum. If only India could return to that golden age. If Nehruvian non-alignment was wrong, if Nehruvian socialism, too, was wrong, surely Nehruvian secularism could also be wrong?

The BJP – a cadre-based organisation closely linked with Rashtriya Swayamsevak Sangh (the National Voluntary Corps) which has twice been banned in independent India – was waiting for just such soul-searching among Indians. The RSS's leaders have expressed admiration for Hitler and Mussolini. They want Hindus to rise, to feel pride in their ancient past; they consider Islam and Christianity as alien faiths. The umbrella organisation, which includes the VHP, the RSS, the BJP, the Hindu Maha Sabha (HMS) and other political fronts, is called the Sangh Parivar. It has been working painstakingly at changing the Indian consensus and to use its political power to transform India's liberal, secular, modernist ethos.

The BJP capitalised on the growing disenchantment with the status quo and stepped into the void, offering the attractive cocktail of nationalism and Hindutva. Its activists painted slogans in cities, saying '*Garv se kaho, ham Hindu hai*' ('Say it with pride, we are Hindus'). Forget the corrupt Congress and the ideologically bankrupt left. Turn to us: we will bring back the golden age of Rama.

Ayodhya, India 2002: the pillars of a would-be temple to Rama are paraded through the town. Credit: Camera Press / Findlay Kember

The BJP has had few supporters in the past. Until the mid-1980s, the BJP (and its earlier incarnation, the Jana Sangh) rarely got over 15% of the vote. In 1984, it had two of the 547 seats in the Indian parliament. That figure rose to 88 in 1989, 121 in 1991 and now stands at around 170, because of electoral alliances it has formed with other parties. In 1996, it became the largest single party in parliament; two years and another election later, it came to power with its allies. When Advani embarked on a *rath yatra* (chariot march) in 1989, sitting in a Toyota truck carrying a bow and arrow, exhorting thousands of Hindus to liberate Ayodhya, he cut a bizarre, comical figure. But he had the last laugh: in three years, the mosque was gone; six years later, he was India's home minister.

The BJP's rise can clearly be traced to the razing of the mosque, which some Hindutva supporters claim has made them feel they have avenged the humiliation they had suffered. Their swagger received intellectual imprimatur. From his rarefied pulpit in Oxford, the late Nirad C Chaudhuri said: 'I say the Muslims do not have the slightest right to complain about the desecration of one mosque. From AD 1000 every Hindu temple has been sacked [by Muslims].'

Other intellectuals backed the braggadocio. Nodding approvingly, VS Naipaul called the mosque's destruction 'an inevitable retribution'. For too long Hindu nationalism had been subjugated; it was now finding its true voice, and this resurgence could only be a good thing, he argued in his book, *India: A Million Mutinies Now*. Hindus should relive what historian AL Basham called 'the wonder that was India'. That meant a time before alien faiths contaminated India.

The central tenet of Hindutva is precisely that. India must recapture its proud past. The world must recognise it and offer India a place at the head of the table. If it won't listen, India will go nuclear (as it did, first in 1974 and then, as a reminder, in 1998).

The BJP is not in a hurry. Like communist ideologues, BJP's leaders think long-term; their vision is to transform the way Indians think over a generation or two. With that in mind, Hindu nationalists have astutely focused on history textbooks. Their strategy is clear. First demonstrate that Indian history is written by westerners with a colonial agenda or left-leaning Indians who distort reality. Then reveal how the historians have deliberately overlooked Muslim atrocities against Hindus through centuries. Then the nationalists will take on India's secular icons – Gandhi and Nehru – for appeasing minorities. And in that chasm the BJP will underscore its message: that Hindus can only be safe in a Hindu India and minorities must live by Hindu rules.

The first target is the building block of Indian history, the esoteric Aryan Invasion Theory. Conventional history says that around 5,000 years ago, Aryans came to India, as immigrants or invaders, and settled around the Indus Valley, creating the Mohenjo Daro and Harappa civilisation. They later came into contact with Dravidians, who lived further to the south and, over centuries, the two groups intermingled, creating the complex Indian society. Islam and Christianity came later, leading to the multi-everything Indian identity today.

If you accept that scenario, you accept the syncretic nature of Indian society, that it is an amalgam of many influences and ethnicities. But if you challenge that view, you can provide an alternative, purist view, which is that there never was an Aryan invasion. According to the revisionists, Hindu civilisation predated the Aryans: India had always been the land of *sanatana dharma* (eternal faith). Invasions, if any, occurred only in the last millennium, first by Islamic invaders, who ransacked temples and killed thousands, and later during the colonial period.

The political import of this alternative view is obvious: if you accept it, you can argue that Muslims and Christians in India are foreigners. The challenge to the Aryan Invasion Theory is thus not an impenetrable debate among Indologists, but a vigorous argument that goes to the heart of the Indian identity. Hindu nationalists have challenged the orthodoxy of Indian history and questioned the work of Max Muellar, Romila Thapar, Dwijendra Narayan Jha, Bipan Chandra and other historians. Leading the charge are David Frawley, an Ayurvedic doctor from the US, Koenraad Elst, a Belgian Hindu philosophy student, NS Rajaram, a former consultant with NASA, Bhagwan Gidwani, a retired tourism official, Shrikant Talageri, a former bank officer, and others. None of them is an historian or an archaeologist.

While the Hindu nationalist revisionists continue to write voluminously, few historians take them seriously. Michael Witzel, professor of Indology at Harvard University, calls their attempts guesswork bolstered by 'actual fraud'. As an example, Witzel shows how Rajaram wants to prove that horses existed in prehistoric India. Now zoology and archaeology tell us there were no horses in India until the early second millennium BCE. But if Rajaram can show horses in India before the Indus civilisation (2600–1900 BCE), then he can presumably 'prove' that *Rig Veda*, an ancient Hindu text, preceded the Indus civilisation because it refers to horses. That would disprove the commonly accepted theory that the speakers of Indo-Aryan languages came from outside. Witzel concludes: 'Apparently, they do not realise how ridiculous all of this reads outside the confines of the revisionists' rewriting of Indian history along autochthonous lines. Their claims are historically impossible and are based on an unsubstantiated reading of the script.' But Witzel, the nationalists argue, is a westerner with an imperial history and a reputation to defend.

After debunking scholars to establish that India was always a Hindu civilisation, the nationalists' next target is the Islamic invasion. Blaming historians affiliated to Jawaharlal Nehru University in Delhi for understating the horrors of Muslim rule in India, the revisionists quote from Al-Beruni and Gulbadan, recounting stories of Islamic rulers taking Hindu slaves and killing Hindu women and children. That may indeed have happened, but what it has to do with Hindus and Muslims in India in 2002 is an issue the revisionists duck.

Secular shibboleths are the next target. Islam, the nationalists assert, is not a religion of peace. Appeasing minorities, they assert, is wrong. After 11 September, they had hoped their rhetoric would gain wider currency but mercifully that hasn't happened. Their work of documenting Islamic atrocities in India, including the destruction of hundreds of temples and the murder of thousands of Hindus, goes on. To set these historical wrongs right, the Sangh Parivar doesn't claim all the temples that were destroyed. It wants only three sites – in the holy cities of Ayodhya, Kashi and Mathura. Elst defends these demands: 'In withholding from the Hindus access to their sacred sites in Ayodhya, Mathura and Varanasi, you also make present-day Hindus pay the price for the defeat of their ancestors by those who indulged in vandalism and destruction. If punishing the progeny of the perpetrators is indeed undesirable, punishing the progeny of the victims is even more undesirable.'

If India has not confronted these demons, the nationalists argue, the fault lies with the colonised Indian mind. The Congress leaders who led India's freedom movement – Gandhi, Patel, Nehru – were all educated in England. They were anglicised and original Macaulayites – a reference to Thomas Macaulay, whose 1835 Minute spread English education in India. Today, Macaulay is remembered in India for writing that a single shelf of a good European library was worth the whole native literature of India and Arabia, and for calling upon imperial Britain to form 'a class who may be interpreters between us and the millions whom we govern; a class of persons, Indian in blood and colour but English in taste, in opinions, in morals and in intellect'. Macaulay's 'children', the English-educated Indian elite, could hardly be expected to understand India.

The BJP, in contrast, is home-grown and genuine, its leaders argue. Despite its apparently pro-business outlook, the BJP remains suspicious of urbanity, of alien influences and cultures, and of multinationals. It coined the famous slogan, 'We want computer chips, not potato chips'. And it doesn't like Christian missionaries either.

Its final target, interestingly, is Gandhi. Not necessarily the Gandhi who asked Indians to boycott foreign goods, but the Gandhi who went out of his way to accommodate Muslims (an HMS activist assassinated Gandhi in 1948), and the Gandhi who made non-violence a powerful weapon. While no BJP leader has openly criticised Gandhi, plays and films which show Gandhi without the halo that Richard Attenborough placed around him have become popular. Other heroes of India's freedom struggle, particularly martial and violent ones like Bhagat Singh and Subhas Bose, are being resurrected.

The timing could not be better. A recent poll in *Outlook* magazine shows that few teenagers have any idea of Indian history. Catching them young and transforming them early would suit the BJP just fine.

If the strategy succeeds, it would make India a Hindu Pakistan. When India and Pakistan became independent, Pakistan was created as a 'homeland for Muslims'. Today, it has become an Islamic state; India chose secularism and democracy. By championing Hindutva, the BJP is making Indians choose their narrower identities. The BJP may appear foolhardy, but we must remember that its goal is not to win only the next election, but the next generation. It can't get more ominous than that. ❑

Salil Tripathi *is a writer and freelance journalist*

LONG LIVE THE PATRIOTIC SYNDROME
SIDHARTH BHATIA

WHATEVER HAPPENED TO THE WORLD'S
LARGEST AND, THEY SAY, FREEST
MEDIA? GONE IN THE NEW WIND OF
JINGOISM AND JOBS FOR THE BOYS

In June this year, *Time* magazine carried an article from its India correspondent, Alex Perry, headlined 'Asleep at the Wheel?' It was a look at the health problems that Indian Prime Minister Atal Behari Vajpayee was allegedly suffering from, and it asked whether he was fit enough to lead a nuclear-armed country of 1 billion people, especially one that was perpetually hostile towards its neighbour Pakistan, also similarly armed.

The article, accompanied by a picture of Vajpayee in a wheelchair, wasn't up to *Time's* famed standards of accuracy, but to judge by the reaction of the Indian establishment it was a crime of monumental proportions. It was, said one worthy, an insult to 1 billion Indians. The leader of the Bharatiya Janata Party, the leading party in the governing coalition, declared there was a 'foreign hand' behind it, the usual term to describe unnamed global forces out to destabilise India. Workers of the Shiv Sena, a rabidly Hindu militant organisation that is a close ally of the BJP, burned copies of *Time*, and newspapers friendly to the regime weighed in with invective against the 'racist and supercilious' attitudes of the writer and the magazine.

The saga ended eventually, but with hints that when Perry's accreditation comes up for renewal he might face problems: in short, he will have to leave India.

The last time this happened was during the national emergency in 1975–77 when foreign journalists, notably the renowned BBC correspondent Mark Tully, were asked to get out of India. That was a dark period for the Indian press: censorship was imposed for the first time in independent India's history, journalists were locked up in jail and newspapers protested by carrying blank editorials. One of the jailed politicians at that time, Lal Krishna Advani, famously summed up the Indian media's capitulation before the emergency: 'You were asked to bend, you chose to crawl.'

Today, as deputy prime minister, Advani is the strongest man in the government, presiding over the home ministry (which controls the immigration department) and widely considered to be a 'prime minister in waiting'. Indeed, for a brief period during the brouhaha over the Perry piece, Delhi's overheated gossip mills were churning out the story that Advani was somehow behind the claims made about the prime minister's health or, at the very least, had conspired to make a big deal of the matter, to give the article a higher profile.

That may not be true, but what is indisputable is that this government has in recent months come down heavily on sections of the media it has found overly critical and the home ministry has been in the forefront of that campaign.

In March, after a pogrom launched by Hindu mobs in BJP-ruled Gujarat, the party and the provincial government severely attacked the media for its coverage which, they claimed, had inflamed passions. Soon after came the unconnected arrest under the Officials Secrets Act of a journalist from Kashmir, son-in-law of a prominent separatist Kashmiri leader. The subsequent revelation that the sensitive documents about Indian troop movements allegedly found on his laptop were available in the public domain has considerably diluted the case against him. (At one stage, police claimed he collected pornography – it turned out to be spam in his mailbox.)

The introduction of the Prevention of Terrorism Act, said to be in response to the threat of terrorism faced by India, is a catch-all piece of legislation that could be used against a journalist who interviews a wanted person, and it has no built-in safeguards. In an ironic twist, the first person arrested under the notorious law turned out to be a politician whose party is a part of the coalition – he had declared his support for the Liberation Tigers of Tamil Eelam, an outfit banned in India.

But arguably the case that has had the most chilling effect on press freedom in India has been that of Tehelka, a news portal founded by journalists that has made a name for itself in investigative journalism (see www.indexonline.org). Its first investigation was in the cricket betting scandal, but that did not create the kind of sensation (*tehelka* means 'sensation' in Hindi) that was launched when, in March 2001, the website revealed the results of an eight-month-long investigation into defence deals.

Using a fictitious arms company, West End, as a cover, journalists posed as defence agents and filmed many politicians, civil servants and defence officers, retired and in service, asking for and receiving bribes, liquor and, in one case, prostitutes in return for getting a contract. The image of the president of the BJP accepting a wad of notes from the putative defence dealer was seared on the collective consciousness of the nation when shown on national television, and a female colleague and companion of the defence minister was filmed promising to facilitate a defence deal in return for a donation to the party. The state-owned TV network, which reaches 90% of the population, chose not to show the footage that every other channel was airing with glee.

After weakly attempting to deny the revelations, the defence minister resigned and the BJP president also quit, all the while claiming he had been framed. The evidence was overwhelming, however, and though many journalists did not care for these tactics – using spy cams and prostitutes was straying too far from traditional journalism – the story was too good to ignore.

The government launched an inquiry, but it had a sting in the tail no one noticed. The commission of inquiry was also asked to probe the motives of Tehelka because, the government and its supporters let it be known, the investigation was at the behest of the website's funders, a financial company with operations in the stock market that had made huge killings when the markets went for a dive after the story became public. It was an ingenious claim and it squarely put the onus on the journalists to prove that their enterprise was an exercise in journalism and not a cunning plan on behalf of their owners. Stories were also floated that the website had 'links' with shady gangsters; and the trump card, used in India whenever anything has to be discredited, was that there was a foreign link. Like many other companies, some of Tehelka's funders invested on behalf of foreign entities, a perfectly legitimate activity in the stock market, and, moreover, there was no law prohibiting foreign investment in websites.

It was soon clear what the government meant by investigating 'motives'. The offices of the financial company, which held less than 15% of shares in the website, were raided frequently and its owners arrested and told not to leave the country. Their once hugely profitable company was shut down.

Worse followed. As government lawyers set about discrediting the portal and its journalists, and the government showed its disdain for Tehelka's damaging revelations by reinducting the defence minister into the cabinet, the security agencies went after the website with a vengeance. With its funding sources drying up – staff went without salaries for months – the portal was already on the defensive but gamely trying to do stories. In the course of investigating a story on illegal poaching of protected animals, a reporter paid off two professional poachers for information. The reporter

SIDHARTH BHATIA

LOOSENING THE TIES

For all its nationalism and its invocation of past Indian glory, this government recently took the monumental step of casting aside a 50-year-old regulation and allowing foreign investment in the Indian media. The stronger domestic groups resisted the move; others, faced with mounting losses and declining market share, welcomed it, indeed lobbied for it. Now, the dreaded 'foreigner' will be allowed to invest up to 25% in Indian print media, provided editorial control remains in Indian hands. Will the new owners have to guarantee that they will not indulge in 'international conspiracies' against India?

was promptly arrested and, soon after, another senior staffer of the portal was arrested for 'trying to assault an investigating officer'. The gloves had clearly come off and the vendetta was in full swing.

By now, one might have expected other Indian journalists to be up in arms. After all, the Indian media have never tired of telling the world how free they are, how unlike other Third World countries where the press is gagged. Yet apart from the occasional article condemning a specific incident, there has been an abject lack of organised protest, an unwillingness to accept the fact that there is a pattern to all this and that this is the emergency all over again without the formal legislative proclamation. Quite simply, the Indian media, while unsparing in its criticism of the government on many issues, has failed to come together to protect its own, or even resist this incremental onslaught.

Many reasons have been advanced for this. The shock of the blatancy is definitely one factor, and journalists, taking their freedoms for granted, have grown complacent and soft over the years. There is also little doubt that the media, while growing in glamour and clout, have correspondingly lost their militancy as journalism has turned into a lucrative profession and the unionism that characterised it is now dormant, if not dead. Owners, while giving handsome salaries to their staffers, have neutralised their radicalism; most, if not all, owners have other business interests they would not want to see affected by too much anti-government action.

But the changing media scene has been compounded by a relatively new phenomenon, the sustained effort by this government to co-opt the media into a wider 'national effort': journalists have become part of the establishment rather than at odds with it. Individual journalists and media organisations have always been wooed by the establishment in India (as much as elsewhere), but in recent years the media as a whole have been brought onside as part of a national patriotic project, creating a climate of consensus where dissent has limited place.

The co-option of the media takes many forms. Never has a government had so many media advisers – all former journalists – and rarely have journalists been accommodated so much in government advisory committees, consultancies and even in the upper house of parliament. The tiny but forcefully vocal community of 'strategic experts', who will quite blithely comment about how 'Pakistan could be obliterated' if it went in for nuclear war while India would only be wounded in parts, have been quite happy to compromise their independence by willingly joining government advisory boards. As a result, the reading public gets a less than objective view from the influential mainstream media. This has gone a long way towards building the generally hawkish atmosphere in the country.

More worrying is the decline in any challenge to the received wisdom on contentious issues such as human rights abuses, especially in Kashmir.

This was seen at its most blatant during the border war at Kargil in 1999 between Indian and Pakistani soldiers (disguised as irregulars) who had infiltrated the area. It was India's first television war and the nation was enthralled by live coverage from the front as its brave boys ousted the infiltrators from the treacherous mountain passes one by one. Soldiers didn't die – they turned into martyrs and heroes, and their funerals, too, were given widespread coverage.

A new mood of flag-waving jingoism, not seen in India for a long time, took over and the entire nation rallied behind the troops. Questions about how this infiltration had happened, as well as any attempt to hold politicians and others to account, were shelved. The coverage was blatantly one-sided and anything that showed Indian soldiers in a poor light was killed; the army's version of events, mostly given in highly controlled briefings in Delhi, was accepted at face value.

Apart from helping a hard-pressed government facing a difficult mid-term election, the propaganda enabled some point-scoring across the border. Indian satellite television beamed the Indian point of view into Pakistani homes and ordinary Pakistanis, already ambivalent about their military's ill-thought-out adventure, were further demoralised by daily contradiction of their own government's claims. At the same time, India banned Pakistan television from Indian cable operators and surreptitiously shut down the websites of Pakistani papers. Pakistan did not reciprocate.

To be fair, the Indian media have not fully bought in to the BJP's agenda wholesale and liberal critics of its pernicious sectarianism abound. But dissent is located strictly within a preordained framework and, on the whole, the media must take their share of the blame for the jingoism that has been let loose on the country.

But now, at last, the worm is showing signs of turning; the prolonged honeymoon could be over. Poor handling of the economy, sectarian riots the government sought to justify and corruption scandals – even in the procurement of coffins for the 'martyrs' of Kargil – have tarnished the reputation of a party that claimed it was different from its predecessors. And as the media become more critical, the government shows it is not averse to using the iron fist. Already rumours are circulating of dossiers on unfriendly journalists the government claims are 'anti-nationals'. Nothing in their experience has prepared the current crop of journalists to face this level of hostility and, unsurprisingly, the profession has yet to come up with an organised response, though the murmurs are growing. Before it does, there will be some serious soul-searching.

In a climate where the middle classes, who number well over 200 million, are consumers of news and therefore of advertising, and who have been happy to be swept away by the new jingoism, it will require confidence to stand apart and break the consensus. The opposition parties, too, have been swayed by the rhetoric of neo-nationalism, often supporting the government unquestioningly in its 'war against cross-border terrorism'. This leaves only the media to ask the questions. Unless journalists themselves realise they must reassert their independence by asking the tough questions they have so signally failed to do in recent years, they will have only themselves to blame for further government attacks.

EVEN BOLLYWOOD . . .

'If I urinate on the border, the whole of Pakistan will be flooded,' declares an Indian soldier in the Hindi film *Maa Tujhhe Salaam* (Mother, I Salute You). The Hindi film factory of Bombay, known universally as 'Bollywood', churns out hundreds of potboilers every year, and this one, made in 2001, is no different, with its songs, garishness and bombastic dialogue. The over-the-

Poster advertising Mother, I Salute You: *the front-benchers didn't like it.*
Credit: Courtesy Neptune Films

top idiom of the average Hindi film is what makes it unique and audiences expect nothing less. The conventional wisdom of this dream factory is that the 'front-benchers' – the industry's term for India's cinema-going masses – do not care for subtlety and want only escapism. And the dream merchants give them just that. Indian commercial film-makers claim to have a finger on the popular pulse and tailor their product to fit the prevailing social mood.

Yet even a few years ago such incendiary dialogue would not have been allowed by the censors. Films were supposed to promote social harmony, not incite racial or communal hatred. Enemies of the nation were unnamed evil-doers rather than clearly identified countries. But that was then, and India today is a very different place; for some time now, the country has been told in no uncertain terms that the greatest threat to it comes from Pakistan, and the not so subtle subtext is that the Muslims of India are a fifth column. Indian film-makers have been quick to latch on to patriotism as the perfect formula to keep the punters happy and, in the last two or three years, films with patriotism as the central theme have been hitting the theatres with clockwork regularity.

Take a look at some of the titles: *Mission Kashmir, Border, Gadar (Revolution), Indian, Maa Tujhhe Salaam, LoC* (an abbreviation of Line of Control, the border that divides India and Pakistan). All these have valiant Indian soldiers fighting the nefarious designs of the enemy – invariably Pakistan – to spread terror in India. Some, like *Gadar*, about an Indian soldier who marries a Muslim girl only to discover that her father is an India-hater, have recourse to history – it is set in the aftermath of the subcontinent's partition in 1947. The film *Border* recreates a battle between the two sides fought in 1971. *Mission Kashmir* delineates the dilemma of a young Kashmiri who turns to terrorism, while in *Maa Tujhhe Salaam* a soldier single-handedly saves India from a terrible fate. All, however, are clear in pinpointing the enemy with different grades of subtlety.

The Indian film baddie has undergone a significant transformation over the years. For a long time, the average villain had nothing on his mind barring seducing the virginal heroine and indulging in petty crime or murder on the side. In the 1970s, the worst thing anyone could do was to indulge in large-scale smuggling, especially of gold and drugs.

A few years later, the politician emerged as the most venal species in the country, followed closely by the corrupt policeman. The disillusionment felt by most ordinary citizens with the instruments of the state was well reflected by scriptwriters and film-makers; the average hero was now the incorruptible cop who stood up to his dastardly bosses (and also managed to woo the leading lady).

With a new mood of neo-nationalism sweeping the country, aided and abetted by rabid Hindu nationalistic forces who have raised the pitch against minorities and blame Pakistan for most of India's ills, popular culture has begun to reflect these concerns. The frequent exhortations against 'cross-border' terrorism and the limited war with the neighbour in 1999, as well as the heightened tension early this year when both nuclear-armed countries stationed over 1 million soldiers at the border, have all contributed to the jingoistic atmosphere in India that is reflected in Hindi cinema as well as on television.

This is not a new phenomenon. In the aftermath of India's humiliating defeat at the hands of China in 1962, Indian film-makers responded by making films detailing the country's anguish at this apparent perfidy (India and China were ostensibly friends before that). What is different now is a new level of crudity, in presentation as well as dialogue, in condemning the named enemy, and the more than symbiotic link with the prevailing anti-minority, especially anti-Muslim, mood.

In the last decade or so, the forces of Hindu militancy have gone on the offensive – literally – against Muslims, beginning with the demolition of a sixteenth-century mosque in 1992 (*Index* 1/2002). The brutal, state-abetted pogrom in Gujarat in early 2002, in which hundreds of Muslims perished, was the latest outburst of that aggression (see pp160–61).

The Bharatiya Janata Party, the central party in the coalition that rules India (and that also administered Gujarat at the time of the killings), and its various sister organisations must take the blame for much of the anti-Muslim rhetoric. Yet it was clear that this strategy had its political rewards: post-1992, it transformed the BJP from a pariah party into the ruling one, and this clearly reflects the acceptance and support of its pernicious propaganda among the burgeoning middle classes, variously estimated at between 200 million and 300 million people. These are the people who buy cars, live lavishly and consume the goods that multinationals are so eager to sell; and if they want pop patriotism, why shouldn't film-makers and television channels sell it to them?

But crudity has its limitations. Most, if not all, patriotic films have come a cropper at the box office, with the audience quick to realise that something more than loud sloganeering and in-your-face flag-waving is needed to make a film worthwhile. The clichéd and formulaic approach of the average Bollywood film-maker is not enough to satisfy a jaded audience.

The cannier film-makers and, more important, the television producers who reach middle-class drawing rooms have realised that these Indians want something more. And they have tapped into an emotional base far more invidious and therefore lucrative.

On the Rupert Murdoch-controlled Star TV satellite channel, urban audiences are nightly treated to the goings-on in an Indian family in the soap *Kyonki Saas Bhi Kabhi Bahu Thi* (When the Mother-in-Law was a New Bride). All the ingredients of a soap are present – jealousy, bickering, plotting and, most of all, tear-jerking melodrama: no different from countless other family soaps, except that this is a large joint family, the kind that has totally disappeared from Indian society. This fictitious family, with its upper-middle-class lifestyle, its impeccably dressed, bejewelled women and its adherence to a conservative social value system, evokes a nostalgia for a well-ordered existence that nothing can disturb – all the women are fair-skinned, there is not a minority character in sight and everyone subscribes to tradition and ritual as good Hindus are supposed to do.

There is probably no family like this in real life: growing urbanisation has meant more nuclear families, more working women and, consequently, greater modernity, which is seen as having killed 'traditional values'. The soap invokes an idyllic world in which everyone knows their place: thus, a female character whose husband dies in a car crash refuses to get married again (widow remarriage was a controversial subject in India over a century ago), while another character gets a gender test done to find out if her unborn child is a boy (such tests are banned in India). Critics have pointed out that all female characters occupy an inferior space in the hierarchy of this fictitious family and have criticised the soap for promoting regressive values; the producers point to its huge audience ratings.

The show has spawned many imitations and even Hindi cinema has been quick to pick up the signals that its chief constituency – the urban middle classes – are sending. It is interesting to note, for example, that India's best-known film star, Amitabh Bachchan, who articulated the angst of an entire generation with his 'Angry Young Man' persona by rebelling against the establishment in the 1970s, now revels in playing conformist characters who espouse tradition and heritage.

By a happy coincidence, these trends fit in with the Hindu right's campaign to return to a time of mythical grandeur, when India – read Hindu India – was a great country and when the social order, underpinned by the caste system, was apparently harmonious. What is even more signifi-cant is the success of these films among expatriate Indians in the West and elsewhere who want to link up with this imagined India located in a different time and space; an India they feel guilty about leaving but that is now accessible to them.

The great Indian dream factory therefore continues to churn out these concoctions of pop patriotism, assured of a ready market. In time, perhaps, it will give way to a new fad as audiences tire of it and producers look for the next big commercial thing. The dictates of the bottom line are, after all, para-mount, and if audiences demand a dose of India–Pakistan amity, that too will be delivered. In the meantime, it is frightening to think that at a time when sanity is needed to restore social equilibrium and harmony in the country and the region, and a balm has to be applied to the hurt of the minorities, movies such as *Maa Tujhhe Salaam* only add to the jingoism and the climate of hatred. For future historians studying this delicate moment in India's history, the role of popular culture in contributing to rising intolerance will be a valuable subject indeed. ❏

Sidharth Bhatia writes regularly on South Asia and is an Associate Press Fellow of Wolfson College, Cambridge University

Publicity photograph for War and Peace.
Credit: Courtesy Anand Patwardhan

MAKING WAR

No stranger to controversy, Indian film-maker Anand Patwardhan is once again confronting attempts by the Indian Censor Board to prevent screenings of his latest award-winning documentary War and Peace. *The Board has so far demanded over 21 substantial cuts in the film before it is released.*

In his August press release announcing the cuts and his intention to appeal against them, Patwardan says of these attempts to ban the film: 'War and Peace begins and ends with the ideas of Mahatma Gandhi. Focusing on the danger of nuclear war in the Indian subcontinent, the video goes on to describe the problems faced by people living near nuclear testing and mining sites, the horror of Hiroshima and Nagasaki, the culpability of the USA in using atom bombs on a nation that was about to surrender, the globalisation of the arms trade. It derives its power and emotional appeal from the growing movement for peace both in India and in Pakistan. Unfortunately, in both countries there is an invisible force that does not want peace, a force that has come to power precisely by spreading divisiveness within the country and the sustained threat of war outside it.

'While a cursory glance at the cuts demanded by the Central Board of Film Certification exposes its blatantly pro-ruling party bias, reverse inference should not be drawn. War and Peace is not a film against any particular party. If the BJP is criticised in places, so is the Congress Party for having tested the first bomb in 1947. Where the Tehelka "armsgate" in which the present government seems embroiled is mentioned, so is the Bofors scam which undid the Congress Party in the past.

'Officials of the Censor Board must be made to understand that their brief cannot be to wield their scissors in the interests of particular ideologies. The Censor Board and all the vital institutions in our country must be freed from the undemocratic grip of "the invisible force".' ❑

JVH

EXPANDING THE AIRWAVES
FREDERICK NORONHA

INDIA CLAIMS TO BE THE WORLD'S
LARGEST DEMOCRACY BUT, UNLIKE
ITS SMALLER NEIGHBOURS, FEARS
TO OPEN UP ITS AIRWAVES TO ITS
CITIZENS

In early 1995, the Indian Supreme Court gave an interesting ruling. It criticised the long-held government monopoly over broadcasting and declared the airwaves to be public property. They were to be utilised for promoting public good and ventilating a plurality of views, opinions and ideas.

This judgement held that the 'freedom of speech and expression' guaranteed by Article 19 of the Indian constitution includes the right to acquire and disseminate information. 'Broadcasting is a means of communication and, therefore, a medium of speech and expression. Hence in a democratic polity, neither any private individual, institution or organisation nor any government or government organisation can claim exclusive right over it. Our constitution also forbids monopoly either in the print or electronic media.'

Despite the judgement, India continued to drag its feet until the late 1990s. Reluctantly, the state-controlled broadcaster All India Radio was given some level of 'autonomy'; for the most part, this meant that the organisation would have to concentrate on earning revenues and foot a growing part of its own bill. And the government cautiously opened up radio to private commercial FM broadcasters. By mid-November 1999, the government announced that the bidding process to set up 140 FM stations in 40 cities had closed after 'overwhelming response', with 349 potential broadcasters finally left in the race for a licence. By early August 2000, 26 companies had received letters of intent from the government. Licences cost millions of rupees and only a few urban centres within India are to be covered. Nevertheless, from being a staid government monopoly Indian radio is making the change to highly commercialised broadcasting.

Contrary to government claims, however, it is clear that their policy has been far from the success they claim. Expressly forbidden by their licences from broadcasting news or current affairs, stations have made a dent in a few cities by rejuvenating interest in radio, but for India's mass radio audience, privatisation and the promised deregulation have made little change: public service, community, educational and development broadcast networks are, so far, the poor relations of privatisation.

And it is only in a few major cities that the commercial FM thrust has picked up. As of mid-August 2002, barely ten commercial FM radio stations had been commissioned in six Indian cities – Bangalore, Indore, Lucknow, Ahmedabad, Pune and five stations in Mumbai (Bombay). Three more companies have paid licence fees to broadcast in six other cities – Bhubaneswar, Cuttack, Jabalpur, Coimbatore, Tirunelvi, Visakhapatnam – but were yet to launch operations. Nine more firms were given an extended deadline until 29 August to launch their operations.

But there are signs that the government is bending to public pressure; it has indicated its willingness to open up broadcasting to the educational sector. No news, of course. In recent months, universities have come up with proposals to launch 'educational radio' stations from their campuses. But policy has so far confined this to the state-run Indira Gandhi National Open University (IGNOU). IGNOU stations have been commissioned at Allahabad, Bangalore, Visakhapatnam, Coimbatore, Lucknow and Mumbai. A seventh station at Bhopal is likely to be commissioned shortly, with another 23 more promised for the financial year 2002/3.

There were other hints in August of a rethink, at least on the educational front. Indian Information and Broadcasting Minister Sushma Swaraj was quoted in the *Times of India* as saying she was giving 'final touches' to a proposal permitting schools, colleges and other educational institutions to set up their own radio stations to cater for a variety of activities. Swaraj added that the idea behind the proposal came from the concept of community radio, popular in many foreign countries. 'The ministry will have some control, especially where content is concerned, but it will be very minimal,' she added, hinting at a persistent concern of the government that opening up the airwaves could expose it to unpalatable criticism.

For decades, India's radio stations have been centralised, government-controlled, over-dependent on relays and lacking in editorial independence. In recent years, a small number of citizens' groups across India have been pushing for something very different, through the community radio model. In July 2002, a meeting in Hyderabad issued the Pastapur Initiative on Community Radio, released at the end of a four-day UNESCO-sponsored workshop. It pointed out that 'a truly people's radio should perceive listeners not only as receivers and consumers, but also as active citizens and creative producers of media content'. It added that community radio should have three key aspects: it should be non-profit making, have community owner-ship and management, and community participation. Community radio is distinguished by its limited local reach, low-power transmission, and programming content that reflects the educational, developmental and cultural needs of the specific community it serves.

Today, it is technically and economically feasible to set up hundreds, if not thousands, of low-powered FM radio stations across the country. What is lacking are laws to permit this and the political will to allow radio to play its full role in a country such as India.

Recent studies suggest that radio in India has a potential listenership of 98.5% of the population. There are some 104 million homes with radio, double the number of those with TV. Radio has a far broader reach than television. Given the low levels of literacy in India and the low purchasing power of the large majority, radio will inevitably retain its edge over the print media and television in terms of outreach.

Media critics such as Sevanti Ninan have posed the relevant questions: 'Why is [the government] so nervous about opening up a medium that has powerful development potential? Are media groups such as the owners of the *Times of India* and *Midday* more benevolent than development groups? Why is a 52-year-old democracy so terrified of positive decentralisation?' ❏

Frederick Noronha (fred@bytesforall.org) is a freelance journalist who writes regularly on development issues

FATAL FRIENDSHIPS

PERVEZ HOODBHOY

FOUR DECADES AND FOUR DICTATORS
LATER, PAKISTAN'S STABILITY, AS
WELL AS THE SURVIVAL OF ITS LATEST
MILITARY RULER, HAVE BECOME
CONTINGENT ON US SUPPORT

White House, Washington 2002:
General Pervez Musharraf watched by George W Bush.
Credit: AFP Photo / Stephen Jaffee

Appearing at a press conference in military uniform in late August, General Pervez Musharraf declared he would remain president and army chief for the next five years, would have the right to name the heads of the three military services, and emphasised that no parliament could overturn his 29 amendments to Pakistan's constitution. 'This is part of the Constitution,' he declared, waving his hand in the air. 'I am hereby making it part of the Constitution.' Convinced of his sagacity and goodwill, Musharraf says he does not want to rule, but must because no one else can reform Pakistan. 'Democratic dictatorship', he says, is what the country needs.

The reaction in Washington was mild – no talk of regime change here. 'He's still tight with us in the war against terror, and that's what I appreciate,' Bush told reporters while visiting Squires Mountain in Oregon. 'He understands that we've got to keep al-Qaida on the run. . . . And I appreciate his strong support.' Indeed, squeamishness has never afflicted America's Pakistan policy. As Deng Xiaoping once famously declared: 'It doesn't matter whether the cat is black or white so long as it catches mice.' Today America's mouse-catcher is flying high.

General Musharraf is the fourth Pakistani general in 40 years to seize power. In 1965, General Ayub Khan – a staunch anti-communist – brought to his nation the dubious distinction of being, in John Foster Dulles's words, America's 'most allied ally'. Then, in 1971, Richard Nixon rallied to the defence of General Yahya Khan, who had run amok and led the country into a catastrophic civil war. But it was the coup of 1977 by General Zia-ul-Haq that was to have the most profound influence, not only on Pakistan but all over the world. Zia brought a messianic zeal to redefine Pakistan as an Islamic state run by sharia law and to Islamicise its institutions. The US was not enthusiastic, but then the Soviets walked into Afghanistan.

From the early 1980s on, Pakistan was to be the hub of a thriving global jihad industry. Financed for a decade by the US and Saudi Arabia, US strategy to drive the Evil Empire out of Afghanistan required marshalling the forces of Islam from Algeria and Morocco to Egypt and Saudi Arabia. The Pakistan army participated enthusiastically – 'Islam, Pakistan, Jihad' were soon emblazoned on banners at recruitment centres, beards proliferated, promotions went with piety and few could be seen to miss Friday prayers. A new ethos was in creation; this was to be an army not just for Pakistan, but to fight the enemies of Islam everywhere.

After the Soviet Union withdrew, and then self-destructed, jihad went into temporary limbo. But, like any military-industrial complex, it too found excellent reasons for not doing away with itself. Fortunately for those initially recruited by the CIA and Pakistan's secret agencies, the Pakistan army still had plenty of use for jihad. It wanted 'strategic depth' (a friendly backyard) for itself in Afghanistan, and sought to wrest Kashmir from Indian occupation without all-out war. Both required setting up a complex infrastructure of Islamic militant groups that freely roamed the country, but whose existence could be officially denied. Some were closely connected with al-Qaida and the Taliban.

Then came 9/11. Faced by a United States bent upon bloody vengeance, Pakistan's military establishment scurried to join the US-led coalition and take up arms against its former creation the Taliban, and their Amir-ul-Momineen (leader of the pious, Mullah Omar). Osama T-shirts disappeared from bazaars in Peshawar. This betrayal was resisted only by a few senior officers with an Islamic bent. They were quickly rendered irrelevant. General Musharraf knew the alternative. In all likelihood the US would 'have done an Iraq on Pakistan', as one highly placed member of the foreign ministry conceded to me in the week after 11 September. He was probably right.

Today, the Pakistan army's jihad philosophy lies buried under the rubble of the World Trade Center. It has taken upon itself a brand new role. The transition has not been painless. Bloody encounters with al-Qaida, beginning after Tora Bora, have exposed internal contradictions. As casualties mount, and hostile tribal reaction to joint US/Pakistani search-and-destroy operations on the Western border increases, officers and men are asking: why?

Inevitably, the anger – visible or otherwise – at having to fight America's war against al-Qaida and the Taliban focuses on Musharraf, a man who received high praise from the United Jihad Council after secret incursions and battles fought against India around Kargil in Kashmir two years ago. Musharraf's successful coup was warmly welcomed by right-wing religious groups in Pakistan. But today he lives in mortal danger, aware that he is silently stalked by the forces that once sided with him.

To be sure, Musharraf claims a reform agenda and the US is happy to believe him. But he is no Mikhail Gorbachev, nor is he a Kamal Ataturk. All his attempts at reform arose under international pressure. Feeble at best, Musharraf's reforms invariably avoid the type of structural changes Pakistan needs to break out of its recurring, worsening crisis.

In 15 years, Pakistan's population will exceed that of the US. The economy, which has grown at around only 3% in recent years, is hopelessly incapable of providing jobs for the exploding population. The education system – which cannot offer any school for four out of ten children and only poor-quality schools to the rest – contributes directly to the growth of *madrassas* promoting jihad and militarism. The problems are vastly compounded by a huge military establishment.

All countries have armies, but in Pakistan things are reversed. Here, it is the army that has a country. Defence expenditures consume between one-third and one-half of the national budget. Over the decades, senior military officers have been transformed into powerful landlords through grants of choice agricultural lands and real estate. Many, if not most, public corporations are headed by retired officers.

Given General Musharraf's diminishing domestic popularity, some here worry about his survival. But a real threat 'from the street' seems impossible. Pakistan's public, disillusioned by Benazir Bhutto's and Nawaz Sharif's kleptocratic regimes, is far too wretched and ambivalent to rise up. Even heavily armed militant groups are no match for the state's firepower. While intrigues and coups are always possible, Musharraf's survival is likely because he won't touch the enormous powers and privileges of the military.

Pakistan's stability, and Musharraf's political and physical survival, have now become contingent upon US support. Ironically, fate has yoked his survival to George W Bush, who could not recall the name of this Pakistani leader at the time of the US presidential elections. Indeed, after Pakistan was declared a US ally, all earlier sanctions were lifted, and international financial institutions rescheduled debts and gave new loans. Currently, foreign exchange reserves are 700% higher than before 9/11. However, this by itself does not indicate that the economy has improved – manufacturing has steadily decreased in the past year and fear of instability has resulted in essentially zero foreign direct investment.

True, General Musharraf is not a religious fanatic and, unlike his predecessor General Zia, has not exercised brute repression. It is also true that his sudden removal – or possible assassination – would be disastrous in a situation where Islamic militant groups wait in the shadows. But Pakistan's army is part of the country's problem; it cannot be a solution. It must relinquish control over civilian institutions, cut back its budget and move Pakistan away from militarism and war. The US must realise that its support for Pakistan's former dictators ultimately boomeranged. But shall it learn from history? ❏

Pervez Hoodbhoy is professor of physics at Quaid-e-Azam University, Islamabad

AND NOW FOR THE GOOD NEWS . . .
ZAMIR NIAZI

CHANGE CAN COME FROM UNEXPECTED
QUARTERS, AS PAKISTAN'S JOURNALISTS
ARE DISCOVERING UNDER THE COUNTRY'S
PRESENT MILITARY RULERS

Even in the world's three 'mature democracies' that boast the freest media, things are not always as they seem. In his *Agents of Power: The Media and Public Policy*, Herbert Altschull comes to the conclusion that the press is 'not its own master' but a tool in a grand design whose contours are shaped 'by vested interests – financiers, multinationals, politics and governments. The press is not a free agent anywhere: neither in democracies, developing countries nor dictatorships. It submits itself to a variety of manipulations while maintaining a façade of 'individuality' and 'independence of opinion'.

How does Pakistan, once again under military rule, measure up to this? On 16 October this year, General Pervez Musharraf will have completed three years of one-man rule. In his first address to the nation on 17 October 1999, Musharraf stated that the media 'formed an integral part of statehood in the era of information technology'. A quarter of a century earlier, another man in khaki, General Zia-ul-Haq, also in his first broadcast to the nation, announced that although he had imposed martial law there would be no press censorship or media restrictions. It took him just nine days to impose press censorship in the 'national interest'. A reign of terror was loosed on the press: hundreds of workers were jailed, newspapers and presses were seized and sealed, four watchdogs were whipped. It was journalism's darkest hour.

The press has been treated as enemy number one by all our dictators, regardless of their persuasion: the 'controlled' democracy of General Iskandar Mirza; the 'basic' democracy of self-appointed Field Marshal Ayub Khan; the 'Islamic' republic of Zia-ul-Haq. The dubious democracies of Zulfikar Ali Bhutto, Nawaz Sharif and Benazir Bhutto were little different. Forget the jackboot: rulers in civilian garb sat over the legacy of the khakis, adopting the same carrot-and-stick approach to control the press. Their limited success was due to a handful of intrepid professional editors – the majority of daily papers are edited by their proprietors – columnists and reporters who stood up and paid the price, a few with their blood.

Bangladesh 1972: a child's drawing recalls the war against West Pakistan in 1971.
Credit: Marilyn Silverstone / Magnum Photos

However, Musharraf remained faithful to his word; even went further. On 2 February last year, he told the nation that not only was he 'a firm believer' in the freedom of the press, he was 'even considering a liberalisation policy for the establishment of private radio and TV channels'. Nor were these empty words. Moreover, for the first time, government-owned TV and radio started 'live' coverage of current affairs instead of pre-recorded programmes that had passed before an internal censor board.

During Yahya Khan's martial law, before the creation of Bangladesh, we witnessed a moment of openness during the 1970 election campaign when the state-owned electronic media gave full coverage to opposition rallies and invited leaders of various political parties to speak without any let or hindrance. However, soon after the election results, which were totally contrary to the expectations of the ruling junta, censorship was reimposed before the start of the military crackdown in then East Pakistan that culminated in the break-up of Pakistan and the birth of a new country, Bangladesh.

The early days of Benazir Bhutto's first government in 1989 saw another brief period of relaxation in control over the electronic media. It proved to be short-lived: Benazir reverted to despotic control over the state-owned media which, in turn, reverted to their time-honoured role of toeing the government line.

Now there is a whiff of fresh air, one reason for which was Musharraf's need in the early days of his takeover to win the support of the international community, notably Bill Clinton, and end the isolation in which he found himself. Ironically, it was the press, taking full advantage of its new-found freedom, that came to his rescue with its bold and outspoken coverage of events at home as well as internationally. It allowed him a breathing space and, surprisingly, the government made no attempt to interfere in the day-to-day functioning of the press. This strategy gave him some respite on the international front.

Meanwhile, most of the press, particularly the mass circulation Urdu-language press, mercilessly took the general to task for his U-turn on Afghan policy, particularly the abandonment of the Taliban, and his policy on Kashmir. The English-language press was less wholehearted in its support, but took a fairly objective critical stance. On the perennial Kashmir dispute, for instance, journalists openly advised the government to adopt a 'pragmatic policy' rather than the 'principled' one that had prevailed for over five decades.

There is, as everywhere, a downside to the new press freedom: the scurrilous and sensational coverage of Urdu-language tabloids such as the *Morning Special* and *Mashriq Evening Special* is a disgrace to the profession and has had disastrous consequences for its victims. Both papers were shut down for a month on government orders but, following the intervention of the proprietors' guild, the order was revoked.

This is not an isolated incident. There are a number of newspapers in small towns that invite the wrath of the local authorities and pay for it. But for the mainstream press, this is the best of times – even though, at the personal level, journalists still suffer from the wrath of those highly placed in the administration or in the country's intelligence agencies (of which we have a gross surfeit) whom they have offended. The boys are 'politely' invited to the office concerned for 'explanation/clarification' and thrashed by goons. A couple of officials have been suspended for this practice, but it continues.

For instance, in August, the editor of the Karachi Urdu daily *Jasarat*, Muzaffar Ejaz, was summoned by an intelligence agency for publishing some 'incorrect' and 'unfounded' information against a certain government department. According to the editor, he was 'detained' for over six hours and grilled by officials in 'abusive' language.

In the same month, Shaheen Sehbai, former editor of the daily *News*, part of Pakistan's biggest newspaper group, had a similar run-in with members of the junta. Last year, Sehbai had a wordy duel with his press baron editor-in-chief, left the paper and departed to the US to start his online weekly *South Asia Tribune*. While still in Pakistan he had annoyed the junta by publishing 'false and unfounded' reports. Now he has once again invited the wrath of the government by circulating similar information from the safety of the US.

In December last year, Musharraf took another courageous step by releasing the Hamoodur Rahman Commission report that had exposed the brutality and barbarism perpetrated by the military junta in 1971 in East Pakistan. In August, during a state visit to Bangladesh, the general publicly expressed his 'regrets' for the 'excesses' committed by his predecessors. No civilian government – there have been nine of them in the intervening 31 years – has found the courage either to release the report or apologise for the crimes committed in Bangladesh at that time.

The brutal murder of Daniel Pearl of the *Wall Street Journal* in February this year by a bunch of fanatics was a black spot on an otherwise more sanguine media outlook. The murderers have subsequently been found guilty and sentenced (*Index Index* p123).

The country is on the verge of general elections, scheduled for 10 October 2002, intended to result in a new form of government known as 'democratic dictatorship'. The federal minister for information recently promised that press freedom would be 'institutionalised' before power was handed over to the new set-up. He advised journalists to protect the traditions that had been built up during the past few years. 'Freedom', he said 'is not only given, freedom must be taken. If this is once given, it would and should be difficult for any government to retrieve.'

It took only a few days to discover from the press itself what this 'institutional structure' might be. Three laws pertaining to the press had been approved by the federal cabinet, it reported: the Newspaper/News Agency/Book Registration Ordinance, the Formation of a Press Council Ordinance – responsible for dealing with public complains against the press – and the Defamation Ordinance.

Journalists have demanded the replacement of Ayub Khan's draconian Press and Publications Ordinance since 1984. Literally hundreds of newspapers and thousands of journalists have fallen victim to it since its institution in 1963. In 1987, the Islamic sharia court declared some of its articles 'un-Islamic' on the grounds that 'it upholds the right to protest and dissent and determines the pattern of a journalist's performance in his commitment to truth'. The verdict made it 'binding' on the media to 'raise their voice against oppression and tyranny'. Disregarding the verdict of his own creation, Zia challenged the sharia verdict in the Supreme Court. Nothing more was done until the caretaker government that followed Zia's mysterious death in a plane crash in 1988 passed an ordinance amending Ayub's press law by removing some of its more offensive articles.

Constitutionally, an ordinance remains in force for three months and can be extended only twice, unless parliament approves it. In the ten years of civilian governments under Benazir Bhutto and Sharif no attempt was made to get the amended ordinance on to the statute books. On the contrary, both prime ministers made ample use of the old ordinance to hound the press.

The drafts of both the freedom of information and press council ordinances were well discussed with professional bodies representing editors, journalists and proprietors – the All Pakistan Newspapers' Society (APNS) and the Council of Pakistan Newspapers' Editors (CPNE) – before publication and the first should have been passed into law in October. However, both bodies 'rejected' them on the ground that the government had made 'certain amendments' in the 'agreed drafts'; they accused it of a 'breach of faith'.

But the government had an ace up its sleeve: its reply revealed that 'on the insistence of the APNS and CPNE, the government has agreed to the *funding* [emphasis added] of the Press Council'! In his rejoinder, the official spokesman gleefully admitted that 'certain minor amendments have been made in the drafts'. Perhaps our press lords have forgotten the hard fact that 'there are no free lunches'.

No newspaper had published the texts by mid-September; no journalist has yet been able to comment.

In conclusion, two comments, both by Indian writers. First, Javed Naqvi, the New Delhi-based senior correspondent of several papers including *Dawn* in Karachi:

> Students of a graduation course asked me to compare the quality of freedom available to journalists in Pakistan and India. I said Pakistani journalists had endured far greater hardship than their Indian counterparts . . . All this is supposed to have steeled them to become better watchdogs against wayward establishments. (The students wanted to know about the Musharraf government.) I said there are

journalists . . . who faced considerable threats to their freedom from the Musharraf government but that did not mean that everyone who wrote against the government was being put in the doghouse . . . There are Pakistani journalists . . . who are respected in India for their moral integrity . . . I could barely name an Indian editor.

Another eminent Indian writer and columnist, and advocate of the Indian Supreme Court, AG Noorani, visited Pakistan at the height of the tension between India and Pakistan earlier this year. In a lengthy interview he said:

I found Pakistanis asking themselves searching questions and challenging conventional wisdom. The press (in Pakistan) is free to an unprecedented degree. One has only to read three volumes . . . (on the state of the press) to realise the degree of change (from the past) and to admire the fight that some put up, no less than the craven submission of some to power that we experienced ourselves (in India) during the emergency in 1975–76. ❑

Zamir Niazi is the author of several books on censorship in Pakistan including The Web of Censorship *and* The Press in Chains, *both published in Pakistan*

A MATTER OF DISHONOUR

MUNEEZA SHAMSIE

At Independence in 1947 there were few educated women in Pakistan and hardly any professions open to them. Today there are women architects, lawyers, bankers, diplomats, civil servants – and there has been a woman prime minister. There is a strong women's movement backed by feminist writing. In urban Karachi, older settlements such as Orangi – once Karachi's largest slum with a population of 1 million – have seen pioneering development work that has led to a 70% literacy rate across gender. The custom of purdah is fading. Women are running small business enterprises or taking up jobs.

On the other hand, the laws of the land provide women with little protection. Lawlessness has spread because of a breakdown of the administrative and political structure and, since the 1980s Afghan conflict, a widespread availability of arms. In most parts of the country women are considered lesser beings. They can be married off, divorced or discarded at will, terrorised in the name of family honour, chastity and religion, or bartered to resolve medieval, feudal squabbles. This attitude has been reinforced by the discriminatory laws initiated or promulgated by the regime of General Zia-ul-Haq (1977–88) in the name of Islam.

For 23 years, activists, lawyers, journalists and other professionals have demanded the repeal of these laws, including the notorious 1979 Hudood Ordinance that does not differentiate between rape and adultery. No government, not even that of a woman prime minister, Benazir Bhutto, or a liberal dictator, Pervez Musharraf, has done so, for fear of offending Pakistan's virulent religious lobby.

'This government does not have the political will to repeal these laws,' said Zohra Yusuf, Council Member of HRCP (The Human Rights Commission of Pakistan), of the present regime. 'The theory is that there will be a backlash, although under US pressure the government has cracked down on some militant parties of religious extremists and has survived that.'

Meanwhile, in an obscure village in the Northwest Frontier region, an illiterate woman reports rape to the police. A district judge decides her pregnancy is proof of adultery. Under the Hudood Ordinance, he sentences her to be stoned to death. Civilised society is outraged. A superior court in

Oranji Township, Karachi: pioneering schools for girls and boys.
Credit: DIL (Development in Literacy, Pakistan)

Peshawer suspends the sentence. The government sets up an official Commission for the Status of Women to examine discriminatory laws. Months pass. The Commission dithers.

On 22 June in Meerwala, another remote village, a 12-year-old boy from a comparatively low-caste Thattal clan is accused of having 'illicit relations' with a girl from the powerful Mastoi clan. A village council, or *jirga,* is held, presided over by the Mastoi. This is an ancient, parallel and more informal system of justice than the state judiciary. To avenge the 'insult', the *jirga* decides that Thattals must be suitably dishonoured. They sentence the boy's sister to gang-rape and then parade her half-naked. But the press reports it. There is another outcry and demands to repeal the Hudood Ordinance. This is not done, although the government does step in and arrest the offenders.

'In this country, for centuries there has been a feudal culture that regards women as possessions,' says Yusuf. 'But for a *jirga to* take such a decision, publicly and blatantly, it has to believe you can get away with it. It is unlikely that the [state] district administration did not know what was happening.'

According to the HRCP, in the Multan district surrounding Meerwala most crimes against women are not reported. Even so, in a six-month period there were 150 reported rape cases, but only 13 offenders were arrested; 40 women were killed for 'honour', but only 15 murderers were arrested. Husbands, fathers, sons and particularly brothers committed these honour killings. More often than not they were used to settle personal scores, to seize a woman's property or for some equally dishonourable purpose.

'The courts are becoming more conservative in interpreting laws,' says Yusuf. 'In honour killings, the judge relies on the provision of "extreme provocation". This government has called honour killings the equivalent to murder, but I am not aware of any specific case or ordinance where this has been applied.'

There was a time when nationalist leaders, including the founder of Pakistan, Mohammed Ali Jinnah, supported pioneering Muslim League feminists against the orthodoxy. The women's movement in Pakistan was spearheaded by the economist and educationist Begum Ra'ana Liaquat Ali Khan, wife of the country's first prime minister. She established the nation-wide women's welfare organisation, the All Pakistan Women's Association, that drafted the 1961 Family Laws Ordinance and pressured President Ayub Khan to promulgate it. The ordinance included clauses that discouraged polygamy, regulated divorce procedures and introduced a minimum mar-riageable age for women. The mullahs held violent protests, but the govern-ment stood firm. Today, this ordinance is still 'under review' by the Federal Sharia Court set up by Zia-ul-Haq to 'Islamise' Pakistan's laws, many of which date back to the British Raj.

In 1981, the full implications of the Hudood Ordinance became ap-parent when a couple, married against family wishes, were accused of adul-tery by relatives and sentenced to barbaric punishments. This galvanised educated, professional women in Pakistan, including Yusuf (then editor of an evening newspaper *Star*) and her media colleagues. They formed the Women's Action Forum and gave it a strong voice in the English-language press. In 1983, WAF came out on the streets in protest because Safia Bibi, a blind girl who was raped, was found guilty of adultery. The legendary sisters, Hina Jillani and Asma Jahangir, both lawyers who had founded Pakistan's first all-women law firm, were pivotal to the movement. They defended Safia Bibi and obtained an acquittal.

'When the Islamic laws were introduced my initial reaction was to go deeper into Islamic law to find a more advantageous interpretation to that of the mullahs,' says Hina Jillani. 'I abandoned this exercise. It's not that one can't find the answers within Islam if one looked, but I realised the issue was political power and the abuse of religion. There were some principles involved. The principle of equality has to be recognised. That equality should be unqualified, unconditional. This should not be subject to any interpretation to suit a particular religious belief or culture.'

Together and individually, the sisters have fought for the rights of women, children and minorities in court. They have faced death threats, slander and armed attacks, initiated or incited by religious fanatics. Jillani also runs Dastak shelter for women; it provides free legal aid. In 1999, one of her young female clients whose only 'crime' was to want a divorce was shot dead in Jillani's office by relatives to avenge family honour. The victim's mother aided in the murder (*Index* 1/1999).

'This whole concept of honour is such a farce,' says Jahangir, now a UN Special Rapporteur. 'I have yet to see anybody feel that their honour has been bruised because their daughter is being beaten black and blue by the son-in-law. I have seen women being sold by their families. Where was honour at that point? It is just hypocrisy and double standards.'

Religious extremists have never won an election in Pakistan, but they have been fostered by successive governments, in particular the military establishment, for political ends. In 1990, the elected government of Nawaz Sharif passed the Law of Qisas and Diyat. This legalised the ancient Muslim custom of giving blood money as atonement for a murder instead of the death penalty, subject to agreement of the next of kin. The sum liable to a woman victim's heir was half that of a man.

Judging by figures given by scholar Tahir Wasti, murders in Pakistan increased over 42% between 1991 and 2000, in no small part as a result of the Law of Qisas and Diyat. Influential persons and terrorists can force the victim's heirs to settle, rather than press charges. If the murderer is the father of the victim, he is often pardoned by the next of kin who are his dependants. Recently, this law was given a grotesque twist, merging it with a tribal custom, *wani*, of bartering women. In a tribal feud, four convicted murderers were spared in exchange for 8 million rupees and eight girls. The *jirga* or *panchayat*, which brokered the deal, included influential landlords, politicians and religious leaders. Two girls of 15 and 18 were promptly married to elderly men in the victim's family. The authorities intervened and rescued them.

Nuzhat Shireen, who belongs to the Aurat Foundation, a group of activists working with poor women since the 1970s, says: 'We would like to see an end to this parallel system of justice through the *panchayat* or *jirga* and to all discriminatory laws. The police must be reformed too, because they are a part of this.'

Last year, Musharraf's government made it mandatory for 33% of seats in the locally elected bodies to be reserved for women – a first in Pakistan's history. The Aurat Foundation has held workshops and training programmes for the elected women. 'These women are well aware of their rights,' said Shireen, 'Many of them have stood for elections because they want to speak out for women.'

For the forthcoming elections in October, the government has revived, and substantially increased, reserved seats for women. The Aurat Foundation and other activists are demanding a 33% representation for women in the provincial and national assemblies. They would also like women to stand for general seats with much greater support from political parties. Shireen says: 'We shall only be able to resolve these problems of discrimination in Pakistan when the government, NGOs and political parties start working together.' ❏

Muneeza Shamsie is the editor of two collections of Pakistani writing in English: A Dragon Flying in the Sun *(OUP 1997) and* Leaving Home: towards a new millennium *(OUP 2001). She is also a freelance journalist*

THE POET IS HEARD IN THE LAND
KAMILA SHAMSIE & AISHA RAHMAN

Pakistan is a country that sprang from the mouth of a poet. Or at least that's one way of looking at history. Whatever one's notion of partition politics, there is no disputing that fact that the first prominent Indian Muslim to proffer the idea of a separate homeland for the Muslims (as opposed to an 'Islamic homeland', an idea that took root after, not before, the creation of Pakistan) was the renowned Urdu poet, Allama Iqbal. In Pakistan today, Iqbal is still a figure of great reverence – the national poet, in whose honour there is a public holiday each year. The content of many of his profoundly philosophical poems would doubtless find little favour with successive governments, but no one, no matter how powerful, would dare speak out against him.

Iqbal is only the most obvious of the Urdu poets who hold such a prominent and – for governments – vexing position in Pakistani society. It's a country with an appallingly low literacy rate, but that's had little effect on the popularity of its poets. Poetry in Pakistan is recognised as an art that is made for performance; at poetry readings (*mushai'ras*) thousands of people turn out to hear their favourite poets – moreover, poems are often set to music and thereby reach an audience of millions. The influence poets wield as a result was most successfully demonstrated when countrywide protests against the government forced the resignation of President Ayub Khan in 1969: in many towns the protests were sparked off by the verses of the popular poet, Habib Jalib. Also, in the wake of the repressive Hudood Ordinances of 1979 (see pp191–93), a number of female poets were a vital part of the feminist movement that fiercely challenged the government – and, in some cases, won important victories. The feminist poets have also been groundbreaking in addressing taboo subjects, such as female sexuality, with candour.

The price poets pay for their influence and popularity is often imprisonment or exile. Faiz Ahmed Faiz was placed in solitary confinement for allegedly being part of a planned coup to overthrow the government; Fehmida Riaz had to go into exile in India as a result of a number of cases brought against her, including one on the grounds of sedition, that carried the death penalty; Kishwar Naheed has faced charges on more than 30 different occasions, including a charge of obscenity for publishing an abridged translation of Simone de Beauvoir's *The Second Sex* under the title *We Sinful Women* (Women's Press 1990).

Intimidation hasn't silenced the poets – quite the opposite. And governments are not above using the stature of the poets for their own ends. When President Musharraf visited India for an all-important summit last year he sent the poet Ahmed Faraz ahead of him as a 'pre-summit emissary'.

KS

MERCENARIES (EXCERPTS)

AHMAD FARAZ

With tears we said goodbye to you
When battle called you away;
Little hope was there of victory, though
Even in defeat we never let you out of our hearts.
You sold your dignity to preserve your life;
Still we tolerated your treachery.

The oppressed of the East were ours too,
Whose blood you wiped on your face.
Did you really go to crush revolt
Or did you go to plunder and rape?
How could you change their fate?
You were too busy trying to wipe them out!

. . .

Still I said you were not to blame,
Just to please the people of the city.
Though my poems were no balm for your wounds
Still, just to comfort the helpless,
For my lost landscape,
For my hopeless, sad people, I sang.

. . .

Little did we know that you, the defeated
Would come to lick our open wounds,
That you who knew the taste of blood
Would break all bounds of cruelty,
That after the killing in Bengal
You'd come and slaughter in Bolan.

. . .

You have seen the processions of people,
Banners of revolt in their hands.
The drying blood on the pavements
Signifies that judgement day is near.
Yesterday we had only love for you
But today the flames of hate are rising in our hearts.

Today even the poet must perform his duty;
In the pen there's blood, not ink.
When your masks came off, then we knew
That you are not soldiers, but hired killers.
It's no longer just the tyrant's head we want,
We demand the blood of all collaborators!

THE LAUGHTER OF A WOMAN

FEHMIDA RIAZ

In the singing springs of stony mountains
Echoes the gentle laughter of a woman
Wealth, power and fame mean nothing
In her body, hidden, lies her freedom
Let the new gods of the earth try as they can
They cannot hear the sob of her ecstasy.
Everything sells in this marketplace
Save her satisfaction
The ecstasy she alone knows
Which she herself cannot sell

Come you wild winds of the valley
Come and kiss her face

There she goes, her hair billowing in the wind
The daughter of the wind
There she goes, singing with the wind.

Translated by Rushksana Ahmed

CENSORSHIP

KISHWAR NAHEED

In those times when the camera could not freeze tyranny for ever
only until those times
should you have written
that history
which describes tyranny as valour.

Today, gazing at scenes transferred on celluloid,
one can gauge
what the scene is like
and the sound
when trees are uprooted from the hillsides.

Whether you are happy or sad
you must breathe
whether your eyes are open or closed
the scene, its imprint on the mind,
does not change.

The tree that stands in the river
always remains wooden
cannot become a crocodile.

For a long time now,
we have stood
on the rooftops of stories
believing this city is ours.

The earth beneath the foundations has sunk
but even now we stand
on the rooftops of stories
assuming life to be
the insipid afternoon's wasted alleyways
with their shattered bricks
and gaping fissures.

Translated by Ruskhsana Ahmed

A PRISON EVENING

FAIZ AHMED ZAIZ (1911–84)

Each star a rung,
night comes down the spiral
staircase of the evening.
The breeze passes by so very close
as if someone just happened to speak of love.
In the courtyard,
the trees are absorbed refugees
embroidering maps of return on the sky.
On the roof,
the moon – lovingly, generously –
is turning the stars
into a dust of sheen.
From every corner, dark-green shadows,
in ripples, come towards me.
At any moment they may break over me,
like the waves of pain each time I remember
this separation from my lover.

This thought keeps consoling me:
though tyrants may command that lamps be smashed
in rooms where lovers are destined to meet,
they cannot snuff out the moon, so today,
nor tomorrow, no tyranny will succeed,
no poison of torture make me bitter,
if just one evening in prison
can be so strangely sweet,
if just one moment anywhere on this earth.

Translated by Agha Shahid Ali ❏

Poems selected by **Kamila Shamsie** *and* **Aisha Rahman**

CULTURE

CONTINUING OUR
FOCUS ON WRITINGS
FROM THE DIASPORA,
WE FEATURE THE
WORK OF A KASHMIRI
POET LIVING IN THE
USA. AND A BRITISH
SCIENTIST EXPLAINS
WHY HE JOINED THE
ACADEMIC BOYCOTT
AGAINST ISRAEL

Ramallah, West Bank 2000: shadows on a wall.
Credit: Larry Towell / Magnum Photos

DIASPORA VOICE

Continuing the theme of our last issue (*Index* 3/2002 *Home and Away: Diaspora Voices*), we feature the work of Agha Shahid Ali. Born in 1949 in Delhi to a family of Shia Muslims from Srinagar in Kashmir, Ali was 12 when the family moved to the USA. They returned to Srinagar three years later, but Ali went back to the US in 1975 and mainly lived and taught there from that time. His summers he spent in Kashmir with his parents: 'I always move in my heart between sad countries.'

He published several poetry collections in the US, among them *Country without a Post Office* (Norton 1997), from which the following poems are taken. Of this collection he said: 'My entire emotional and imaginative life began to revolve around the suffering of Kashmir.' Of the experience of living abroad, he once said: 'I wish all this had not happened: this dividing of the country, the divisions between people – Hindu, Muslim; Muslim, Hindu – you can't imagine how I hate it . . . At least here [in the US] we have been able to make a space where we can all come together because of the good things.'

Ali died on 8 December 2001 of a brain tumour.

JVH

POSTCARD FROM KASHMIR

Kashmir shrinks into my mailbox,
my home a neat four by six inches.

I always loved neatness. Now I hold
the half-inch Himalayas in my hand.

This is home. And this is the closest
I'll ever be to home. When I return,
the colours won't be so brilliant,
the Jhelum's waters so clean,
so ultramarine. My love
so overexposed.

And my memory will be a little
out of focus, in it
a giant negative, black
and white, still undeveloped.   *(for Pavan Sahgal)*

THE LAST SAFFRON

Next to saffron cultivation in interest
come the floating gardens of the Dal Lake
that can be towed from place to place

1

I will die, in autumn, in Kashmir,
and the shadowed routine of each vein
will almost be news, the blood censored,
for the *Saffron Sun* and the *Times of Rain*

will be sold in black, then destroyed,
invisibly at Zero Taxi Stand.
There will be men nailing tabloids
to the fence of Grindlay's Bank,

I will look for any sign of blood
in captions under the photos of boys,
those who by inches – after the April flood –
were killed in fluted waters, each voice

torn from its throat as the Jhelum
receded to their accounts and found cash
sealed in the bank's reflection.
I will open the waves, draw each hushed

balance, ready to pay, by any means,
whatever the drivers ask. The one
called *Eyes of Maple Green*
will promise, 'I'll take you anywhere, even

in curfew hours,' and give me a bouquet –
'There's a ban on wreaths!'

2

I will die that day in late October, it will be long ago:

He will take me to Pampore where I'll gather flowers and run back to the taxi, stamens – How many thousands? – crushed to red varnish in my hands: I'll shout: 'Saffron, my payment!' And he'll break the limits, chase each rumour of me. 'No one's seen Shahid,' we'll hear again and again, in every tea house from Nishat to Naseem. He will stop by the Shalimar *ghats*, and we'll descend the steps to the water. He'll sever some land – two yards – from the shore, I, his late passenger. Suddenly he'll age, his voice will break, his gaze green water, washing me: 'It won't grow again, this gold from the burned fields of Pampore.' And he will row the freed earth past the Security zones, so my blood is news in the *Saffron Sun* setting on the waves.

3

       Yes, I remember it,
the day I'll die, I broadcast the crimson,

so long ago of that sky, its spread air,
its rushing dyes, and piece of earth

bleeding, apart from the shore, as we went
on the day I'll die, past the guards, and he,

keeper of the world's last saffron, rowed me
on an island the size of a grave. On

two yards he rowed me into the sunset,
past all pain. On everyone's lip was news

of my death but only that beloved couplet,
broken, on his:

'If there is a paradise on earth,
It is this, it is this, it is this.'

                    (for Vidur Wazir) ❏

WHEN IS A BOYCOTT ABSOLUTELY NECESSARY?

PATRICK BATESON

WHEN, IF EVER, IS A BOYCOTT
JUSTIFIED? WHAT ARE THE PRACTICAL
AND MORAL CRITERIA THAT DETERMINE
WHEN THE TIME HAS COME?

As the Israeli–Palestinian conflict worsened, Hilary and Steven Rose, she professor of social policy at Bradford University, he professor of biology at the Open University, wrote to a large number of friends and colleagues asking whether they would put their names to a letter recommending a boycott of Israeli academic institutions. My own feeling was that Israeli reprisals against the Palestinians after the suicide bomb attacks dealt with the symptoms rather than the causes of the violence. It is naive of the most passionate advocates of 'the war against terror' to suppose that Israel can kill the Hydra by chopping off one of its heads, and implausible that Israel will ever achieve the Herculean task without generating ten more heads for every one destroyed. Before the country has alienated all its friends, leaving itself in a more perilous position than if it had attempted to deal with the major sources of discontent, Israel would benefit from a thorough analysis of why it has stirred up so much hatred.

If I had a reservation about signing the boycott letter, it was that I did not know what Israeli scientific colleagues in the peace movement would feel about it. Would they find such a letter helpful? I sensed they must be feeling terribly isolated and did not want to add to their misery. So I wrote to a number of Israeli friends to discover their reactions. Inevitably, I got a mixed response, but I was particularly impressed by the message from one colleague. She wrote to Steven Rose:

> Pat Bateson told me about your letter to the newspaper that you
> hope will exert pressure on my crazy government. I think this is a
> good idea – we need some form of intervention. I am answering
> immediately, so at present I can talk only in my own name, but I
> believe some colleagues in my department . . . will share my feelings.
> I believe you should publish your letter whatever Israeli academics

feel. Some may be too attached to their grants to be happy with
what you are doing.

On the strength of this, I decided to sign the letter that duly appeared
in the *Guardian* on 5 April with the names of more than 120 academics and
research workers. The letter read as follows:

> Despite widespread international condemnation for its policy of
> violent repression against the Palestinian people in the Occupied
> Territories, the Israeli government appears impervious to moral
> appeals from world leaders. The major potential source of effective
> criticism, the United States, seems reluctant to act. However, there
> are ways of exerting pressure from within Europe. Odd though
> it may appear, many national and European cultural and research
> institutions, including especially those funded from the EU and the
> European Science Foundation, regard Israel as a European state for
> the purposes of awarding grants and contracts. (No other Middle
> Eastern state is so regarded.) Would it not, therefore, be timely if at
> both national and European level a moratorium was called upon any
> further such support unless and until Israel abides by UN resolutions
> and opens serious peace negotiations with the Palestinians, along
> the lines proposed in many peace plans including, most recently,
> that sponsored by the Saudis and the Arab League.

Colin Blakemore, Richard Dawkins and I are Fellows of the Royal
Society and were singled out from the signatories for especially vehement
attack. We have all been involved in controversial issues in the past and are
not afraid to stick our heads above the parapet. I have never been subjected
to such a volume of hate via email: I was accused of being anti-Semitic, a
Nazi, sub-human, etc. A senior editor at *Nature* made the usual anti-Semitic
accusations and strongly implied that I might as well not think about
sending a paper to his journal. I was also accused of using my office
inappropriately. In fact, I had been asked to give my private address:
the Provost's Lodge at King's College, Cambridge, is where I live.

I wrote back to the less abusive protestors and the debate often took on
a more civilised character, though some of my US colleagues, in particular,
remained unforgiving, finding the whole idea of the proposed boycott
utterly repugnant. Jewish friends in the UK said, more in sorrow than in
anger, that they wished I hadn't signed the letter but listened to the

arguments and, even if they didn't agree, respected that people might choose the moratorium to jolt the conscience of a country.

Was that necessary? Here again is the voice of the same friend and colleague in Israel whose views had persuaded me to sign in the first place:

Thank you for your letter and for your concern. It is not the hate reactions that I get from the right-wingers that are distressing to me – I am used to those. I am shocked by the amazing hate reactions that I am getting from my left-wing colleagues who interpret my support of the *Guardian* letter as an act of treason, as spitting in the face of the Israeli academic community, as an act justifying and encouraging anti-Semitism, as killing the spirit of science in Israel and so on. I am really shocked and dismayed by these irrational responses, and at first I was not prepared . . .

I am really disappointed by my left-wing colleagues, although I am getting over the initial shock. Their reaction is so full of self-defence and self-righteousness that I find it unbelievable and somewhat disgusting. I am also amazed at the level of tribal loyalty of the academic community – a lot of the people who condemn me are in favour of some form of sanctions on Israel – but not in their back yard, not on the holy academic community! And I am also angered by the petty warnings of some people that I shall pay an academic price . . . I hope that this reflects unjustified worry on their part, but if this is what people really think might happen, well, they should be ashamed of the system.

But, Pat, these really are small matters. We live in a terrible reality. The bomb that exploded yesterday was very near to where I live and where I often do my shopping. I worry about my family and friends constantly and I am enraged by what we [Israelis] do to the Palestinians who suffer ten times more than we do. I need not tell you what I think about Sharon's government, how strongly I oppose it. I agree with your analysis of the situation and I think the recent resolution of the European Parliament is excellent – very good for both sides. I love Israel and I worry deeply about what my society is becoming.

Some Israeli friends supported this position but others, perhaps predictably, dismissed such views as those of 'communists' and 'trouble-makers' who were beyond the pale of Israeli society. Archbishop Desmond

Tutu, when he got to hear of the proposed boycott, supported it and added that, in his view, the intellectual boycott of South Africa had played a part in the downfall of apartheid. The relevance of this analogy is disputed and I shall return to the genuinely interesting and important question of the circumstances in which a just boycott is possible.

What are the arguments? I have always been impressed by the intelligence of my Israeli colleagues and by the torrent of well-articulated arguments that pour from their lips and pens. Now the full measure of their verbal skill was deployed against me, Blakemore and Dawkins. Richard Dawkins was so impressed that he stated publicly he regretted signing the *Guardian* letter. Rarely were the arguments downright silly, but I did encounter the claim that the Sharon policy of reprisals was working – emailed to me just before another bomb was exploded.

The most common question put to me was: why pick on Israel when so many other, more horrible things are happening in the world? What about the Russian treatment of Chechnya or the Chinese treatment of Tibet? My response was that the unresolved issue of Israel and Palestine, probably more than any other, is likely to generate world conflict. The manifestly unjust treatment of the Palestinians motivates the Islamic world to distrust and hate the West and generates precisely what the West fears most: the terrorism that could disable civilisation. And Israeli intellectuals are much more likely to be in a position to influence the political process in their own country than are Russian or Chinese intellectuals in theirs.

Another question was: would not a moratorium on funding to Israeli institutions damage the pursuit of knowledge that is neutral and has nothing to do with politics? I was asked this by a *New York Times* reporter who initially wanted to know whether I was keeping Israeli students out of my own college. I said I had signed the *Guardian* letter in a private capacity. In any event, the moratorium was not directed against individuals; I would strongly disapprove if its spirit were interpreted in that way. On the matter of the neutrality of science I provocatively mentioned Mengele.

'Are you likening Israeli scientists to Mengele?' she asked.

'Certainly not,' I replied. I explained to her that I merely wished to make the point that Mengele's horrific experiments on concentration camp prisoners were conducted in the social context of an equally horrific ideology, a terrible fact that argues against the assumption of the neutrality of science.

Nevertheless, she managed, in her article, to imply that I was suggesting a link between Mengele and Israeli scientists. Unsurprisingly, that little piece of mischievous reporting triggered a fresh round of abusive emails.

A somewhat similar view to that of the *New York Times* reporter was published in *The Times* of London on 14 August in an article by Susan Greenfield. She opened as follows:

> We university mandarins are supposed to be reflective and logical: above all we are, presumably, expected to think through the consequences of our actions beforehand, and to place the highest priority on the unfettered pursuit of knowledge and promulgation of scholarship. I deplore the recent call by British academics for a boycott of Israeli cultural and research contacts: it simply flies in the face of what academics, and scientists in particular, should be about.

I thought this was grandly priggish and naive. By a process known as 'affiliation bias', scientists consciously or unconsciously tailor their published findings to the wishes of their paymasters, whether they be the tobacco or the food industries, civil servants making procurements for national defence or pharmaceutical companies. Of course, it can and should be argued that this is regrettable, undesirable and should not tarnish the ideal of honest sharing of information. But the impact of society on science is all too evident. Moreover, influences flow both ways and the impact of scientists on society can also be very considerable. If their funding is threatened by the actions of their own government, their initial response will certainly be to protest volubly that they have nothing to do with political decisions, but then they can start to exert the real influence they do possess.

Greenfield poured especial scorn on her two Oxford colleagues, Blakemore and Dawkins, characterising them as 'wannabe statesmen'. Having built a divisive fence, she went on, they now seemed to wish to sit on it. 'This type of vacillation does nothing for the current shifty image of scientists with the general public.' Blakemore and Dawkins are perfectly capable of responding in kind, but I felt that her argument was shallow and, indeed, I suspect that the public perception of shifty scientists, if it is real, is more likely derived from strong pronouncements based on inadequate evidence such as those Greenfield is inclined to make herself. That said, I too have felt ambivalence about the recommended moratorium on funding for Israeli academic institutions because it does, indeed, run counter to the ideals – if not the practice – of our profession. But the debate needs to be treated with proper seriousness and not dismissed as vacillation.

I promised earlier to return to the issue of justified and unjustified boycotts. This is a matter about which a genuinely interesting debate can be held. I have started such a discussion with a very dear Jewish friend who disapproved of my signing the original *Guardian* letter. He thinks that contemporary Israel is not like South Africa under apartheid. Many South African academics were complicit in the racial policies of their government and benefited personally from them. Israel is a democracy and its academics are only harmed by the policies of their violent right-wing government. Whether or not my brave Israeli colleague who stood out against the pressures to conform would agree with him, the issue is an important one. If we agree that boycotts can be instigated with justice on certain occasions (and I accept that many would not agree), can we specify what constitutes proper grounds for this? ❏

Patrick Bateson *is professor of ethology and provost of King's College, Cambridge*

THE VARDAR SHORES OF PEACE

MICHAEL FOLEY

The Stone Bridge over the River Vardar in the middle of the Macedonian capital, Skopje, divides more than just the old city and the new: it divides two communities, the Albanians and Slav Macedonians.

On one side, the Albanian, are the minarets and domes, the bazaars and the Ottoman architecture. Small boys try to sell you lighters and ballpoint pens, men in white skullcaps play backgammon and drink tea. Some women are veiled. This side of Skopje is Asia and Muslim. A walk across the stone bridge, built on Roman foundations, and one walks into modernity.

The 'new' Skopje rose out of the ruins of the earthquake in 1963. To suffer an earthquake that left 100,000 without homes was bad enough; to suffer twice over with the neo-brutal rebuilding of the city under a 1960s communist regime compounded the tragedy. The city was rebuilt in concrete, with highways cutting swathes through it. Today, apartment blocks are streaked with water stains. Here and there a balcony has fallen, giving a building the look of a mouth missing a tooth or two. Paving has subsided and grass and weeds are growing between the cracks. The street furniture, the traffic lights, direction signs, manholes, are rusty. Scaffolding usually means something is being held up rather than repaired. Green spaces running along the centre of roads or between buildings are full of weeds. More recent buildings are little better, especially churches, whose architects seem to specialise in their own particular form of brutalism.

Along the embankment of the Vardar in central Skopje, young Macedonians sit looking across the slow-moving river towards the mountains that surround the city, at the domes and minarets. They sit outside the new trendy bars: the Irish bar with its dark wooden interior; the New York-style bars with cocktails; the sophisticated bars decorated in chrome and mirrors. Given that few are wealthy in Macedonia, it would be invidious to suggest that on one side of the Vardar sit the wealthy looking over at the poor on the other, but that is what it looks like to a visitor. On one side the Orient, poor and exotic; on the other, the bars and banks of a richer, more powerful people. Albanians account for 70% of social welfare. Macedonia was always the poorest part of Yugoslavia and has hardly

Skopje 2002: view across the Muslim quarter of the old city.
Credit: Michael Foley

prospered since independence in 1991. Since the outbreak of violence last summer, what little economic activity there was has slowed to a trickle.

Macedonia is a strikingly beautiful country. Eating at a former monastery in the mountains overlooking Skopje, it is easy to forget that quite close is a village where The Hague War Crimes Tribunal is investigating the deaths of Albanian villagers.

It is still a tense country, despite the peace deal. Driving from Skopje to Ohrid you pass what Macedonian friends say are policemen. They sit in sandbagged emplacements with heavy machine guns poking out. They wear camouflage and body armour and check cars carefully. Since the Framework Agreement was signed, violent incidents, border shootouts and bomb blasts have continued to take place on a regular basis.

Whenever there is an incident, NATO and EU officials appear on television saying the agreement is in place: there is no war. Macedonian journalists say there is a difference between incidents and war. Anyway, they say, most incidents take place within the Albanian community, between different guerrilla factions, emphasising, again, the separateness of the two communities.

If any Macedonians ever read this, they will throw their eyes heavenwards in frustration and say that such an analysis is typical of Western journalists who have misunderstood the Macedonians and the Albanians since the violence last year. Macedonians are a friendly people and are great company. However, they do feel aggrieved. The treatment of the ethnic Albanians has been appalling but, as far as many Slav Macedonians are concerned, the Albanian minority has achieved concessions by terrorist means. Outside the parliament building in Skopje, there is a permanent protest against constitutional changes.

Macedonians believe the international media have been unfair to them. At a meeting of the Journalists' Association, called to discuss a new code of conduct and partly intended to stop the attacks the ethnic media make on each other, one journalist asked if there was any way to stop the foreign media from supporting 'Albanian terrorism'. The Macedonians do have a point. Western journalists covered the plight of the Macedonian Albanians as an extension of the war in Kosovo, as if Albanians in Macedonia had suffered the same degree of ethnic cleansing. Albanian guerrilla leaders were portrayed as romantic figures, even though the NATO General Secretary, Lord Robertson, has described the Albanian National Liberation Army as 'a bunch of murderous thugs'.

Macedonians feel they have few friends. Bulgarians to the north-east claim Slav Macedonians are Bulgarians. Macedonians believe Albania and Kosovar Albanians want to make Macedonia part of a Greater Albania. The Greeks, of course, oppose Macedonia even being called Macedonia and insist the country be called, awkwardly, the Former Yugoslav Republic of Macedonia, or FYROM.

When ethnic violence erupted, the international community rushed in to find a solution as fast as possible; there are so many conflicting claims that any conflict in this small country could ignite the whole region, bringing in Serbia, Kosovo, Albania, Greece, Bulgaria and even Turkey. Since a peace was brokered by Western diplomats last year, foreigners have been present in the form of consultants, monitors, mediators, facilitators and even soldiers. And since the Framework Agreement was signed, the international community has been trying to force one compromise after another on the two sides. The carrot for the people of Macedonia and their political leaders is aid money. Earlier this year, €307 million was committed to the country for development and reconstruction. Whether all this effort has dealt with the country's deeply rooted problems of inter-ethnic tensions, corruption, nepotism and organised crime is a moot point.

Some observers have talked of the two main ethnic communities living in separate parallel worlds. Albanians and Macedonians pass each other in the streets, deal with each other in shops, but that is it. There is no interest in the culture, the music, the literature or drama of the other side.

This parallel world extends to politics. The 15 September general election saw two distinct and separate campaigns: one within the Macedonian community, another in the Albanian. The other smaller ethnic groups – there are so many that the French coined the phrase *salade macédoine* for their mixed, multi-vegetable salad – pick up seats where they can. Macedonia is one of the few, possibly the only, country where there have been Roma members of parliament.

As much as any other institution, the media conform to this parallel universe. There are the Macedonian media and the Albanian media. They both cover the same events, but from totally opposing viewpoints. What unites them is a cavalier attitude to sources: they run stories without sources, publish rumours as fact, include unsourced comments, put quotations into people's mouths and insert opinion directly into the middle of a news items. Journalists do not even train together. At the journalism school at Skopje's university there is only one Albanian student.

There is a huge amount of media for a country of about 2 million people. A spokeswoman for the Macedonian Institute for the Media estimated that there were around 130 radio and television stations, including pirate stations, and about 50 newspapers. TV stations and newspapers are either supported by the state or by political and business interests, none of which is any guarantee of independence. It goes without saying that there is little concept of public service media. Given that on top of all this journalists are inexperienced and badly paid, the question of whether the Macedonian media were at all capable of covering the election competently had to be asked. At least one researcher involved in an EU-funded media monitoring exercise said he thought not.

Journalists are aware of the problems, but few of the international bodies that are involved in journalism training or media support have addressed either ownership or pay and conditions. The journalists, through the Association of Journalists of Macedonia and the International Federation of Journalists, have formulated a code of conduct and have begun to implement it. The code is the first serious attempt to confront issues such as a lack of professionalism and solidarity, hate speech and problems associated with ethnicity. However, even such worthy and genuine initiatives are problematic: the council charged with implementing the code has no Albanian journalists taking part in its deliberations. ❏

Michael Foley *is a journalist and teaches journalism at the Dublin Institute of Technology. He worked as an adviser to the Association of Journalists of Macedonia on formulating its code of conduct*

RECESSION BLUES

ANDREW GRAHAM-YOOLL

January 2002 | Sex and the city

The great macho libido is crestfallen – by about 50%. And that is official; or as official as any survey can be. A recent article in a Sunday edition of *La Nación* quoted a study by experts at the Clínicas Hospital who reported that 'sexual desire has declined in Argentines due to the crisis'. The first expostulation was one of disbelief, but 'Come off it!' seemed quite inadequate in the circumstances. If such an august journal said half Argentina's males were off the job, some more appropriate commiseration was needed. A less formal headline in *Pagina 12* (where else?) closed 2001 with a quote from broadcaster Fanny Mandelbaum: 'Due to the crisis, people fuck much less.'

The report in *La Nación* quoted Dr Osvaldo Mazza, head of the department of urology at the Clínicas. He said: 'When society deprives man of the chance to work, produce, provide and protect, abilities that he brings with him from the cradle, this curtails his sexual capacity.'

What a distressing way to see a great summer slip by. The season of love and mating opportunity is fizzling out all about us. Somehow, the idea of 'No sex, please, we're British' seemed an appropriately English joke about themselves, and ran for ages as a West End play. That went well with the self-deprecating folklore that included Nancy Mitford's *Love in a Cold Climate* and produced a wealth of Anglophobe jokes. But it is hard (sorry, no pun or reference intended) to imagine the Argentine male admitting to such a shortcoming (ditto) or making light of an issue that has been vital to *porteño* society's fantasies about itself.

The male is at a loss. There is a need for alternative distraction: exhausting family activities and new hobbies to explore new areas of interest. For couples who enjoy the night life, the problem could be met head on by joining the current craze for tango. There the national male could work out his fantasies by doing standing up what he would like to do or has forgotten how to do lying down.

This crisis-ridden activity (sex, not tango) has produced complications. No man nowadays can go to Wednesday-night-out-with-the-boys to discuss an erotic feeling. It would be in bad taste as he would be seen to be a liar, or unique in current society, or a being from elsewhere impersonating the boys' old mate: a stranger. In this fashion-driven city, it is out of fashion to feel horny. In fact, you don't have male company mentioning genitalia except in medical terms.

My own survey took me to see *The Vagina Monologues*, at the Teatro La Plaza. The audience, as reported by critics elsewhere, was largely female, apparently there to learn about something they had never seen. The minority male portion of the house looked quite glum, especially when one of the actresses, a Valkyrie-like blonde, performed a series of gasps and hoots to represent the longest ever orgasm on stage. Instead of exciting, the performance was belittling. A remembrance of things past.

In view of the adverse rumours, a visit to the heart surgeon was in order, to find out if there is any danger of popping my clogs when on the job as a result of taking Viagra. I left assured, and in possession of two free samples which, at 32 pesos for four in the drug store, are not easily affordable in these cash-less days of cash-only sales. The local variety is offered as Pfizer's 'Sildefil', which is blue like the 'V' one. And there is one edifyingly called 'Magnus', produced by the Argentine laboratory Sidus. This one is wine red, but you are told on the prospectus not to drink alcohol before the pill. Giving up the booze as part of the foreplay eliminates a tradition. Afterwards, drinking is OK, or smoking, or asking for the remote control, as the American poet Robert Pinsky wrote.

It is very uplifting to have science come to the rescue in this Argentine summer of discontent.

April 2002 | Bullets, banks and beggars

There are two bullet holes in the steel panel under the Banelco ATM keyboard at the Galicia bank branch in San Cristobal. They are unconventional but appropriate reminders of summer in Buenos Aires. The hold-up was on 14 February. But nobody around there remembers the date, although the events are very real in the local memory. There have been hundreds, or too many, bank raids in this long fraught summer of 2002. A policeman on duty was shot in the head that day, but nobody remembers now if he survived. Who wants to know? Who gives a devalued peso for a policeman's life these days?

In the lower south, such as Barracas, the scavenging dogs compete with scavenging people for the contents of the rubbish bags and boxes. Late at night, small, thin, dark men, often accompanied by children or by a very pregnant woman, push supermarket trolleys or pull barrows loaded high with paper and carton, or they sit on the load and drive emaciated-looking horses. The men, the children, the pregnant women drive rods through rubbish bags, looking for glass or metal or whatever.

Uptown, the people, and the dogs, look for food, mostly outside the burger joints on Corrientes Avenue or the Florida pedestrian way. In Retiro, the dogs dart between buses to reach a bag dropped on the sidewalk or at the bus stop by a bottle washer from the bars and stores that make the once-grand railway terminal feel like a souk. One morning, there was a dead dog by the torn bags. You wonder if some morning there might be one of those small, skinny, dark scavenger people dead on the pile of scattered rubbish.

This long summer of 2002 that now sinks in buckets of rain, in the fourth long year (46 months say the business dailies) of hopeless recession, begins to smack of biblical suffering.

The Romanian beggar who walks the streets among the embassy residences and elegant cafés near Avenida Libertador told one of his benefactors that he was leaving Buenos Aires. Argentine generosity had dried up and there seemed no point in staying. If one leaves, will all those others, entire families of Romanians who flit among the tourists at the San Telmo market on Sundays, also pack up? For some, it will be a relief: no more whining women carrying barefoot infants sucking at nipples that look like saucers, or diminutive children demanding coins in a peremptory tone. What have we come to if even the beggars are emigrating?

It seems hard to accept that there are 6 million poor in and around Buenos Aires – 12 million nationwide – in a population of 36 million. This summer we constantly echo the question put by Mexican writer Carlos Fuentes: 'What is it about Argentines that they have to do these things to themselves?'

The sound of the summer may well be the aggressive, quite humourless *cumbia villera*, which tells a thing or two about the country, or Rafaga's pop tropical, turned into our latest export commodity, *cumbia de las pampas*. That is according to the entertainment supplements. For most of us, though, the sound of the summer of 2002 that will rattle down the years is the pot-banging at midnight, from December onwards. But perhaps the worst sight of all will be the hand-banging on metal and wooden shields protecting banks against their customers: people slapping their hands on galvanised sheets, often sliding to the ground in tears. A public catharsis.

The individual tragedies are heart-rending: people have lost their savings, people have been swindled by politicians, policies and banks four times or more in half a century. The dollar rate was a fiction in 1955 when it was 1.70 pesos in the last days of Juan Perón. Alvaro Alsogaray cheated state employees out of a chunk of their wages with the 9 de Julio Bonds. Raúl Alfonsín imposed 'forced savings' in the mid-1980s and hyper-inflation wiped out what was left in the bank. Antonio Erman González introduced the Bonex foreign exchange bonds on 2 January 1990. Domingo Felipe Cavallo brought in the convertibility on April Fool's Day, 1991, and people lost a high percentage of their savings in the two pirouettes. And then Cavallo's *corralito* froze savings dramatically in December 2001. After two weeks and four presidents, President Eduardo Duhalde said he would fix that – and devalued the peso, cheating people out of what was left.

Why do people go back to banks? Do they trust them? Or is it greed that has made people believe, against reality, that this time they could get rich?

The architecture of banks will change. Banks used to have fortified neo-classical lines to give the appearance of security. Then marble gave way to glass and steel (imported from Brazil), as branches proliferated and plastic replaced cash in the age of electronic banking. Banks will probably become vaults again, security developed from the metal armour installed against the protesters. The idea of vaulted estate agents is puzzling, for that is what banks will become as they put on the market the thousands of properties they will repossess from customers who cannot pay their mortgages.

The graffiti on bank walls are collectors' items: 'Danger, Banking Area' read one on Diagonal Norte early in the year. The scrawls were painted by otherwise respectable, now desperate members of the middle class.

With over 20% unemployment (20% of how many? The real rate is probably higher), decline is evident in the middle class. Its members are impoverished by the loss of savings, capital and jobs. What is left of that thriving class, the well-heeled 3%, can be found at the elegant La Biela restaurant, in the posh Recoleta district, taking late breakfasts on Sunday morning. The more battered former members can also be seen on the street, as on Avenida Belgrano. A well-dressed woman sold coffee to cab

drivers and pedestrians. She had been a secretary and was sacked. Her
husband sold cold soft drinks from a picnic fridge. He had once owned
a small clothing business that went bust. They are broke.

The remnants of failed businesses can be found all about the south
side of the city. Parque Patricios, Boedo and Barracas . . . Closed butchers,
clothiers, small carpenters and foundries. Families turned wood or metal on
two lathes that produced enough income for a comfortable life and summer
holidays in Mar del Plata. The premises have been dark for years. The
question as you pass these places is whether this Argentine generation
will ever see a recovery.

August 2002 | Silent witness

She was a pretty girl, mid-teens. She stopped her barrow to load some
old newspapers. The top one was a *Clarín* supplement about photographer
Sebastiao Salgado. The headline: 'Beautiful poverty' (*Bella miseria*). A truck
driver shouted, 'Wanna fuck, *cirujita*?' Then he drove at her cart, knocking
it over. The girl swore, righted the cart and refilled it.

All the wretchedness and the banality of Argentina's decay was there.
The scavengers and their trail of litter are subjects of revulsion to the people
who sweep the sidewalk in the morning. But look at it this way: the *cirujas*
(from *cirujano*, surgeon, hence 'trash surgeons') scrape a living from recycling
rather than go into crime, which is the only other growth occupation.

'Beggars of the new millennium are better educated and younger,' the
headline read, as if we could be proud of our better class of down-and-outs.
That was in the newspaper *La Razón*, to soften the drop as we plumb our
present depth of regression. The statistics say there are now 6.2 million
people underemployed or jobless, 45% of the workforce. The 'informal
sector' has taken labour out of the statistics. But even the 'informals' are
in crisis: the 'rent a mob' lot are not paying the 20 pesos they did last year.
Crowds would be hired by political thugs to burn a few tyres on the
highway and snarl traffic for a day. And there was a sandwich thrown in.
Now it is only ten pesos, and not as often and no sandwich. And ten pesos
after 250% devaluation is not much. People are glad to get the ten and say
nothing. Think of devaluation as a form of censorship.

The poor come out at night, so they are not seen. And not seen much
either are the rich who have not fled to Miami. They flaunt their foreign
funds in the foyers of the posh hotels, the only place they find safe from
the crime wave that has taken hundreds of lives, including those of 67

policemen killed in Buenos Aires in the half-year up to the end of July 2002. There were 55 police murdered in Buenos Aires in the whole of 2001. People don't care about dead police. They were hated for so long under military despots that there is not even pity for their dead. People forget that police represent the level of order in a society, and if cops are corrupt, ignored or dead, they represent no order. Like now.

Drivers get across the city quickly. Little traffic: the high price of fuel has made people leave cars at home. You hardly see the new poor, the vanishing middle class. One day soon, Argentina will get its George Grosz to portray our social contradictions. Grosz (1893–1959), the German Dadaist, drew the wealthy and the military of the 1920s as fat and bespectacled, and the poor as one-legged walking cadavers.

The poor are like the 'disappeared'. You don't talk about them until told it is safe. Then we shall go around saying, 'I knew somebody who was "poor". You mean you didn't know?' as we did in the 1980s, after the despots. Some day about 2010, when preparing the festivities for the second centenary, we shall take speech out of its cell and discuss the poor, as we dared talk about the atrocities.

We shall probably never talk about middle-class poor, too embarrassing. Their lot seems much worse because they can't even scavenge. The middle class will starve, because of a disease called dignity. They don't know how to be poor. A biologist who lost his job and had his apartment repossessed says that members of the middle class, the dregs of their dignity draped in a suit, go to the city airport at night. They get a few hours' kip in the improved installations. It is warm and dry, and there are no fleas from tramps. They pull a little case on wheels and mingle among the real passengers and try to look as if they had missed their plane. They really miss a lot. The unemployed biologist swears it is true.

If you don't want to believe this, you can take refuge at an elegant restaurant, filled to capacity at midweek. That is the other Argentina, the rich one we boast about, which helps us deny there is hunger and that children are suffering malnutrition and leave school to beg for food, not even coins any more. We hardly talk about hungry kids. Think of hunger as a form of censorship.

Some forms of rescue remain. *Clarín* reported on 21 April that a support group had been formed for families of young people who emigrate. The relatives behave like the bereaved. This was a country of immigration. The German hospital ran a seminar on 'Secondary prevention of depression

George Grosz (1893–1959), Eclipse of the Sun.
Credit: AKG London

in a country in crisis'. The Pirovano hospital offered a course on survival. *La Nación* ran an article with guidelines for people who have to pay kidnap ransoms.

A woman went to the Durand hospital to have a breast lump extracted for testing. She was told by the doctor to take the substance to the lab herself as there were no porters. She could not take the syringe because, though it was disposable, it had to be reused. The substance for testing was put in alcohol in a plastic cup and two empty Redoxon tubes and carried, open, in the rain, to the basement lab.

That's normal, said the doctor. To see real decadence we should have watched a TV show called *Titanic* on 10 May, when a taxi driver was ridiculed for returning 17,000 pesos left in his cab by a woman who paid no reward. Ridicule by TV is a form of censorship. ❏

Andrew Graham-Yooll *is chairman and former editor of the* Buenos Aires Herald

These articles appeared in the January, April and August issues of the Herald *magazine*

WWW.INDEXONCENSORSHIP.ORG
CONTACT@INDEXONCENSORSHIP.ORG
TEL: 020 7278 2313 • FAX: 020 7278 1878

SUBSCRIPTIONS (4 ISSUES PER ANNUM)
INDIVIDUALS: BRITAIN £32, US $48, REST OF WORLD £42
INSTITUTIONS: BRITAIN £48, US $80, REST OF WORLD £52
**SPEAK TO TONY CALLAGHAN ON 020 7278 2313
OR EMAIL TONY@INDEXONCENSORSHIP.ORG**

Index on Censorship (ISSN 0306-4220) is published four times a year by a non-profit-making company: Writers & Scholars International Ltd, Lancaster House, 33 Islington High Street, London N1 9LH. *Index on Censorship* is associated with Writers & Scholars Educational Trust, registered charity number 325003 **Periodicals postage:** (US subscribers only) paid at Newark, New Jersey. Postmaster: send US address changes to *Index on Censorship* c/o Mercury Airfreight International Ltd Inc., 365 Blair Road, Avenel, NJ 07001, USA